CHALLENGE in Eastern Europe

CHALLENGE
in Eastern Europe

12 Essays edited by
C. E. BLACK

Prepared under the auspices of the
MID-EUROPEAN STUDIES CENTER
of the National Committee
for a Free Europe, Inc.

Foreword by Joseph C. Grew

KENNIKAT PRESS
Port Washington, N. Y./London

CHALLENGE IN EASTERN EUROPE

Copyright 1954 by the Trustees of
Rutgers College in New Jersey
Reissued in 1971 by Kennikat Press by arrangement
Library of Congress Catalog Card No: 75-118427
ISBN 0-8046-1400-8

Manufactured by Taylor Publishing Company   Dallas, Texas

ESSAY AND GENERAL LITERATURE INDEX REPRINT SERIES

Foreword

It was after his return home to England that John Donne wrote: "No man is an island, intire of itselfe; every man is a peece of the Continent, a part of the maine; if a Clod bee washed away by the Sea, Europe is the lesse, . . . any man's death diminishes me, because I am involved in Mankinde."

In the three centuries since Donne, the world has begun to learn the simple lesson that nations, like men, are their brothers' keepers. In today's world, where the distance from Boston to Berlin is shorter in time than was that from Donne's London to Liverpool—where men, or ideas, or total destruction can cross a continent or an ocean in a day—American interest encompasses the world.

The Monroe Doctrine, Wilson's Fourteen Points, the Truman Doctrine, Korea, and the forthright declarations of President Eisenhower all illustrate how United States foreign policy, in the nation's self-interest, has become progressively committed to a greater geographical periphery in a shrinking world.

From the economic, political, and strategic aspects, Eastern Europe is of vital importance to the Free World. The economic health of Western Europe ultimately depends upon a free intercourse among all the countries of Europe, and until that situation once again prevails, America must, to some degree, help the West European economy. Meanwhile, the economy of captive Eastern Europe is being systematically and ruthlessly exploited for the benefit of Soviet Russia.

Politically and strategically, a permanently Communist Eastern Europe would be an American disaster. The Soviet power monopoly in the area has transposed Russian armed forces and communist ideology hundreds of miles nearer to the production and population centers of the West, affording the Soviet Union a strategic zone of hundreds of thousands of square miles and millions of human beings.

The United States has a moral obligation to help restore to the captive countries of Europe and their unhappy peoples our common cultural, religious, and political heritage. For it must always be remembered that these peoples are captives —that they did not freely choose Communism, but had it brutally or deviously thrust upon them.

Millions of American citizens or their forefathers came to this country before the First World War in the pursuit of some aspect of freedom that was denied them in the Eastern Europe of their time. But the current Communist oppression is absolute. Today, the people are subject to a new and universal tyranny which dims the minor past injustices of Old World empires to insignificance.

In the larger view, America cannot willingly accept a world, or a Europe, half slave and half free. The slave half of Europe must someday be free, or the free half of Europe too may be enslaved.

In the past, a large segment of the American public has seemed to be almost willfully ignorant of the peoples comprising Eastern Europe, and it may be held that this lack of knowledge contributed to the postwar Communist tragedy. More recently, the study of the area has been greatly developed in the United States and at long last is tending to assume its rightful place in American thinking. That knowledge is power has held good for two thousand years. Knowledge remains one of freedom's major weapons.

America has assumed the leadership of the Free World in taking up the Communist challenge to individual liberty and national independence.

To sustain the hope of freedom in half a continent; to learn and to contribute to truth and knowledge; in enlightened self-interest to dedicate ourselves and our country to freedom's cause and restitution—

This is the *Challenge in Eastern Europe.*

JOSEPH C. GREW

Preface

Eastern Europe—the region embracing Albania, Bulgaria, Czechoslovakia, Hungary, Poland, Rumania, and Yugoslavia, and for certain limited purposes the Soviet zones of Germany and Austria as well—has long been familiar to students of European history. To Western public opinion in general, however, this region has become known chiefly as a result of the two world wars, for which it provided some of the major diplomatic problems and military battlefields.

Despite the significant role of Eastern Europe, the Western democracies have tended to regard it primarily as a region of inherent economic poverty and political instability. They have failed either to recognize the extent to which its problems reflected their own policies, or to see it as an area vital to their security. This lack of understanding of the problems and significance of Eastern Europe was most conspicuous at the end of the Second World War. At that time decisions were reached and concessions made by the West on the basis of assumptions that were not firmly grounded in the realities of this region. Important lessons were eventually learned, but not until great harm had been done to the peoples of Eastern Europe and consequently also to the welfare of the Western democracies.

The purpose of the essays in this volume is to review the record of the recent past in order to interpret the many-sided challenge presented by Eastern Europe. They describe this region in its transition from agrarian underdevelopment and political strife toward a more complex society, a more productive economy, and a more stable political system. The end of this process of transition is not yet in sight, and it has in most respects been set back by the policies of the Communist regimes since the Second World War. At the same time Eastern Europe remains a region of dynamic developments that have remained in many ways beyond the range of Western understanding.

These essays reflect the considerable diversity in experience and points of view of the authors. Some have wrestled with the problems of Eastern Europe as responsible members of governments both before and since the Second World War. Although they are acquainted at first hand with the policies of the Communist regimes, they write less from bitterness than from a desire to interpret for the West the lessons of their experience. Others bring to their subjects such objectivity as is afforded by academic study, and view Eastern Europe with a degree of abstraction difficult for those whose families and careers are directly involved. Still others combine academic study with some measure of personal experience that has permitted them to test the values that printed volumes do not always convey.

These diversities of background and viewpoint are merged in the common desire to interpret the challenge offered by Eastern Europe to the leaders of the Western democracies. Underlying these essays is the belief that a careful survey of the problems of this region is a first and essential step in the search for solutions in a democratic spirit. Although no blueprint for meeting the challenge of Eastern Europe is here attempted, an understanding of this region essential to the drafting of such a blueprint is offered.

With one exception, these essays were presented in a somewhat different form as lectures at the Institute of Public Affairs and Regional Studies of the Graduate School of Arts and Science at New York University in the summer of 1953. They were prepared under the auspices of the Mid-European Studies Center of the National Committee for a Free Europe, Inc. The assistance provided by the Center, both material and editorial, was vital to the completion of this volume. The editor is responsible in matters of planning and organization, but the views expressed herein are those of the several authors.

C. E. BLACK

Princeton, New Jersey
November, 1953

Notes on the Authors

C. E. BLACK is Associate Professor of History at Princeton University. From 1943 to 1946 he was with the Department of State in Washington and in Eastern Europe. He was a member of the United States Delegation on the United Nations Security Council Commission of Investigation Concerning Greek Frontier Incidents in 1947, and was on the faculty of the National War College in 1950-51. He is author of *The Establishment of Constitutional Government in Bulgaria* (1943); co-author, with E. C. Helmreich, of *Twentieth Century Europe: A History* (1950); editor of *Readings on Contemporary Eastern Europe* (1953); and a contributor to *A Handbook of Slavic Studies* (1949), *Negotiating with the Russians* (1951), *European Political Systems* (1953), and *The Threat of Soviet Imperialism* (1954).

HUBERT RIPKA was Minister of State in the Czechoslovakian Government-in-Exile from 1940 to 1945, and Minister of Foreign Trade from 1945 to 1948. A graduate in history from the Charles University in Prague, in the interwar period Mr. Ripka served as editor of two prominent Prague dailies, *Narodni Osvobození* and *Lidové Noviny,* and of the political and literary weekly *Prítomnost.* His numerous writings on current affairs include *Munich, Before and After* (1939), *East and West* (1944), and *Czechoslovakia Enslaved: The Story of the Communist Coup d'État* (1950).

ARNOLD J. ZURCHER is Professor of Political Science and heads the Institute of Public Affairs and Regional Studies at New York University. During the Second World War he lectured at the School of Military Government in Charlottesville, Va., and since 1945 he has been Executive Director of the Alfred P. Sloan Foundation. Mr.

Zurcher has written extensively on political problems, and in the field of European government he is the author of *The Experiment with Democracy in Central Europe* (1933); co-author of *Propaganda and Dictatorship* (1936), *The Governments of Continental Europe* (1940), and *Postwar European Federation* (1943); and editor of *Constitutions and Constitutional Trends Since World War II* (1952).

STANISLAW MIKOLAJCZYK went into exile in 1947 after serving for two years as Vice-Premier and Minister of Agriculture in the Polish Provisional Government. He was a leader of the Polish Peasant Party for many years, and from 1930 to 1935 he represented that party in the Polish parliament. He was a member of the Polish Government-in-Exile as Deputy Prime Minister and Minister for Home Affairs from 1941 to 1943, and as Prime Minister in 1943-44. Mr. Mikolajczyk is now Chairman of the Polish National Democratic Committee and President of the International Peasant Union. He is also the author of *The Rape of Poland: Pattern of Soviet Aggression* (1948).

LADISLAV FEIERABEND was for many years a leader of the cooperative movement in Czechoslovakia. In the interwar period he served as General Manager of the Board of Czechoslovakian Agricultural Cooperatives, Vice-President of the Export Board, and President of the State Grain Monopoly. He was Minister of Agriculture in 1938-39, and Minister of Finance in the Czechoslovakian Government-in-Exile from 1941 to 1945. He is the author of *Le commerce cooperatif du blé* (1932) and *Agricultural Cooperatives in Czechoslovakia* (1952).

BRANKO M. PEŠELJ was associated with the Croatian Peasant Party from 1925 to 1953, and has been an officer of the International Peasant Union since its founding in 1947. He practiced law in Zagreb from 1932 until his departure from Yugoslavia in 1945, and since arriving in the United States he has been affiliated with Radio Free Europe and the Mid-European Studies Center. Mr. Pešelj received a Ph.D. degree from Georgetown University in 1950, and has written extensively on the peasant ideologies and agrarian movements in Eastern Europe.

GEZA TELEKI was Minister of Education and Culture in the Hungarian Provisional Government in 1944-45. He is now Associate

Professor of Foreign Affairs at the University of Virginia, and he has been affiliated with the Mid-European Studies Center. Mr. Teleki is known for his work in the field of economic geography, and before the Second World War he was Professor of Economics at the Kolozsvar University and Director of the Paul Teleki Research Institute in Budapest.

JAN H. WSZELAKI resigned in 1945 as Minister Counselor of the Polish Embassy in Washington, D.C., after a career of twenty-six years in the Polish diplomatic service. He was educated at the Moscow Economic Institute and the École des Sciences Politiques in Paris, and has had a special interest in the economic development of Russia and Eastern Europe. From 1935 to 1942 Mr. Wszelaki served as economic adviser to the Polish Ministry of Foreign Affairs, and during the Second World War he was an active participant in studies in European federalism carried on in London and at Oxford. He is the author of *Fuel and Power in Captive Middle Europe* (1952), and of articles in scholarly journals.

HENRY L. ROBERTS is a member of the staff of the Council on Foreign Relations, on leave from the Department of History at Columbia University. During the Second World War he saw duty in Eastern Europe with the United States Army. Mr. Roberts is the author of *Rumania: Political Problems of an Agrarian State* (1951); co-author, with Paul A. Wilson, of *Britain and the United States: Problems in Cooperation* (1953); and contributor to *The Diplomats, 1919-1939* (1953).

JACOB B. HOPTNER is Research Director of the Mid-European Studies Center of the National Committee for a Free Europe. From 1943 to 1947 he was with the American Red Cross Mission in Italy and served as Special Representative of that organization in Yugoslavia. Mr. Hoptner is a graduate of the European Institute of Columbia University, and is Associate Editor of the *Harvard Slavic Studies*.

KARL W. DEUTSCH is Professor of History and Political Science at the Massachusetts Institute of Technology. During the academic years 1952-54 he took a leave of absence to serve as Research Associate at the Center for Research in World Political Institutions at Princeton University. As an officer in the Department of State and other government agencies, Mr. Deutsch directed several studies in international politics and attended the United Nations Conference on International Organization at San Francisco in 1945. He also was a member of the Interuniversity Research Seminar on Comparative Politics of the Social Science Research Council, and is an Associate in the University Seminar on Organization at Columbia University and a Fellow of the American Academy of Arts and Sciences. Mr. Deutsch is the author of *Nationalism and Social Communication* (1953), *Political Community at the International Level* (1953), and a forthcoming *Interdisciplinary Bibliography on Nationalism, 1935-53.*

Contents

PART ONE

THE POLITICS OF
EASTERN EUROPE

1 Eastern Europe in Historical Perspective

C. E. BLACK

The study of Eastern Europe is a recent development in the Western Hemisphere and represents a long delayed recognition of the significance of this region in world affairs. Although the peoples of this area have participated for many centuries in the varied problems of European politics, it is only in recent years that their importance as distinct national entities has been brought into the focus of the American world outlook.

It should, of course, be recalled that in the eighteenth century, under very different circumstances, the Western Hemisphere had good reason to be aware of Eastern Europe. In the persons of a Kosciuszko and a Pulaski this region participated in the liberation of the American colonies, and in the early years of the republic a Thomas Jefferson followed with well-informed interest the republican movement in Eastern Europe. Yet for the greater part of the nineteenth century the peoples of this area were dominated to one degree or another by the governments of the Habsburg, Hohenzollern, Romanov, and Ottoman dynasties, and the relationship of their destiny to that of the Western Hemisphere was in large measure lost to sight.

It was nevertheless not entirely by chance that President Wilson took the initiative during the First World War in proclaiming that a just settlement in Eastern Europe was a prerequisite to world peace. Not only were Americans in many walks of life becoming aware of the importance of this region, but Wilson himself had at one time given some attention to its problems. As early as 1877, as an undergraduate at the College of New Jersey (now known as Princeton University), Wilson wrote a paper on "Prince Bismarck," which reflected his interest in the role of Eastern Europe in the international relations of that period; but this was only a student's essay, and it touched on Eastern Europe no more than peripherally. It was as an international statesman that Wilson came forward in 1918 to proclaim in his Fourteen Points three principles, among others, that he considered fundamental to a peaceful settlement. These principles were: national self-determination for the peoples of Eastern Europe (Points X-XIII), free and equal trade (Point III), and a general association of nations (Point XIV).

This image of a just settlement was only partially achieved in the peace treaties for, although the new frontiers followed reasonably closely the national principles, the equally vital requirements of free trade and collective security were in large measure neglected. What is significant about Wilson's program is not the ultimate failure of the peace settlement, since his own program was implemented only in part, but the fact that he correctly stressed the three central issues affecting the destiny of Eastern Europe. Throughout modern history, the peoples of this region have struggled with the problems of national liberation, modernization, and regional organization, and in reviewing their history these three categories provide a useful framework of analysis.

Of these three problems, that of national liberation is certainly the one that has concerned the peoples of this area most continuously. As minority groups, the peoples of Eastern Europe tended to suffer from discrimination at the hands of the governments whose territory they inhabited and, once they were infected with the spirit of the enlightenment, national liberation came to be regarded as the solution to all their problems. Significant reforms were indeed carried out in the nineteenth century within the existing political framework, but the road to reform was obstructed by many obstacles. Although national liberation almost inevitably means revolution and war, it appeared to many Eastern European leaders to be preferable to the available alternatives. The diplomatic history of Europe was, in fact, punctuated by great crises as one province after another broke loose from the Ottoman empire, and when this process culminated in the First World War and the liberation of the remaining peoples of this region, it was widely regarded as a logical step in human progress.

The leaders of Eastern European opinion did not regard national liberation as an end in itself, but rather as the best means for promoting the modernization of their peoples. This aim was stated in many different ways, some speaking of education, others of freedom, and many more of economic welfare. This is certainly a much broader objective than the principle of free and equal trade enunciated by Wilson, but that principle was an essential prerequisite to modernization in the view of the American president. In general terms it would not be unfair to say that the goal of Eastern European leaders in the last two centuries has been to raise the spiritual and material level of their peoples to the European standard established by England, France, Germany, and their smaller neighbors. This interpretation of their goal is certainly very generalized, yet it represents more accurately the aspirations of this region than do the specific programs of individual leaders or schools of thought. The fact that this objective has not yet been attained is fundamental to an understanding of the problems of Eastern Europe, and much of the political extremism of this region can be traced to the frustrations resulting from this failure.

The most obvious reason for the failure to achieve a European standard, and probably also the most important, has been the persistent necessity of giving priority to national security over human welfare. This problem has, of course, been faced by all modern states, but it has affected the peoples of Eastern Europe to an unusual degree. It would not be too much to say that the insecurity of these states, due more to regional factors than to size, has been the source of most of their difficulties. Of the various solutions that have been attempted, including national opportunism, alliances with great powers, regional pacts, and participation in the League of Nations, none has met the special needs of the situation.

I

The European wars resulting from the French Revolution and the Napoleonic conquests infected the leaders of the Eastern European peoples with the modern spirit of nationalism and liberalism, but the peace settlement concluded in 1815 did little to satisfy the hopes that had been aroused. The peoples of this region remained under the firm rule of the Romanov, Habsburg, Hohenzollern, and Ottoman dynasties, and before long the process of national liberation came to occupy their principal energies. Of the many national groups in this region, only the Serbians and the Montenegrins achieved any measure of independence before 1815, although the Magyars occupied within the Austrian monarchy a position of special influence. The remaining nationalities in this region had not yet taken the first steps towards independence. The struggle for freedom lasted for a full century, and was a complex process in which the rivalries among the nationalities frequently occupied as much energy as the struggle against the dynastic governments.

The development of nationalism and liberation in Eastern Europe was the product of many influences. Within the larger framework of the enlightenment, the peoples of this region were stimulated by the philosophy of nationalism developed by Herder and his school and by the ideas of the French Revolution disseminated through cultural channels and by Napoleon's armies. The Poles, Czechs, and Magyars were most strongly influenced by this new spirit at first, and until the middle of the nineteenth century liberalism took precedence over nationalism. In this period a Czartoryski, a Palacky, and a Széchenyi worked for reforms within the political framework established in 1815, and their policies produced significant results. It was only after the defeat of liberalism in the abortive revolutions of 1848 that nationalism came to predominate, and this nationalism was rapidly hardened by the opposition that it encountered. By the end of the century only the Magyars had achieved the substance of their national aims, and this at the expense of becoming among the most rigorous oppressors of their own non-Magyar minorities. The peoples of Southeastern Europe achieved independence only to a limited degree before the First World War, while the Poles and Czechs remained under firm imperial rule. The approximate distribution of these nationalities at the turn of the century is illustrated by the table on page 8.

Of all the oppressed peoples of Eastern Europe, the Poles were the most numerous and their situation in 1815 the most acute. Possessors of a proud tradition of government dating back to the later middle ages, and at one time the third in area and fourth in population among the European powers, they had suffered domestic disintegration and territorial partition in the eighteenth century. In the peace settlement of 1815 the largest segment of Poland was in-

Principal Eastern European Nationalities Before the First World War *

(APPROXIMATE FIGURES IN THOUSANDS)

	Austria Hungary [a]	Russia [b]	Germany [c]	Rumania [d]	Serbia [e]	Monte-negro [f]	Bulgaria [g]	Albania [h]
POLES	5,000	7,931	3,086	—	—	—	—	—
MAGYARS	10,100	—	—	—	—	—	—	—
CZECHS	6,550	—	—	—	—	—	—	—
SLOVAKS	1,950	—	—	—	—	—	—	—
SLOVENES	1,300	—	—	—	—	—	—	—
CROATIANS	2,625	—	—	—	—	—	—	—
SERBIANS	1,925	—	—	—	4,048	—	—	—
MOHAMMEDAN SERBO-CROATIANS IN BOSNIA	650	—	—	—	—	—	—	—
MACEDONIAN SLAVS	—	—	—	—	500	—	100	—
MONTENE-GRINS	—	—	—	—	—	516	—	—
RUMANIANS	3,200	1,122	—	7,136	—	—	—	—
BULGARIANS	—	173	—	200	—	—	4,153	—
ALBANIANS	—	—	—	—	—	—	—	800

* Fully satisfactory statistics on the nationalities of Eastern Europe for this period are not available, owing to inadequate census data as well as the imprecision of the concept of "nationality." The above figures refer only to the nationalities that emerged as independent states, or dominant members thereof, after the First World War. They omit the Germans, Ukrainians (Ruthenians), Turks, Italians, and others who formed a significant part of the population of this region in 1914. The following are the sources used:

a Robert A. Kann, *The Multinational Empire,* Vol. II, p. 305; based on census of 1910.

b Brokgauz-Efron, *Entsiklopedicheskii Slovar,* Suppl. Vol. II, App., p. xii; based on census of 1897.

c *Statesman's Yearbook,* 1914, p. 890; based on census of 1900.

d *Ibid.,* p. 1213, estimates of 1913.

e *Ibid.,* p. 1282, estimate for 1913, author's estimate of Macedonian Slavs.

f *Ibid.,* p. 1090, estimate for 1913.

g *Ibid.,* p. 727, estimate for 1914; author's estimate of Macedonian Slavs.

h *Ibid.,* p. 621, estimate for 1913.

corporated in Russia as a nominal "Kingdom." Cracow became a free city under the joint protection of Russia, Prussia, and Austria, while western Poland became the Prus-
sian province of Posen (Poznan), and the province of
Galicia was ceded to Austria. For a brief period it seemed
that the Kingdom of Poland might develop a degree of
autonomy under Russian rule, but the firm suppression of
the insurrection of 1830 brought an end to this hope. The
mid-century revolutions were echoed in all four parts of
Poland, and in each section ended with a further tighten-
ing of the imperial regime. In German and Russian Poland
minority rights were increasingly disregarded in the latter
half of the nineteenth century, and the city of Cracow lost
its freedom through Austrian annexation. Only in the Austrian province of Galicia did the Poles develop a significant
degree of self-government in this period, and in this atmosphere the Polish national movement was able to develop.

The Czechs and the Slovaks almost lost their identity
after the annexation of the Kingdom of Bohemia by the
Habsburgs in the seventeenth century, but in the revolutionary era they regained interest in their national culture. In
the first half of the nineteenth century they were infected
by the new spirit of nationalism and contributed such leaders as Dobrovsky, Šafařik, Palacky, and Havliček. However,
here as elsewhere, the revolutions of 1848 brought defeat
and retrenchment. As the Austrian government became more
decentralized, the Czechs won increasing rights of local self-
government, and by 1900 the questions of Czech autonomy
and the Czech language had been raised by such leaders as
Masaryk and Kramař to issues of European importance.
The Slovaks, under the harsher rule of the Magyars, did not
fare so well. Small in number and living in the underdeveloped reaches of the Carpathian mountains, the Slovaks
lacked the cultural heritage of the Czechs. Nevertheless, under Štúr, Šafařik, and Kollar a Slovak national renaissance

took place, and in the generation before the First World War a bitter struggle was waged against Magyar rule.

The exceptional character of Hungary's position was derived both from its traditions of provincial administrative autonomy, which can be traced to the thirteenth century, and from the fact that it had within its boundaries substantial Slavic and Rumanian minorities. Although the Hungarians, or Magyars, were less a minority than a member of the ruling group, they were by no means satisfied with the somewhat ambiguously defined rights of self-government granted when the Austrian Empire was created in 1804. The Hungarian nobility became an important force for reform within the empire and contributed many leaders to the liberal movement. Under the moderate guidance of Széchenyi important reforms were accomplished, but the more radical nationalist program of Kossuth was defeated in 1848-49 by the combined efforts of Austrian and Russian troops. Both the Magyar and the non-Magyar peoples were discriminated against in the period of Austrian centralism that followed, but with the military decline of Austria the privileges of Hungary were reasserted. The Austro-Hungarian compromise of 1867, negotiated under the wise statesmanship of Déak, gave Hungary a constitutional position equal to that of Austria within the empire and a political influence that was frequently greater despite certain economic disabilities.

Although Croatia enjoyed a degree of autonomy in Hungary after 1868, having in fact occupied the position of a dependency of Hungary intermittently since the eleventh century, it still suffered many limitations. The experience of Napoleonic rule in 1809-13 and the growth of Gaj's nationalist movement under the name of Illyrianism brought Croatian national feeling to the point where it could no longer suffer with equanimity the cultural and political restrictions imposed by the Magyars. The neighboring

Slovenes, under Austrian rule, developed a national program under the leadership of Kopitar. The government of the German Austrians was certainly milder than that of the Magyars, but in the years before the First World War the Slovenes, like their Croatian cousins, had reasons to feel that their political development was being unjustifiably restricted by Habsburg policies.

The temper and direction of Croatian and Slovene nationalism was increasingly influenced by the successful efforts of the Serbians and the Montenegrins, who were also Serbian in language. Before 1815 both peoples had struck their first blows for independence from Turkish rule. Within the Habsburg empire, an important minority of Serbians was divided between Austrian, Hungarian, and Croatian rule, and was augmented in 1878 when Bosnia-Herzegovina came under the joint administration of Austria and Hungary. This province had a mixed population of Croatians, Serbians, and Mohammedans who were largely of Serbo-Croatian origin. In the eighteenth century significant concessions had been made to the Serbian minority in Hungary, but subsequent events led to a decline in their position and after the compromise of 1867 the situation was ripe for a national protest.

It was nevertheless in the Ottoman empire that the Serbian national movement, inspired by Obradović and Karadžić, found its most active rallying point. The Montenegrins gained recognition of their independence from Turkish rule in 1799, and the Serbians, starting with their first uprising in 1804, took advantage of every weakness in the Ottoman system to wrest increasing political independence and territorial aggrandizement. The years 1817, 1829, 1856, 1878, and 1913 mark the important stages of Serbian growth, and these developments were watched with warm interest by the South Slavs within the Habsburg empire. The question of South Slav national rights now became linked with the struggle of Austria-Hungary and Russia for hegemony in the Balkans, and the annexation of the Slav-inhabited Ottoman province of Bosnia-Herzegovina by the Habsburgs in 1908 was as important an event in South Slav politics as it was in European diplomacy. In view of Serbian indignation at this Habsburg stroke, it is not surprising that Sarajevo, the capital of Bosnia-Herzegovina, became the site of the incident that detonated the First World War.

In the Turkish territories south of Serbia, the Macedonian Slavs inhabiting the valleys of the Vardar and Struma rivers spoke a language closely related to both Serbian and Bulgarian. During the greater part of the nineteenth century, Serbian efforts were concentrated on the national struggle, and within Turkish territory Macedonia became tied to Bulgaria by administrative and political bonds. The absence of a clearcut Macedonian nationality made this province a source of a bitter rivalry between Serbia and Bulgaria that greatly hampered the national movements of the two contestants in the generation before the First World War.

To the east of Serbia, the Bulgarian national renaissance was somewhat delayed by the greater tenacity of Ottoman rule. By the middle of the century the national movement was nevertheless fully developed in its literary and religious aspects, and in 1878 the Russian-Turkish war brought political independence. Unlike the Serbians, whose territory was expanded gradually through the century, the Bulgarians were given immediate hope of a full realization of their territorial aims when the Russians appeared able in the spring of 1878 to impose their will on Turkey. The revision of these initial peace terms a few months later, as a result of British and Austrian pressure, resulted in a greatly reduced Bulgaria and in a nationalist movement that was stimulated to an unusual degree by this frustration. Despite its preoccupation with territorial aggrandizement, the

Bulgarian government nevertheless made significant social and political progress in the years before the First World War.

The situation of the Rumanians was similar to that of the Serbians in that one part of their people lived under severe limitations within the Habsburg empire, while across the border in Turkey their co-nationals gained the substance of national independence by the middle of the century. The Rumanians in the Habsburg empire lived primarily under Hungarian rule after the compromise of 1867, and despite certain political concessions they never gained full national recognition. The vigorous struggle led by Vaida-Voevod and Maniu against political and cultural discrimination had a significant impact on the balance of forces within the empire but failed to achieve any concrete success before the First World War. The Rumanians in the Turkish provinces of Moldavia and Wallachia, adjacent to the Russian frontier and overlapping into the neighboring Russian province of Bessarabia, were able, because of this strategic position, to extract important concessions from the Ottoman government. By 1829 they attained autonomy under a Russian protectorate, and the Treaty of Paris in 1856 created the conditions under which they were to gain full independence within a generation. Like Serbia, this free Rumanian state was to exert a powerful attraction upon the discontented Rumanian minority within Austria-Hungary and eventually contributed to the disruption of the empire.

The Albanians fell under Turkish rule in the fifteenth century after the brief but heroic resistance of Skanderbeg, and during the period of Turkish rule they contributed many distinguished personalities to the Ottoman civil service as well as a dynasty to the Turkish province of Egypt. It was not until the neighboring Greeks and Serbians gained their independence and began to covet the lands of the Albanians that an active movement for national liberation developed

among the latter. At the same time the strategic position of
Albania with respect to the Adriatic made it an object of
imperial interest on the part of Austria-Hungary and Italy.
When the Albanian liberation movement got under way,
it thus had to guard against a variety of dangers, and finally
in 1912 during the Balkan wars it became the last state in
Europe to proclaim its independence from Turkish rule.

This rapid glance at the national movements in Eastern
Europe in the century before the First World War gives
particular attention to those peoples that achieved their
independence as a result of that conflict. At the same time,
important issues of political and religious rights that were
associated with the national movements but did not play an
equally important role in the political outcome of the First
World War have not been discussed. The Germans also
had significant national minorities in this region, but their
national movement took a different direction. The same
may be said of the Jewish minorities that played an important role in the lands inhabited by the Poles, Magyars,
and Rumanians. Their position, especially in Russian Poland, was frequently worse than that of other minorities,
and their liberation movement took the form of Zionism.
It is important to recognize that there were many influential groups in Eastern Europe that for one reason or another
preferred increased autonomy within the existing political
framework to complete liberation. Indeed, the peoples of
this region made important social and economic progress
in the century before the First World War, and when independence was won it soon became apparent that some of
the nations with the highest level of attainment were those
that had remained longest under alien rule.

Much has been said in criticism of the peace settlement
in Eastern Europe at the end of the First World War, but
it must be allowed that the principle of national self-
determination was applied with considerable consistency.

With certain notable exceptions involving injustice to new German, Magyar, and Ruthenian minorities, the boundaries were drawn about as close to linguistic frontiers as economic and geographic viability permitted. The trouble lay less with the peacemakers than with the principle of national self-determination, especially when applied without the two compensating factors stipulated in Wilson's program: free trade and international organization. The shortcomings of this un-Wilsonian settlement were serious, and cast a long shadow over the next generation. Central among these shortcomings was the exaggerated emphasis on the spirit of exclusive state nationalism, a natural but in the end disastrous consequence of the prolonged concern with national liberation. This spirit, in its postwar manifestations, became an obstacle to the solution of the many boundary disputes, raised protective trade barriers around the new states to the point of self-strangulation, and prevented the organization of a sound system of collective security.

II

Although the hope of the Eastern European leaders for the spiritual and material development of their peoples was placed increasingly in national liberation, it should not be forgotten that in the century after 1815 the peoples of this region made significant gains in the process of modernization. This process, considered as the expansion of human rights within a framework of increasing productivity and distribution in all branches of the economy, developed at an uneven rate in the different parts of Eastern Europe. In the broadest sense, modernization may be considered as the transition from a feudal and agrarian to a democratic and industrialized society, and in this region it involved certain characteristic steps. The most important of these steps were: the growth in human rights, of which the political were by far the most important; the increase of educational opportunities and general culture; and the development of the economy through agricultural improvement and the expansion of industry and trade.

Political freedom in Eastern Europe before the First World War ranged in degree from negligible rights, as those of the Slovaks in Hungary or of the Poles in Russia, to independent states with constitutions of strongly democratic tendencies, as in certain countries of Southeastern Europe. The latter had been influenced by Western models, and made provision for parliamentary government based on wide suffrage. The constitutions of Serbia, Rumania, and Bulgaria, drafted in the latter half of the nineteenth century by native statesmen experienced in the ways of Western constitutionalism, were founded on a genuine faith in democracy. It is true that royal or ministerial authoritarianism and resort to rough methods were not uncommon in these countries, yet the social egalitarianism already prevailing in Serbia and Bulgaria was a strong force for democracy in these countries. Although illiteracy and political inexperience remained a serious obstacle to orderly government, the generation before the First World War offers significant examples of governments being changed by orderly democratic procedures. Illustrative of the difficulties under which popular elections with universal male suffrage were conducted is the fact that in the Bulgarian election of 1880 only 32 per cent of those eligible to vote cast their ballots, in contrast to about 80 per cent in France and Belgium and 60 per cent in Germany and Italy in the period 1875-80.

Hungary had a longer tradition of constitutional government than did the Balkan states and after 1867 was in most respects an independent state, but its social structure was more conservative and its desire for political democracy less evident. Moreover, the Magyar achievement of political autonomy was marred by the oppressive treatment of the non-Magyar minorities. Thus in a parliament that as late as 1910 represented scarcely more than one quarter of the adult male population, the Magyars who numbered just over one half the population, apart from Croatia, had 405 seats to 8 for the Slovak and Rumanian minorities. The Croatians were represented by 40 deputies when mutual Croatian-Hungarian affairs were under discussion. The Czechs and the Poles in the Austrian provinces developed an aristocratic form of local self-government in the latter half of the nineteenth century and contributed distinguished statesmen to the Austrian government, and at least the Czechs gained experience in the techniques and responsibilities of democracy in local government and in unofficial organizations. Similarly in the Polish-inhabited lands of the German and Russian empires, little opportunity was available for gaining experience in electoral and parliamentary procedures.

Educational opportunities in Eastern Europe were steadily improved in the century after 1815 despite frequently hostile government attitudes. The greatest progress in this field was made in the Czech-inhabited provinces of the Habsburg monarchy, where general compulsory education was introduced in 1869. In Hungary popular education was started somewhat later, and illiteracy among the Magyars declined rapidly. The schools, however, were used as a vehicle for the Magyarization of the non-Magyar minorities of Hungary and, as a consequence, the great majority of Slovak and Rumanian children were compelled to get their education in the Magyar language. In Hungary, discounting Croatia, there were four times as many Magyar-language schools as non-Magyar and five times as many Magyar schoolteachers. The Slovenes under Austrian rule and the autonomous Croatians fared a great deal better, while in independent Montenegro, Serbia, Bulgaria, and Rumania, national school systems were developed insofar as meager resources permitted. The Poles fared differently in their three parts. In

Austrian Galicia they underwent a great cultural revival in the latter part of the nineteenth century, and this was the only area in which schools and universities using the Polish language could develop freely. The Polish population in Prussia lived under better educational conditions than did their co-nationals in Russia, but in both countries they were subjected to vigorous programs of denationalization.

The state of popular education in Eastern Europe is revealed by illiteracy figures for the years 1920-21, before the new independent states had exerted an influence on education. The rate of illiteracy for males and females of school age and over was 7 per cent for Czechoslovakia, 15 per cent for Hungary, and between 30 and 40 per cent for Poland and Yugoslavia. The rate was between 40 and 50 per cent for Rumania and Bulgaria, and in Albania it was much higher. These figures may be compared with illiteracy rates of under 1 per cent for Great Britain and Germany, 6 per cent for the United States, and about 50 per cent for Russia.

It is worth noting that the low level of literacy in most of Eastern Europe did not prevent the development of a high level of culture among educated persons. The universities of Prague, Cracow, and Budapest were the most distinguished among many of high level, and very significant contributions to European culture in the arts and sciences came from this region. The "intelligentsia," as those with higher education and professional skills were referred to, provided both the leadership of the national movements and the statesmen of the nations born at the end of the First World War. As individuals they were the equals of the political leaders of the great powers and included in their number many great Europeans.

Agricultural improvement, or the increase in productivity and in the welfare of the population dependent on agriculture, is a complex process. In Eastern Europe, it involved in particular the release of the peasants from feudal

servitude, the adoption of improved techniques of agricultural production and marketing, and the improvement of
the lot of the individual peasant through land reform and
the combined efforts of the landlords and the state. Most of
European Turkey had never known feudalism in the Western sense, and the peasants of Serbia and Bulgaria emerged
early as independent landowners with a sound understanding of their own interests. In many areas of Rumania,
Austria-Hungary, and the Polish sections of Germany and
Russia, however, the peasants were freed from feudal restrictions only to sink into a deeper misery, sometimes called
"neo-serfdom," that stemmed from lack of capital and the
resultant economic dependency on the landlords. As a consequence, while independent peasant political parties began to develop among the Czechs and southern Slavs shortly
after the turn of the century, the peasants in Russia in 1905
and in Rumania in 1907 resorted to the desperate method
of revolution.

The agrarian backwardness that characterized the greater
part of Eastern Europe was a great challenge to social and
political philosophers, and it was not surprising that the
First World War left in its wake attempts at radical solutions by leaders acting in the name of the proletariat or the
peasantry. The recommendation of the economists, in the
presence of this agrarian poverty and overpopulation, was
that agricultural improvement be accompanied by the extension of industry and trade. In the areas where large landowners exercised full political control, this recommendation
was not welcomed as the landowners tended to favor fiscal
policies that kept the price of grain high and the peasant
poor. In other areas, however, important industrial development took place. Thus, the Austrian provinces of Bohemia
and Moravia, with their preponderant Czech population,
accounted for a little over one half the entire industrial output of Austria-Hungary. This production included coal and

iron as well as consumer goods and benefited by the large market that the empire provided. Significant industrial development also took place in Hungary and in other parts of the empire. Similarly, in Russian Poland important industries were developed, but these suffered from the discriminatory policy of the Russian government and from the lack of communications.

Capital for the economic development of this region came chiefly from France until the 1890's, when German and Austrian capital became increasingly active. In Eastern Europe in general, and particularly in the Balkans, loans had as much a political as an economic incentive. Since the credit of Serbia, Bulgaria, and Rumania was poor, the bondholders were able to insist on a variety of controls to assure payment. Although a substantial amount of this capital was used to finance armament and eventually wars, investments of permanent value were also made. Notable among these was the railroad from Vienna to Constantinople, completed in 1888, which with its branches formed the backbone of the transportation system of Southeastern Europe.

III

Collective security and economic interdependence, as these terms are understood today, were certainly among the motives of the various plans for regional organization proposed for Eastern Europe in the century before the First World War. Yet the nineteenth century was for Europe an age in which war was the exception rather than the rule and national frontiers were not the barriers to trade and to the movements of peoples that they have since become. Although motives of power politics in the modern sense were always present, regionalism in this era was also concerned with the reconciliation of national differences through federal arrangements and with the broader cultural relationships of peoples with a common linguistic heritage. The most readily identifiable of these proposals are those associated with the Panslav movement, the plans for the reorganization of the Habsburg empire, and the federation schemes of the independent Danubian states. None of these projects embraced the entire region of Eastern Europe as it is understood today, but all were inspired by ideas relevant to the problems faced by this region in the twentieth century.

The many-sided Panslav movement in its modern form can be traced to the new interest in Slavic history and languages shown by German scholars at the end of the eighteenth century. A realization of their cultural heritage was soon aroused among Slavic intellectual leaders, and it exerted a powerful stimulus to nationalism among the Poles, Czechs, and Croatians. Certain Polish thinkers in the first hopeful years after the settlement of 1815 favored Polish-Russian cooperation as a basis for Slavic unity, but in a few decades the Poles were seeking the aid of their fellow Slavs in the West against Russian oppression. The map and statistics of Slavic peoples published by the Slovak scholar, Šafařik, in 1842 were widely greeted as a revelation of Slavic strength, and in the revolutionary year of 1848 a congress was held in Prague to rally the peoples of the Slavic world. This rather haphazard gathering revealed the political weakness of Panslavism, but it produced some noble statements of individual and national rights and strengthened the self-confidence of the Slavic peoples as to their contribution to European civilization. In publicizing the views of the non-Russian Slavic leaders at the height of their liberal phase, the congress thus served a purpose. Although Slavic nationalism took precedence over liberalism in the latter half of the century, the ideas expounded at Prague in 1848 were never entirely forgotten.

Much more was heard about Panslavism between 1848 and 1914, but during this period it was used primarily as a weapon of Russian expansionism. The Slavic movement evolved in Russia early in the century under the name of Slavophilism and, with the founding of a Slavic committee in Moscow in 1857, it entered a Panslav phase. In 1867 non-Russian Slavs were summoned to a congress in Moscow in connection with a Slav ethnographic exhibition, and at this meeting it was not difficult to discern the expansionist tendencies of Russian Panslavism. During the Russian-Turkish war of 1876-78, this movement developed into an outburst of emotional imperialism, and much was said of bringing all Slavs together under Russian rule. European power politics prevented an undue extension of Russian influence in 1878, but Panslavism came to serve Russian policy and was directed increasingly against the Habsburg empire. This trend was particularly evident at the third Panslav Congress held in Prague in 1908. Although the Russian constitutional reforms of 1905-06 made a favorable impression on non-Russian Slavs and brought about some real concessions to the Polish minority, Russian foreign policy never gave up the idea of pushing the Russian frontier to the West. Had the Tsarist regime survived the First World War it would certainly have demanded that large parts of Eastern Europe be annexed or brought into a satellite relationship, and a liberal Russian government might also have favored the Westward expansion of Russian influence.

The multinational empire of the Habsburgs offered the most challenging problem to the federalists, and the proposals for its constitutional reorganization were varied and ingenious. Of the many ideas arising out of the revolution of 1848, the most comprehensive was the constitution drafted by the freely elected Austrian assembly. After this assembly was transferred from revolutionary Vienna in October 1848, it met for four months in the Moravian town of Kremsier and drafted a federal constitution that had the twin virtues of coming from a free assembly and of granting equality to all national groups in the empire. Under this scheme thirty-nine nationally homogeneous districts (*Kreise*) were to be created within the existing crownlands of Austria. The lower chamber of a bicameral parliament was to be elected by universal male suffrage, thus guaranteeing to the different nationalities a voice in national affairs, and the individual districts were to have extensive rights or local self-government. The Kremsier assembly was dissolved before the draft constitution was formally adopted, but many students believe it plotted a course that might have saved the empire had the Germans become reconciled to the fact of their numerical minority.

Two decades of experimentation with various forms of centralism failed to strengthen the empire and, with the Austro-Hungarian compromise of 1867 and the agreement between Hungary and Croatia in the following year, a new era of federalism was inaugurated. The balance established within the empire in 1867, though modified by concessions to the Poles and Czechs in Austria, favored the Magyars to a point that the Slav and Rumanian minorities could not tolerate permanently. In the face of Magyar resistance, constitutional amendment was not practicable before the defeat of the empire in 1918, but many proposals for reform were put forward. The Austrian Social Democrats, for instance, adopted a program in 1899 that called for creation within the empire of autonomous and nationally homogeneous territories with extensive rights of self-government. Nevertheless, their own party split into its several national components before 1914. Other proposals called for the division of the empire into as few as three and as many as fifteen federated states, and many hoped that re-organization along such lines would draw towards the empire the Slav and Rumanian peoples on its periphery and thus strengthen its international position. None of these proposals had a serious chance of success, however, and when the empire was finally defeated it disintegrated into its national units.

The independent states of Southeastern Europe faced problems that were different from those of the Habsburg lands, and their alliance and federation schemes were designed to meet the realities of power politics. Once the grandiose plans of the 1848er's had been forgotten, one of these being a proposal for a federation stretching from Poland to Serbia, new schemes were developed around the vigorous Serbian ruler Prince Michael Obrenović. Several agreements were concluded in the 1860's among the Serbian, Montenegrin, Rumanian, Bulgarian, and Greek national leaders with the aid of Russian diplomacy, but these efforts were soon overshadowed by the Russian-Turkish conflict. In the long run, the territorial rivalries among the Balkan states proved to be the principal obstacle to their cooperation, and even the successful Balkan Alliance that defeated Turkey in 1912 disintegrated within a year into interallied war. What is significant is that the initiative throughout this period lay with the great powers, and the federation and alliance plans that got beyond the drafting stage were in general those backed by Russia or Austria-Hungary. The principal reality in international relations was the search for security on the part of these two powers that drove them to regard expansion into Southeastern Europe as a guarantee against political humiliation and military defeat. However, the balance was too close for either to succeed in this game, and it was left to a world conflict to clear the stage for a new order.

IV

This brief review of certain key problems of Eastern Europe in the century before the First World War raises many issues familiar to students of current history. If the problem of national liberation was substantially solved by 1920, the solution created about as many difficulties as it settled. The development of events since the First World War demonstrates clearly that nationalism in itself, despite the liberal and idealistic intentions that originally inspired it, has offered only a limited solution to the problems of this region. Much of what it contributed in culture, education, and self-confidence, it took away in international distrust and in self-defeating particularism.

After the First World War economic nationalism, which existed in considerable measure, offset such gains as had resulted from the casting off of the old restrictions. It may be asked whether a good many of the countries of this region could not have prospered better under the old political framework and, in some cases, even whether they have been as well off as they were before the war. Moreover, if one compares the decades of strife since the war with the century of relative peace that preceded it, one is tempted to ask whether the great effort to reorganize Eastern Europe on a national basis did not in fact retard the process of modernization and jeopardize the regional security of these peoples.

Yet it would be a mistake to conclude from these difficulties that a solution attempted along entirely different lines would have met with success. Since the ruling dynasties refused to grant political rights to their minorities, the struggle for national self-determination was an essential step in the process of transition from a relatively simple agrarian society to one that offered the great opportunities and high standards of European civilization. The program suggested by Wilson in 1918 provided for national self-determination together with free trade and international organization. The program that was actually implemented ignored the latter two provisions and must indeed be considered a failure of liberal leadership.

This failure, so apparent when the Nazis overran Eastern Europe after 1938, led many persons to believe that Communism offered a simpler and sounder solution to the problems of this region. They envisaged an agricultural system organized in collective farms, an industry stimulated annually by large state investments wisely allocated, a distribution of commodities justly administered on the basis of work and need, and a regional organization of states based on the good will of brotherly comrades and administered by the wisdom of the big brother in the East. This program has now been implemented, and it has exhibited many shortcomings. It may indeed have succeeded in increasing industrial production, especially in products required for the Soviet economy, but the costs of this accomplishment in living standards and in political freedom have been exorbitant. The Communist regimes have returned the peoples of this region to a system of imperial exploitation much harsher than anything they knew before the First World War, and have brought them regional security only at the price of slavery.

The challenge faced by Eastern European leaders today is to reconstruct for this region a liberal and democratic program that will avoid the mistakes of the past and place emphasis on the freedom and opportunities of the individual rather than on the exclusive security of the national state. It is a sad fact that today consideration of such a program plays so small a part in the work of the national committees formed by exiled statesmen from Eastern Europe and in the official and unofficial broadcasts beamed to the peoples of this region. The reorganization of land tenure and the improvement of agricultural methods; the development of industry along lines best suited to available raw materials and markets; the reduction of the barriers that now exist to the movement of trade, peoples, and ideas; the recasting of political institutions along lines as democratic as is justified by the political maturity of the various countries; and, perhaps most important of all, the creation of supranational organs of government within the region or within Europe as a whole—these and related problems are given little consideration today by those who claim to be interested in the welfare of this region. The future of Eastern Europe lies not with the strong and vociferous but with those, whether at home or abroad, who can formulate the wisest answers to the complex challenge of this region.

2 The Liberal Tradition

HUBERT RIPKA

This essay will endeavor to show that liberalism has its own tradition in the countries of Eastern Europe and that the liberal regimes set up in this area succumbed not so much to internal factors as to the unfavorable international situation. In other words, the development of liberalism in this region between the two world wars was a part of the course of liberal democracy in Europe as a whole.

I

It is necessary first to define liberalism. This force will not be interpreted here as a political ideology of certain political parties or social classes. Although, historically speaking, liberalism has been identified most often with the so-called middle classes, its ideology has a far wider basis. It aims above and beyond the demands of one social class to a political and social order of all society which is based on liberty, equality, and the reign of law. It is in this sense that liberalism will be dealt with in this essay.

It would be impossible to understand the liberalism of any one country if it were discussed only in terms of the political parties which profess liberalism or which, more precisely, adopt only those elements of liberalism which further their own political aims. Regarded in this light, England, where the Liberal Party is the weakest among the principal political parties, would not be a liberal country. Similarly, in France, Italy, and Belgium, liberalism has not been limited to the so-called liberal parties. The situation was the same in the countries of Eastern Europe.

In Czechoslovakia there were only two liberal parties (the National Democrats and the National Socialists), but liberal ideology greatly influenced the Agrarian Party, the Social Democrats and, to a large extent, the Czech Catholics. In Poland, the National Democratic Party was, at first, the only party to accept any of the liberal principles (it endorsed particularly economic liberalism), but the Polish Agrarian and Socialist parties were influenced strongly by liberalism. In Hungary, the Liberal Party was small and without any influence. A similar situation prevailed in Bulgaria, but liberal aspirations for greater freedom and for more civil rights were not limited to members of the Liberal Party. In Rumania, the Liberal Party was very strong, but it was hardly more "liberal" than Maniu's National Peasant Party. In Yugoslavia, the Radicals and the Democrats who found their support chiefly among the Serbians and the Slovene liberals stood for certain principles of political and economic liberalism, but it is a recognized fact that the Croatian and Serbian Agrarians, as well as the Radicals and the Democrats, fought in the name of liberal democracy against dictatorship. In Bulgaria, the Agrarians of Stambolisky represented a party devoted to democratic principles.

The position and influence of liberalism in Eastern Europe is best illustrated by T. G. Masaryk. His own political party was numerically insignificant but Masaryk, as the most prominent liberal in this region, influenced not only the

Czechs and the Slovaks, but also neighboring peoples, particularly the Yugoslavs. A large proportion of the Croatian, Serbian, and Slovene politicians from the Yugoslav provinces that had formerly formed a part of Austria-Hungary were educated before the First World War in the school of Masaryk's liberal thought. Among these men was Stjepan Radić, who later was to become leader of the Croatian Peasant Party.

Liberalism in Eastern Europe, and this is true for other countries as well, cannot be identified only with the so-called middle classes or with supporters of the free enterprise system. The middle classes, with the exception of those in Czechoslovakia and Austria, were not numerically or economically strong or influential. The capitalistic economic order was strongly defended, not only by the liberals, but by pronounced conservatives among whom were those who began to support authoritarian regimes in the 'thirties. The peasants, insofar as they did not adhere politically to parties of the conservative right, were usually very devoted and often even radical supporters of democracy. Similarly, a great number of socialistically oriented workers and intelligentsia, in supporting political democracy, were influenced by ideas of liberalism. Many liberals, usually those belonging to the intelligentsia, were sympathetic to socialistic tendencies. This socialistically-minded liberalism, which had its counterpart in France among the Radical Socialists or the so-called "Independent" Socialists, and in Britain among the British Fabians, was best represented in Czechoslovakia by T. G. Masaryk and his disciple, Eduard Beneš. Both men, although they rejected Marxism, accepted many ideas of the socialistic school of thought. This liberal socialistic orientation was the basis of the Czechoslovakian party of National Socialists whose adherents were chiefly recruited from the small bourgeoisie, the intelligentsia, and the workers. The National Socialists endeavored to combine liberalism with socialism, in the belief that political democracy should be accompanied by "economic democracy."

The importance and influence of liberalism in this region did not, therefore, rest with any particular political parties or social groupings which gave themselves the liberal label or which explicitly professed liberal principles. The influence of liberalism lay in the force of the liberal ideology which exercised influence on the whole national community.

It is often held today, due to the conception of liberalism held in Anglo-Saxon countries and, to some extent, in other countries of Western Europe, that the influence of liberalism in the Eastern European countries was not of great importance. This is accounted for by a theory that the so-called middle classes were weak and that the popular masses, predominantly peasant, had a low social and cultural standing. Czechoslovakia is cited as an example to support this analysis. It is said that Czechoslovakia was able to maintain her democracy because she had an influential and prosperous middle class and because the cultural level of her population was approximately the same as the cultural level of the West. There is no doubt that a weak middle class and a low social standard among the popular masses were serious handicaps to the development of liberal democracy in the agricultural countries of this region. Liberal democracy required, from the social and economic points of view, not uniformity and equalization, but a diversified and well-balanced social structure and an economy with a fair degree of balance between industry and agriculture. Above all, liberal democracy required the "liberal spirit," a combination of a desire for freedom, a devotion to political and social rights, and an eagerness for justice. The existence of liberal democracy, therefore, cannot be defined in terms of social and economic requirements alone.

In support of this premise, several examples can be cited. Before the First World War, in the small Serbia of King

Peter I, there was much more freedom, in spite of the social and cultural backwardness of the people, than there had been under the dictatorship of the Crown in the '30's when the economic and social level of the country was much higher than in prewar years. It is sufficient to compare the liberal Radical, Nikola Pašić, with the unprincipled opportunist Milan Stojadinović (whom Ciano praised as a "true fascist") to realize that the betterment of economic conditions did not prevent the disintegration of democracy in Yugoslavia. Between the two world wars, Poland progressed economically and made great strides in industrialization, yet from 1926 on she was subjected to the semidictatorship of Pilsudski.

In Hungary, after the First World War, the economic situation was not much better than it was in Austria. Yet, in spite of both this and the reactionary regime of Admiral Horthy in Budapest, some vestiges of liberalism survived even the Second World War. In Austria, in spite of the substantial influence exercised in Vienna by the Social Democrats and by the liberal bourgeoisie, a semidictatorial regime was installed in 1934. Germany's economic and social structure was more advanced than that of Czechoslovakia. The grave economic crisis of the '30's caused wide unemployment in both these countries, yet the small Czechoslovakian Republic remained faithful to liberal democracy until she fell before Nazi aggression, while in Germany Hitler was already in power in 1933.

These examples are surely sufficient to show that the strength or weakness of liberalism in Eastern Europe did not depend solely, or even mostly, upon economic and social conditions. These were certainly very important factors, but of more importance were the psychological climate and the political tradition within each individual nation. Czechoslovakia remained democratic until her fall because, ever since the Hussite revolution in the fifteenth century, the substantial majority of both Czechs and Slovaks had been "liberal-minded" even if they had not expressed this through formal Liberal parties. In Hungary, there was a long tradition of liberalism which had been inspired by the Golden Bull of 1222 and which, in the penetrating words of the British historian, Hugh Seton-Watson, maintained "within the Hungarian ruling class . . . a kind of Whiggish liberalism which permitted a measure of intellectual freedom." This explains why Hungary was able to preserve some, if not all, of her parliamentary formalities. On the other hand, in Poland and, to a great extent, in the Balkan countries, the tradition of nationalism pushed liberal tendencies into the background. Austria, whose desire for independence was not sufficiently strong, became a victim of strong pressures exercised by both her fascist neighbors.

In addition to special political conditions in the individual Eastern European countries, international influences and a combination of outside forces greatly affected the development of liberalism in this region. It should be remembered that the prospects for liberalism were favorable only as long as Western democracies exercised leadership in Europe and that the decline of liberalism was in direct proportion to the rise of fascism in certain important European countries. The decline of liberal democracy in Eastern Europe was, therefore, a reflection of the general crisis of liberalism in the whole of Europe.

II

Liberalism in Eastern Europe was related, historically and ideologically, to liberalism in the West, although each had developed certain distinctive features.

The liberals of Eastern Europe, like those of the West, saw as the fulfillment of the political ideals of liberalism a democratic regime based on free elections and on the principle of checks and balances whose purpose is to keep the government under the control of parliament and of the free electorate. They hoped for a regime which would guarantee all the classical civil rights and which would preserve the independence of the courts. To achieve this, these liberals, regardless of political party, fought against authoritarian tendencies and dictatorial regimes.

Liberals in Eastern Europe, unlike those in the West, were not ardent supporters of the type of economic liberalism that is based on competition in a free market and admits only the least degree of state control. These liberals had in common with the supporters of the capitalist system a belief in the economic and social advantages of the principle of private ownership, but only a few among them had a clear-cut conception of the free enterprise system with its economic and social consequences, as it is accepted in the United States or in other Western countries. This difference of conception between Western and Eastern European liberals can be explained easily. In Eastern Europe, modern capitalistic enterprises (in this area predominantly agricultural), and particularly large-sized enterprises, were in an early stage of development. They were somewhat further developed in Czechoslovakia and Austria, and in the '30's began to attain some stature in Poland and Hungary. Under these circumstances and in the face of the limited resources of individual private entrepreneurs, it is understandable that the Eastern European liberals, desiring the industrialization of their countries, sought state support. They asked protection from the state in the form of high customs tariffs, financial subsidies, and currency, credit, and other protective measures. Thus, from an economic point of view, they were influenced far more by the German than by the Western European attitude. German liberalism, guided by the protectionist theories of G. F. List and by Bismarckian power politics, definitely favored building capitalism with the direct and permanent assistance of the state.

Contrary to many Germans, Eastern European liberals remained true to political democracy but, in the field of economic policy, they were in accord with German views, giving preference to state interference and support rather than to free competition and individual initiative.

Differences in the economic development of Western Europe and the United States, on the one hand, and of Germany and Eastern Europe, on the other hand, influenced the thinking of socialists in these countries and account for the differences in their outlook and their method of political action. While Western socialists sought to realize their aims by their own concerted self-help action (in Anglo-Saxon countries and Scandinavia particularly through trade unionism and political influence exercised in parliaments, in Latin countries either through revolution or political infiltration of public institutions), German and Eastern European socialists tended more and more towards economic and political statism. Moreover, the agrarians of Eastern Europe, like the liberals, socialists, and Christian (Catholic) Democrats, also asked for state action to further their economic and social aims. This tendency to look towards the state for aid in economic matters explains why many liberals, particularly in Czechoslovakia, favored vast social reforms benefiting the working class. It is also worth mentioning that the representatives of the liberal-minded bourgeoisie in Czechoslovakia were always in favor of the highly progressive social legislation enacted in that country.

The tendency to ask the state for support in economic matters was a characteristic of the nationalism of Eastern European liberals. On the whole, however, the nationalism of liberals and of many others in this region was no more intense than the nationalism of similar groups in any of the Western countries, and among the liberals themselves there were great differences in interpreting liberalism.

In Eastern Europe, liberalism was more closely connected

with nationalism than it was in the West. This can be attributed chiefly to the fact that beginning with the nineteenth century national liberation found most of its protagonists and representatives among the liberal-minded intellectuals and statesmen. Consequently, almost all the liberals of this region appear as "national liberals." The fusing of liberalism and nationalism continued even after the First World War, chiefly because the Eastern European nations felt that they were endangered by the imperialistic designs of Germany, Italy, and Russia. The nations of this region, faced with such a danger, sought the protection of one or another of the European powers.

The historical development of these nations from the nineteenth century on, their geographic location, their special interests and dissimilar historical traditions—all these factors were instrumental in the growth of nationalism, an intense power which greatly influenced all the contemporary political trends (liberal, socialistic, agrarian, Catholic, etc.). Although nationalism impeded efforts for closer cooperation between the Eastern European nations, it proved to be a powerful force against both Nazi and Soviet imperialism.

It would be a mistake to assume that all Eastern European nationalism was chauvinistic. In this region, as elsewhere, there were two schools of nationalism: one of liberal, tolerant, internationally-minded patriotism; the other, of overbearing, aggressive chauvinism, or provincially limited nationalism. Western influence was predominant in the first trend; German and, to some extent, Russian in the second.

The Eastern European liberals, like the other political groups, were divided between these two trends. As a striking example, one can cite the ideological and political differences between two Czechoslovakian liberals: Thomas G. Masaryk and Karel Kramář. Masaryk, who of all the Eastern Europeans was the most deeply imbued with Western liberalism, was opposed from the start to chauvinistic nationalism. All his life he advocated and pursued, to use his own expression, "European and world politics." He attempted to reach an agreement with Germany as to the problem of the German minority within Czechoslovakia and to solve other nationality problems to the satisfaction of all. He hoped that Czechoslovakia would become another Switzerland.

Kramář, on the other hand, linked Czechoslovakian national interests with Tsarist Russia. He persistently defended the concept of Czechoslovakia as a "national state" in which the Czechoslovakians would be the leading people and minorities would be delegated to a secondary position. His policy was openly anti-German. He envisaged, in the terms of romantic Pan-Slavism, a great Slav federation headed by a "democratic Russia." Viewing the League of Nations and all international institutions with skepticism, he warned the nation to rely on its own strength. Basically, Kramář's theories were defensive. In practice, they would have served as protection against German imperialism.

A similar difference existed in Rumania between the Bratianu brothers, the leaders of the Liberal Party, and Titulescu, the famous Rumanian Minister of Foreign Affairs. Titulescu did not belong to any political party, but his philosophy was definitely liberal. Politically, the Bratianu brothers were liberals in the sense that they defended parliamentary freedom against constitutional monarchy and opposed autocratic ambitions of the prince, later King Carol. Economically, they linked liberalism with the interests of the commercial and banking class. They strove to industrialize the country but, at the same time, they barred foreign capital. In this regard, their economic nationalism was most apparent.

Titulescu, unlike the Bratianu brothers, combined his

genuine patriotism with sincere internationalism. He was an ardent supporter of the League of Nations. He advocated the principle of collective security. He tried to establish better relations with Soviet Russia. It was he who coined the phrase, "the spiritualization of boundaries." However, he was unable to win sufficient following in the ruling circles, and King Carol, who opposed his broad-minded policy, forced him to resign in 1936.

Poland serves as a clear example of the dominance of nationalism over other political and social trends. In the nineteenth century liberalism attracted many of the Poles who were living in exile, especially those in France. Polish liberals worked enthusiastically with Mazzini in the "Young Europe" movement, and many of them took part unselfishly in the revolution of 1848. However, the great national struggle for the liberation and unification of Poland came to assume first place in the interests of all Polish patriots. Roman Dmowski, a prominent Polish statesman, had been devoted to the principles of liberalism in his youth but, during the national political struggle, he became a passionate nationalist of very conservative leanings. After the re-establishment of Polish independence, liberalism strongly influenced certain small Polish groups, for instance the Democratic and Labor Parties. In the latter, the Catholic influence was strongly felt. Ignace Paderewski, the famous pianist, who contributed greatly to the liberation of Poland in the First World War, belonged to the liberals.

The absence of a pronounced liberal trend and tradition in Poland was undoubtedly one of the reasons why Polish democracy, despite the liberal constitution of 1921, succumbed to the nationalistic pressure of Marshal Pilsudski, who established a semidictatorial regime in 1926 which lasted until the fall of Poland in 1939. The principal defenders of Polish democracy were the Agrarian Party, the Socialists, and the Christian Democrats. Naturally, nationalism was strong even in these parties. It must be remembered that even the ardor of Polish Catholicism had its roots in Polish nationalism: Catholicism was a defense against the Eastern Orthodox Russians as well as against the Protestant Prussians.

The Polish National Democratic Party, which represented the middle class and the intelligentsia, became chauvinistic and violently antisemitic in spite of its original liberal aspirations. It fought against Pilsudski's dictatorship more for reasons of power politics than for ideological reasons. From 1930 on, this party inclined, and especially its younger members, more and more towards fascism. Nationalism suppressed the liberal elements of this party almost entirely.

In Poland, where nationalism was more extreme than in the other Eastern European countries, liberalism was limited mostly to certain intellectual groups. One important group had its headquarters at the University of Cracow, with Professor Estreicher as its leader. Liberalism influenced the agrarians and socialists of Poland inasmuch as these groups much preferred democracy to dictatorship.

The case of Poland brings to mind very forcibly a factor which as a rule is not given its due: that is, the dependence of the nations of Eastern Europe upon the other nations of Europe and the rest of the world. The freedom of these nations is dependent on the freedom of all other European nations, including Russia.

It can be said, therefore, that liberalism can prosper in these countries only if the climate of Europe is favorable. As soon as a regime of any of the big powers on the European continent tends towards aggressive expansionism or becomes totalitarian, by definition imperialistic, the liberty of all European nations, great and small, is threatened, and liberalism finds itself in mortal danger.

History clearly proves the accuracy of this analysis. In

the second half of the nineteenth century, a "liberal" climate prevailed in Europe. At that time liberalism penetrated even into Tsarist Russia. The belief that Russia has an inherent tendency toward despotism and slavery leads one to forget that liberal ideas found excellent propagandists and defenders there; to mention but a few: Radishchev, Pestel, Herzen, Soloviev, Milyukov, Chernov, and the Decembrists. In the nineteenth century, liberal tendencies were growing in strength and influence in Eastern Europe and contributed considerably to the struggle for national liberation. The victory of the liberal Western democracies in 1918 led to the liberal democratization of almost all Eastern Europe.

III

The obstacles faced by liberalism in Eastern Europe included both the threat of Communist, and later of fascist and Nazi, interference and the efforts of domestic authoritarian groups that saw in dictatorship the answer to the problems of this region. In spite of these highly unfavorable circumstances, democratic liberalism maintained itself even when dictatorial governments were formed. A courageous opposition fought these regimes without fearing the persecution to which it was exposed. It is easy to prove that Pilsudski and, later, Beck in Poland, Horthy in Hungary, Carol in Rumania, Boris in Bulgaria, Alexander and Paul in Yugoslavia, and Dolfuss and Schuschnigg in Austria, were opposed by democratic forces stronger than, or at least as strong as, the forces which Hitler, Mussolini, and Stalin were meeting in their respective countries. In Germany and Russia and, to a large extent, in Italy, the dictatorial regimes were totalitarian and therefore opposition was almost impossible. But the fact that in Eastern Europe only limited dictatorships were established shows that antiliberal, antidemocratic trends were hampered by the opposition of democratic forces. In this great struggle, many liberals, especially in Yugoslavia, Rumania, and Austria, were lured into the services of dictatorial regimes, and thus doomed themselves to failure.

It would be unjust to discount the actions of either Constantin Bratianu or Titulescu because of the opportunist Tatarescu who placed himself at the disposal of King Carol, or to forget the courageous Ion Duca who, for his uncompromising liberal principles, was assassinated in 1933 by the fascist terrorists of the Iron Guard. In Yugoslavia, there were a number of radicals and democrats enlisted in the service of the royal dictatorship. They thus distinctly deviated from the radical democratic tradition which, especially before the First World War, was represented by Nikola Pašić, famous for his revolutionary struggle against the dictatorial desires of the Obrenović rulers. Pašić was influenced not only by Western liberalism, in which the democratic Serbian King Peter I was educated, but by the revolutionism of the Russian Populists. The influence of the Russian revolutionaries was also strong in Bulgaria, especially in her agrarian movement. For some of those who associated with King Alexander's dictatorship, Foreign Minister Marinković for instance, there may have been extenuating circumstances, for those men were led by fear of the decomposition of Yugoslavia.

Nevertheless, as in Rumania, some earnest liberals in Yugoslavia courageously opposed the royal dictatorship. Because of Stoyadinović, who put a shame on the liberal tradition of the Radical Party, one must not forget Aca Stanojević, a friend of Pašić, or Miša Trifunović who did not fear imprisonment and refused any collaboration with the dictatorship. In the opposition remained also Slobodan Jovanović, an influential professor of Belgrade University, who in the Second World War became the Premier of the Yugoslavian government in London. Against the royal dictatorship were also leaders of the Democratic Party: Ljuba

Davidović and Božidar Vlajić among the Serbians, Večeslav Vilder, a disciple of Masaryk, among the Croatians, and Milan Grol among the Slovenes. The famous Svetozar Pribičević distinguished himself for his courageous opposition to the Alexander dictatorship; he may be counted justly among the founders of Yugoslavia. He also was under Masaryk's influence, and it was through Masaryk's personal intervention with King Alexander that the interned Pribičević was allowed to go into exile. Pribičević gave an example to many others by repudiating his devotion to the Karadjordjević dynasty and becoming a radical republican. The royal dictatorship was opposed also by the Croatian Peasant Party, headed by Vladko Maček, and by the Serbian Agrarian Party, headed by Dragoljub Jovanović. The democratic opposition to the royal dictatorship has been cited in order to point out that when Titoist communism calls itself an "organic" result of the Yugoslav internal development, it does not make any allowance for the strong liberal tradition of Yugoslavia. In Hungary, C. Rassay was the most distinguished defender of liberalism.

The Bulgarian liberals played a prominent role in their country before the First World War but, in compromising with King Ferdinand, they were partly responsible for the unfortunate policies that led to the defeat of 1918. In the period between the two wars they were pushed into the background by nationalists and reactionaries such as Tsankov. Nevertheless, some Bulgarian liberals tried to preserve their own tradition. In 1924 Genadiev paid for his courageous devotion to liberal ideas with his life. Through the efforts of Malinov and Mušanov, the democratic regime was resumed at the beginning of the 'thirties, but the military *coup d'état* in 1934 installed a "progressive dictatorship." King Boris took advantage of this in order to establish his own dictatorship. The opposition of the liberals to this dictatorship was weak in comparison with that of the Agrarian Party which still followed Stambolisky's tradition.

The Agrarian and the Socialist parties and some Catholics, as well as the liberals, carried on the struggle against dictatorship in Bulgaria, Rumania, Poland, and Hungary. They fought for real democracy in the sense of the best liberal tradition. In Austria the Social Democrats were the main force opposing clerical fascism. It is interesting that in Hungary the conservative aristocrats opposed fascist trends. Szálasi, who led the important Arrow-Cross movement, was the most conspicuous of these men. Count Bethlen and Count Teleki also opposed the Nazi pressure, and the latter's efforts were climaxed by his symbolic suicide in 1941.

The opposition to dictatorship and to fascism or Nazism was motivated differently in the individual Eastern European countries and was carried on by different political parties. Notwithstanding these differences, the original inspiration to opposition lay in two main ideas: a longing for freedom and a patriotic devotion to national independence. Pure democratic liberalism is the expression of these two ideas, both of which prove convincingly that the love of freedom was deeply rooted in these countries. Internal antiliberal forces alone would not have been able to crush democratic aspirations. Whenever the elections were more liberal than usual, for instance, in Rumania in 1928 or in Bulgaria in 1931, the democratic parties won. In Poland, Pilsudski's followers, who represented only a small minority of the nation, were well aware that the only means by which they could maintain their regime was political terror. In spite of the pressure of the reactionaries and the influence of fascists and Nazis, the remnants of liberalism in Hungary survived until nearly the end of the Second World War. In view of these facts, it is clear that the liberal democratic forces could have mastered internal difficulties successfully had they not been broken or dangerously weakened by the foreign forces of fascism and Communism.

Czechoslovakia bears witness to this thesis. In Czechoslovakia, as in the other countries, there existed antiliberal, reactionary, nationalist, and fascist trends which attracted certain of the bourgeoisie and rich farmers. These forces were held in check by the democratic thought and genuine patriotism of a great majority of the nation, including the so-called middle classes and the intelligentsia. Nearly everybody followed the principles of the great democrat, Masaryk. Conditions were more favorable to democratic liberalism in Czechoslovakia than in the other Eastern European countries, because this nation was highly industrialized, even in agriculture, because her social structure was happily balanced between industry, agriculture, and bureaucracy, or intelligentsia, and because the cultural level of her people was high. The middle classes, strong in numbers and in social value, and the progressive farmers, who owned middle-sized farms, were reliable support for the liberal democratic regime. The Social Democratic Party, headed by Hampl, Bechyně, Meissner, and Dérer, was influenced spiritually far more by Masaryk than by Marx. The Agrarian Party had liberal-minded leaders among whom Antonín Švehla and Milan Hodža proved to have statesmen's abilities. The Catholic Party, under the wise leadership of the great patriot Jan Šrámek, was progressive in social matters. In Slovakia the process of democratization met with greater difficulties. Slovakia, because of its agrarian structure, resembled the other Eastern European countries more than it did the industrialized Bohemia. However, the transformation of Slovakia into a democratically functioning part of Czechoslovakia proves that other Eastern European countries could have developed in a similar way had democracy been given enough time to exercise its influence upon them.

It is certainly to the credit of Czechoslovakia that she

continually improved her democratic regime during the twenty years of her existence and that her democracy was destroyed only by an attack from without by Nazi Germany. Nevertheless, the other countries of Eastern Europe, economically, socially, and culturally less progressive, cannot be blamed if, in the antiliberal climate of the '30's, they were unable to develop into genuine democracies. The people in these countries did not long less for freedom and for social progress than did the people in other parts of Europe or on other continents. If the unremitting struggle for freedom of the Eastern European countries and their difficult geographic position were kept in mind, the liberal striving of these countries and their aptitude for democratic development would be judged more favorably than is sometimes the case.

In Germany, which was probably economically and technically the most highly developed country on the European continent and which had a high cultural and social level, liberalism was no more influential than in the agrarian countries of Eastern Europe. It was certainly infinitely weaker than in Czechoslovakia. In Germany and in Italy, democracy did not succumb to foreign, but to internal, antiliberal forces. In Russia, liberalism undoubtedly was far weaker than in Eastern Europe.

IV

The development of liberalism in Eastern Europe in the period between the two wars shows clearly that this force was far stronger there than in Germany, Italy, or Russia, and that it attained real success in Czechoslovakia. There were conditions in Eastern Europe that favored the development of liberalism into an influential spiritual, political, and social movement. The most promising forces in this regard were the striving of these nations for freedom and social progress and their genuine patriotism. The success of Czechoslovakian democracy gave substance to the hope that other countries in Eastern Europe would gradually become democratized. Development in this direction, however, was suddenly halted by the European crisis and by the rise of totalitarian dictatorships in the three great neighbors of the small nations of Eastern Europe. In 1938 the expansion of aggressive Nazism destroyed the Czechoslovakian democracy which, until then, had been an isolated island of liberalism east of the Rhine.

This essay has demonstrated that liberalism has its own tradition in Eastern Europe and that, after the liberation of these countries, it will surely play an even more important role than it did before. Liberalism is not a thing of the past. It is the most dynamic force in the present struggle for the liberation of man and for a community of nations based on the reign of law and mutual service. The greatness of liberalism, as Masaryk maintained, lies in its effort to make Jesus, and not Caesar, rule the world.

3 Authoritarian Forms of Government Between the Wars

ARNOLD J. ZURCHER

I

Leading political philosophers of the mid-nineteenth century occasionally looked askance at representative government and at what appeared to be the inevitability of its development into the prevailing form of political expression. Its association with the democratic franchise gave thinkers like John Stuart Mill an occasional qualm; that association caused him, and others like him, to cast about for such qualifications of the franchise and of representative parliaments as would insure the integrity of the intellectual minority both in the institutional expression of the public voice and in the treatment accorded to nonconformist opinion. Others cast an apprehensive eye toward the growth of representative institutions because of the stimulus they allegedly gave to the use of the ballot by men without property or other permanent stake in the community or without civic responsibility or intellectual attainment that might qualify them to be a part of the policy-forming tribunals of the community.

By and large, however, the advance of representative institutions and the concomitant of universal suffrage were regarded with equanimity and were usually hailed with en-

47

thusiasm. For most observers such institutions heralded an advance in civilization; they were an indication of the general increase in civic capacity and in knowledge. These advances represented one step in the inevitable progress toward the betterment of mankind which some of the more optimistic philosophers of the French Revolutionary period—men like Condorcet—had suggested would prevail, once liberty, equality, and fraternity had become the triple pillars of social morality. Even Mill, hesitant as he was to accept full manhood suffrage and the quantitative implications of majority rule, considered the growing acceptance of universal suffrage and of democratic representative institutions as an eventual gain for mankind. Their challenge to civic responsibility, so he felt, would raise the level of education and citizenship and would improve the moral capacity of the average citizen. Such views were shared by those of Mill's nineteenth-century predecessors who were apologists for representative institutions, by Jefferson, Paine, and many of their equally illustrious contemporaries who inaugurated the nineteenth-century political enlightenment. Intrinsically, and because of their effect upon human capacity and moral stature, representative institutions seemed a necessary corollary of the law of progress with which these thinkers premised their interpretation of history.

But events of the past four decades have hardly sustained the optimism inherent in such views of man's political future. Belief in civic perfectability, thought to inhere in representative institutions, has suffered rude jolts as one state after another has revealed a fatal weakness in its representative bastions. Regimes have arisen, over a large portion of the earth, which deny the need of their own legitimation by the uncoerced consent of the governed. The dictatorial usurpers have not merely monopolized power and authority but, with a degree of cynicism unmatched even in the chronicles of Machiavelli, they either have flaunted every symbol and institution of representative democracy or have deliberately perverted these symbols and institutions. Aided by the centripetal implications of modern technology, they have monopolized all avenues of information and communication and conscripted every form of cultural, educational, or economic organization; hence, these contemporary dictatorial regimes, in contrast to those of former times or to the regimes established by Napoleon, are all-embracing in form and their dictatorship can best be described by the adjective, "total."

Since the First World War, totalitarian dictatorships have reared their unlovely forms so frequently that it might well be asked if they are this century's peculiar contribution to the art of government. Such a suggestion may be unduly pessimistic; at the same time, it can hardly be denied that the cancerous growth of totalitarian dictatorship in the twentieth century appears to have made an illusion out of the previous century's belief in progress. Our experience seems to be a reaffirmation of the cyclical interpretation of political development which was the philosophical premise of Polybius and of the apologists of republican Rome. In our generation, at least, such a premise seems somewhat more realistic than the concept of the onward march of history towards ever more moral and more scientific forms of political society. Somewhere in our thinking, it seems, we must allow for the possibility of reaction.

II

Historians, philosophers, and perhaps even statisticians, may eventually supply definitive explanations of this century's rude rejection of the ideas of progress associated with representative institutions and of its relative tolerance of totalitarianism. At this stage, however, any explanation of this phenomenon can be only tentative. One current explanation attributes the decline of free institutions and the rise of dictatorships to causes which are largely impersonal in nature. This is the rather popular thesis that the total state is the logical culmination of economic collectivism and the consequent decay of the free-market economy. Applying a somewhat Marxian-like corollary, this thesis suggests that economic freedom, meaning essentially a *laissez faire* economy, is the basic determinant of every other freedom; hence, as governmental interventionism has grown, we have moved, so it is contended, toward the conscription of every other freedom and the denial of free government itself.

Such a thesis, however, is only superficially plausible. Whatever affinity collectivism may have for totalitarian dictatorship—and there can be no doubt that there is an affinity and a dangerous one—there is little evidence to support the view that our contemporary total dictatorships came into being because of the decline of a free-market economy. The record appears to show that fascist and Communist dictatorships alike came into existence because of the overt action of a monopolistically-minded minority who carried out a *coup d'état* and, having thereby gained control of the traditional sources and institutions of political power, proceeded to oust all other groups. To be sure, economic freedom disappeared in each of these dictatorial regimes, and rather promptly too; but it disappeared after the reins of government had been seized and the ensuing monopoly of political power could be used as means for overcoming the free economy. The idea that an established economy, regulated and operated by the government, makes the destruction of political freedom inevitable and leads directly to a public monopoly of all forms of organized social life finds no substantiation in the history of contemporary dictatorship. In other words, *no* country, formerly free, has become a total dictatorship as a result of what is popularly known as "creeping socialism."

In the case of Eastern Europe, authoritarian forms of government were generally established as a result of a *coup d'état* carried out by groups already possessing power. In some cases, royal authority provided the basis for the seizure of power. Thus in the modified authoritarian regime set up in Hungary in 1920, Admiral Horthy served as regent on the vacant Habsburg throne, while in Yugoslavia and Rumania, royal authority was implemented by the existing bureaucracy and military establishment. In Bulgaria, on the other hand, the *coups* of 1923 and 1934 were carried out by military and civilian leaders without royal authority and only in 1935 was King Boris able to gain control of the government. The regimes of Zogu in Albania and Pilsudski in Poland were likewise the result of civil-military collaboration, and the former did not proclaim himself king as Zog I until he had held power for three years.

Thus the *coups* in these nations were largely the actions of court camarilla or military cliques. They reflected relative inexperience with the techniques of parliamentary government and weak social structures. In part, they may also be attributed to the immense difficulties experienced by political leaders in their attempts to solve the complex domestic and international problems which existed in these states after the First World War. In any case, the resulting authoritarian regimes were essentially of the limited type; they did not, at least at the outset, approximate the totalitarian thoroughness of the succeeding dictatorships which came with the advance of fascist or Communist power.

In the expansion of totalitarian control, war and external aggrandizement have also played their parts; that is, whenever a dictatorial system managed to entrench itself in a major center of national power, it immediately sought to create an area of satellite states. Upon these the dictatorial system was imposed in order that they might be the more effectively controlled. Such was the history of Italian Fascist and German Nazi imperialism; such, also, is the story of Russian Communist totalitarianism. A whole ring of states in Europe and Asia have lost their independence and have been added to the totalitarian area because Soviet Russia and its instruments have so willed it, and because they have used force and sabotage to achieve it.

III

The immediate origins of contemporary dictatorships are thus clearly traditional. Like most tyrannies of the past, our twentieth-century tyrannies are the product of usurpation and conquest, of the *coup d'état,* and of military aggrandizement. But in reminding ourselves of this rather obvious fact, questions arise as to why the usurper and the tyrant have been so successful in our age and why free institutions have proven so vulnerable to their attack. That question can probably never be answered satisfactorily; nevertheless, it is possible to point to various unique circumstances and conditions which weakened or discredited free institutions or otherwise aided the would-be usurpers.

Of these the most obvious has been the fondness of this century for global war. In almost all belligerent countries, and especially in those that were defeated or unprepared to wage war, the economic and social disruption wrought by war produced social tensions and political extremism for which the normal integrative processes of free government often proved inadequate. War, moreover, eroded the integrity of the popular institutions of government. Constant emergencies, the need for decisive action at any cost, and the emphasis upon secrecy, caused men to discount the legislative and normal deliberative functions of such government if, indeed, it did not cause them to hold such functions in contempt; as a consequence, it was an easy step from government by discussion to government by decree, or to what has come to be known popularly as "crisis government." [1] This was the case among the most advanced continental European democracies such as the United Kingdom, France, and Italy. Even in these relatively stable homes of representative institutions, the summary procedures of wartime brought about a decline of confidence in the processes of representative institutions and a lack of faith in the symbols and methods of popular government. That one of these states went the way of fascism, at least temporarily, should not, therefore, be a surprise.

Finally, both global conflicts opened the floodgates of revolution in countries whose social systems were unstable and thereby provided a golden opportunity for any power-hungry minority to impose its will. The Soviet dictatorship is an obvious example of the political effect which war and its occasional aftermath of revolution have had upon our times.

The depression of the '30's also contributed to the weakening of representative institutions. In almost every country, remedies and palliatives for this economic phenomenon called for unorthodox policies and demanded state intervention to relieve social distress. These requirements created situations which were beyond the normal scope of governmental power; the debate thus engendered, the hesitation to put remedies into operation, and the ineffectiveness of many that were placed in operation, combined to raise suspicions about the capacity of democratic government to cope with such emergencies. Coupled with the Communist canard that the free economic institutions of democracy inevitably bring on depressions, the fumblings of those who were taking countermeasures, understandable though these

---

[1] Lindsay Rogers, *Crisis Government* (New York, 1933); Clinton Rossiter, *Constitutional Dictatorship* (Princeton, N.J.: Princeton University Press, 1948).

might have been, aggravated the popular suspicion that democracy and representative institutions were inadequate to deal with the elementary problem of economic security, if, indeed, these institutions did not themselves bring on this problem.

The talking point most used by the Communist and other total dictatorships today is the wholly unjustified assertion that representative democracy cannot cope with the problem of guaranteeing elementary economic security, and that, if this problem is to be solved, mankind must suffer the harsh tyranny and arbitrary discretion of dictatorship. Until we succeed in extirpating from the minds of men the association of dictatorship and security, born largely of the depression and the aftermath of war and appealing especially to countries with little technological development, the future of representative institutions will be none too bright.

What has just been said does not apply directly to the earlier authoritarian regimes of Eastern Europe since these, as already pointed out, came into being for the most part in the 1920's and hence antedated the depression. Nevertheless, this economic debacle aggravated the trend toward authoritarianism in these parts. In the cases of the second Bulgarian *coup d'état* in 1934 and King Carol's assumption of power in Rumania in 1938, economic influences can be discerned. The decline in trade and employment in the early '30's bore a distinct relationship to the weakening of the democratic regime in Bulgaria, and the incoming authoritarian regime adopted statist methods to meet these problems. Moreover, the depression weakened the resistance of the region as a whole to Nazi economic penetration, and the influence of the Western democracies declined as the world markets for the exports of Eastern Europe disappeared.

Another factor that paralyzed the democratic will and advanced the cause of reaction, especially in Eastern Europe, was the extreme nationalism that characterized many political and military leaders. In this region, diversion of state expenditures from armaments to social welfare and gestures of friendship to neighboring countries were regarded by many as a form of treason. The schools and the press preached incessantly that the vindication of a nation's territorial aspirations was a value of the highest order, and authoritarian leaders, acting in the name of such doctrines, generally met with little resistance. It was frequently only a small group of liberal-minded professional men, and in some cases the peasant parties, that placed a high value on social and economic improvement and resisted the authoritarian trend. Thus nationalism, which a century earlier had formed the vanguard of liberalism, now became its most treacherous enemy.

Any account of the vulnerability of free institutions must also comment on the peculiar and often fatal tolerance which democratic governments have exhibited during the past two or three decades towards those who have overtly threatened its existence. Those who governed free states hesitated to deny traditional rights to Communists, fascists, and others even though these groups clearly intended to use such rights to facilitate their own seizure of power. Many pages of recent history have chronicled this dismal story, especially those which tell of the success of German and Italian fascism and of Lenin's bid for power in Russia. Not until 1930 did the political leadership of the Weimar Republic muster the courage to ban street demonstrations, uniforms, vigilantism, and other abuses of the traditional rights of association and expression. By that time, however, Hitler had already sealed the fate of the Republic. He triumphed, even as Mussolini and Lenin had done before him, because the legal regime failed to deny him the opportunity of perverting the privileges of a free state. Among the narrower and more tangible causes of the great reaction, the paralysis of the democratic will and its failure to protect itself from the abuse of its own freedoms is quite likely to acquire more, rather than less, stature among historians.

Another factor which contributed to the vulnerability of representative institutions was the tendency toward what Mirkine-Guetzevitch has called "the rationalization of power." By this term is meant the efforts of constitution makers in certain continental European democracies to shape parliamentary institutions in accordance with too logical formulas. In so doing, they repressed the influence of historical and local forces, thereby slowing down or preventing the adjustment of model institutions to the precise needs and traditions of a particular country. The net effect of this "rationalization of power" was to make representative regimes more vulnerable to the forces of reaction.

Evidence of this trend towards rationalization existed in many areas of government—in the choice and composition of cabinets, in the rules governing ministerial responsibility, and in the procedure of legislatures. It was particularly apparent, however, in the proportional electoral systems which were adopted all over continental Europe after the First World War. So conscientious were the artificers of the proportional representation systems that they sought to represent every facet of opinion with mathematical exactitude. The effect, demonstrated in country after country, was to encourage the fractionizing and splintering of organized political opinion. This occurred to such an extent that the problem of forming governing majorities and providing clear and authoritative mandates for political leadership was greatly complicated.

It is possible that the damaging effects of proportional representation upon parliamentarianism have been unduly magnified. Nevertheless, even a cursory glance at almost any continental representative system between the two world wars will suffice to show that proportional representation encouraged the growth of minor parties and of personal followings and that it stimulated the creation of political groups with militant, uncompromising ideological programs; because this system was in part responsible for such developments, it may also be held responsible for discouraging normal integrative processes among the parties at the polls and in the chambers and for complicating the problem of securing constitutional governing majorities.[2] Indirectly, therefore, proportional representation, the most obvious institutional expression of the trend towards the "rationalization of power" in the interbellum period, bears some of the responsibility for parliamentary weakness and totalitarian success.

It must be conceded at once that, in complicating the problem of integrating political opinion in representative democracies, proportional representation merely supplemented other more fundamental causes. Chief of these was the fact that just after the First World War representative democracy, especially in Europe, had to accommodate itself to the coming of age of powerful new forces on the left of the political firmament. This new left was composed of the forces of Marxian socialism, often in alliance with organized labor. The growth of this element was formidable because of recently enacted ultra-democratic franchise laws and the generous electoral laws of the proportional representation variety.

Historical evidence of this phenomenon is quite clear. The German government which expelled the Kaiser in 1918 was a coalition of Majority and Independent Social Democrats, and the Majority Social Democrats subsequently became the most important party unit in the coalition which

[2] Ferdinand A. Hermans, *Europe Between Democracy and Anarchy* (Notre Dame, Indiana: University of Notre Dame Press, 1951), pp. 52-53, and 66 ff.; same authority in Arnold J. Zurcher, ed., *Constitutions and Constitutional Trends Since World War II* (New York: New York University Press, 1951), pp. 132-133.

created the Weimar Constitution. In England, Labor struck out alone in 1918 with the definite intention of capturing the government, a goal which was first realized under Ramsay MacDonald in 1924. The Socialist Party of Italy became the largest political aggregation on the peninsula in the first postwar elections of 1919. Comparable developments took place contemporaneously in almost every European country, large or small. The Marxian and labor left ceased to form minority elements which architects of cabinets could afford to relegate to the opposition; after 1920, because of its growing electoral and parliamentary power and the corresponding attenuation of the forces of the historic left and center, this new left became a desirable, if not necessary, component of governing majorities.

It was the rise of this new left that further complicated the problem of security majority coalitions in Europe's parliaments just after the First World War. It is possible that, as the claims of the new political force became adjusted and the leadership became accustomed to responsibility, the normal process of compromise and conciliation among parties might have reasserted themselves and the authority of government might have been restored. Such a theory is at least a plausible one.

Unfortunately, the new left was largely the product of the militant, uncompromising Marxist ideology. As late as the First World War, large elements of international Marxism still held their traditional loyalty to the concept of a class monopoly of political power. They rejected sincere collaboration with so-called "bourgeois" parties and often closed their ranks to any of their own number who defied this precept. In short, they looked askance at coalition and compromise, the two indispensable institutions of representative government in a plural society.

The monopolistic temper and tactics of the Marxian left have persisted, nor are they confined to the Communists.

They continue to inspire radical elements among the moderate socialist groups who have long since formally renounced their intransigence. Occasionally, as in the case of contemporary Italy, this monopolistic temper pervades the whole organization of what passes for moderate socialism and makes this group nothing more than a wing of the Communist Party. However expressed, this persistence of Marxian intransigence has contributed significantly to the decline of the integrative faculty in contemporary parliaments and to the relative absence of political consensus. The resulting uncertainty or occasional paralysis of political democracy will have opened the door more than once to reaction and to the *coup d'état*. It was the paralysis of the cabinet in liberal Italy in 1921, brought about in part by the defection of the Marxist left, that opened the door to Mussolini; in Germany likewise, the uncertainty and intransigence of Marxian groups contributed appreciably to Hitler's rise to power.

Democratic weakness, of which the above-mentioned causes provide a partial explanation, is but one factor contributing to the recent advance of totalitarianism; the other cause is the dynamism and inherent strength of totalitarianism itself. The totalitarian dictatorships of our age possess all the advantages of traditional dictatorships, the most important being a political discretion largely unimpeded by public opinion or by standing law; contemporary dictatorships have the additional advantages of power and control that result from the permeation by the state apparatus of all the organized productive and moral forces of society. The result is a behemoth that defies, with almost no risk to itself, anyone who dares resist; those whom it does not defy successfully it can usually corrupt. Indeed, once successfully established, it is virtually immune to internal threat.

Moreover, once either a fascist or a Communist totalitarian system has come into being, it has invariably been successful in corrupting or destroying peripheral free states and in introducing dangerous fifth columns into almost all free governments. As noted earlier, this has been one of the principal factors contributing to the spread of totalitarianism. Poland is a Communist totalitarian state today not because the majority of Poles or even a sizable minority are Communist but because Soviet Russia has dragooned Poland into becoming a totalitarian satellite. Italy has the largest Communist party among the free states because the nourishment and perpetuation of such a party in Italy is an objective of Soviet foreign policy. If totalitarian Communism disappears in Soviet Russia, it is a safe assumption that totalitarian Communism will disappear or become a negligible factor in the rest of the world.

IV

Three decades of experience with authoritarian systems have made the free world somewhat pessimistic. As suggested in the first pages of this essay, our faith in the persistence of free representative institutions, so strongly held in the nineteenth century, has been badly shaken by this experience. So badly has that faith been shaken that some observers doubt that free political institutions can survive. Certainly there are millions today whose loyalty is at least ostensibly given to dictatorship and authoritarian institutions and not to the free institutions of a representative democracy.

Nevertheless, the outlook for the stability of representative institutions is perhaps not as dismal in this first decade of the second half of the twentieth century as it was at certain times during the earlier half. For one thing, we have learned how to make the free world less susceptible to the threat of reaction. Thus, in the constitutional reconstruction which has been taking place since the Second World War, democratic states have undertaken various steps to overcome some of the structural and related weaknesses that previously made them vulnerable to totalitarian attack. France, Italy, and other states have made efforts recently to reward the moderate parties by modifying electoral laws and to penalize the extremist, and especially the totalitarian, parties. This is an important step forward even though states like France and Italy continue to experience difficulty in mobilizing governing majorities.

Contemporary democracies indicate also an increased awareness of the need to protect themselves from those who use freedom for purposes of subversion. Their actions indicate that they have learned how to deal with the menace of internal subversion. There is little chance, for example, that any nation will ever again submit to the abuse of its democratic freedoms as did Germany or Czechoslovakia in the prefascist period. The new wisdom is well expressed in Article 18 of the present Bonn Charter which declares that whoever abuses the various freedoms of the representative state "in order to attack the libertarian democratic basic order, forfeits these basic rights."

But the constructive developments required to overcome the great reaction do not lie wholly, or even chiefly, in the area of constitutional and administrative reform. Of even greater significance are the measures which have developed in the diplomatic and military fields. Here, too, there is much on the credit side of the ledger. Whatever the Second World War may have contributed to the advance of the totalitarianism of the left, it did do away with the two abominable tyrannies of the right, those of Mussolini and of Hitler. This was a great gain for freedom and has caused large areas to be reclaimed for representative institutions even if in Germany and Italy the none too pleasant odor of fascism lingers on.

There remain the tasks of producing effective resistance to the Communist tyranny and of finally subjugating it.

How effective the politico-military struggle directed against that tyranny has been up to now is open to question. Since Sir Winston Churchill's speech at Fulton, Missouri, and the announcement of the Truman Doctrine in 1947, both of which were seminal events in mankind's recognition of the true face of communism, numerous measures to counteract and contain the Soviet menace have been taken, and, as the Korean War will testify, those measures have not stopped short of the use of overt force. The free world at last has come to understand the lengths to which it must go if it sincerely wishes to prevail over totalitarianism of the left. This is progress.

The endeavors to bring about a truce in Korea (1953) and to neutralize other Communist acts of aggression indicate that the free world still believes that negotiation and compromise may bring about a peaceful communism and ultimately a decaying communism. It must be admitted that this is a hope arising from fear of the awful destruction of atomic war rather than from confidence that the totalitarianism of the left will really agree to co-exist with the free world. Moreover, the lesson taught by our experience with fascism also runs counter to such a hope; this lesson seems to say that only military defeat in major war can really destroy totalitarian dictatorship when such has become established as the government of a first-class power. It is to be fondly hoped that the Soviet reaction can be controlled and ultimately destroyed by measures short of war—that Poland, Czechoslovakia, and all the nations now in thrall can be freed and that free institutions can be restored in them without a third world war. It remains to be seen, however, whether this will be possible.

In this discussion of efforts to prevent Communist expansion, mention must be made of another development in the international arena favorable to the future of free political institutions. This is the effort being made, especially in Europe, to promote various forms of economic and political integration among the nations. The growing unification of Western Europe, symbolized by the Council of Europe and especially by the European Coal and Steel Community, is potentially the most important contribution of this generation to the future of free political institutions; such integration promises for free political institutions a greater chance of being able to fill the demands made upon them. It promises, among other things, greater military security at less cost and offers the hope of expanding markets and production, and hence, greater economic prosperity; to the extent that greater integration can achieve these ends, it ameliorates the difficulties of representative institutions and promotes confidence in them.

In the long run, however, even the most favorable developments in the international arena are of less importance to the future of free political institutions than the restoring and holding of man's loyalty to the democratic ideal. In other words, the battle for free institutions, like all battles, is one for men's minds. It is on that battleground that the struggle for free institutions with totalitarianism must finally be fought and won.

In this struggle, the forces of freedom have made great gains; but they have not done so well as they eventually must if they are to prevail. If the battle is to be won, men must be brought to see how hollow and devoid of truth is the claim of Communist totalitarianism that it represents the cause of the masses. Men must be made to understand that the Communists' claim that their system is indispensable to raising the material level of the rank and file and to gaining national independence for colonial people is a cruel hoax. At the same time, the historic ideals associated with representative government, or with what we call democracy, must regain their place among the beliefs of men. To achieve that end, the free institutions of representative democracy must be re-identified with conceptions of progress and with the hope that man may be delivered from conditions which he deems unjust—from poverty, bigotry, discrimination, and national subjugation. Only if the symbols of democratic institutions are once again associated in the minds of men with the conceptions of justice and progress, can those same institutions regain their dynamism and resume the march which Hitler, Stalin, and their minions interrupted in the first half of this century.

4   "People's Democracy" in Theory and Practice

STANISLAW MIKOLAJCZYK

I

After the Second World War, Communist dictatorships were imposed by the Soviet Union on a number of European countries that had been under German occupation. This form of dictatorial government was called "People's Democracy." The reasons for this arose out of the political foundations and tactics of the Soviet Union, out of the internal situation of the Soviet Union as well as out of the situation in the occupied countries.

The Ribbentrop-Molotov pact of 1939 not only encouraged Hitler to start the Second World War by an armed invasion of Poland, but assured him of both an armed ally in the invasion and partition of Poland and an important supplier of food, raw materials, and gasoline. At the time of the pact, Stalin intended to await a more favorable situation in order to assure himself of the fruits of the final victory.

At the end of First World War, the Bolsheviks had counted on successful Communist revolutions in the countries of Europe, but none occurred. The Communist regime of Béla Kun in Hungary fell within a few months, and the Bolshevik hordes who marched upon the West met their defeat at Warsaw in August 1920. In the interwar period, several attempts to provoke Communist revolutions also failed and Communist hopes faded. Not until the Second World War was an opportunity furnished for the Kremlin to establish Communist regimes in Europe.

Hitler's unexpected invasion of Soviet Russia in 1941 made it impossible for the Kremlin to expand its influence at leisure and compelled the Soviet Union to join the camp of the Allies. As an ally of the West in this war and fighting Hitler for its very existence, Soviet Russia gained credit for the heroic qualities of its soldiers. At the same time, under the influence of pro-Soviet propaganda, public opinion in the West came to believe that Soviet Russia had been converted into a state that respected democracy and civil liberties. It is nevertheless clear that during the war the Soviets never renounced their designs regarding Europe and always put their political objectives above war strategy. For example, in Teheran Stalin resisted all war plans not based on the invasion of France.

Stalin believed then that the Western Allies would shed much of their own blood on Hitler's Atlantic Wall, and that even if they landed successfully their march to the East would be so delayed that in the meantime he would be able to extend the Soviet sphere of influence far into Europe. In Teheran and later in Yalta, Stalin took advantage of the atmosphere and of the inexperience of the West with Communist tactics and achieved conditions which favored the implementation of his far-reaching plans concerning Eastern Europe. The policies favored by the Western Allies in the interest of the common cause and in the hopes of speedy victory and better international cooperation were cynically exploited by the Kremlin and used as a basis for the expansion of influence and for the establishment of communism in many other countries.

Apart from the Teheran and Yalta conferences, there are countless examples concerning every one of the countries at present behind the Iron Curtain which prove that the Soviets were preparing themselves systematically in various sectors of life for the domination and communization of these countries. Nevertheless, in order to prolong the period of appeasement immediately after the Second World War, the Soviets attempted to maintain the pretense that they were observing international agreements. They were anxious for a speedy disarmament of the large Allied armies standing in Europe and for the rapid conversion of the war industry of their allies to peace-time production.

The aid of UNRRA, war surpluses, and other credits from the West were at that time indispensable to the countries of Eastern Europe because Soviet aid—apart from noisy propaganda—expressed itself in these countries only in a systematic destitution of industrial equipment and stocks of raw materials. This was carried out under the pretext of confiscation of German assets which belonged as "war booty" to Russia. The Soviet Union hoped for the cancellation of the Lend-Lease obligations and calculated that it had the opportunity of obtaining from the United States a loan for its internal needs in the amount of ten billion dollars.

II

Under these circumstances, in order to lull public opinion in the West, Communist propaganda preferred to call the regimes imposed on the occupied countries People's Democracies instead of frankly calling them "socialist states based on the dictatorship of the proletariat." This gave them a basis for maintaining that the "system of people's democracy" was not a Communist system but a new type of democracy which did not yet have all the characteristics of Western democracies only because these nations were backward and because, except for Czechoslovakia, they had lived before the Second World War under totalitarian or semi-totalitarian regimes and were not sufficiently mature for a Western democratic system. This kind of explanation was not only accepted by fellow travelers but also helped to appease the conscience of the Western leaders co-responsible for international agreements with Soviet Russia and for leaving these nations to Russia's mercy.

The West was not well acquainted with the social and political changes which had taken place in these countries within the last fifty years and which had made themselves apparent in the struggle for freedom and democracy before the war, in the fight against Nazism and fascism during the war, and in the struggle against communism since the war. This continual struggle not only proves the political maturity of these nations but also demonstrates such great self-sacrifice and determination that the question arises whether, despite the setbacks caused by violence and terror, their zeal for the cause of democracy does not surpass that of many who enjoy the blessings of true democracy in the West. The propagation of People's Democracies in the countries of Eastern Europe helped the Communists to stifle the echoes of the struggle of these nations who were defending their freedom and independence under very difficult and heretofore unexperienced conditions. The theme of People's Democracies also enabled the Soviets to stifle the protests of these nations where the Red Army and the NKVD were murdering, arresting, and deporting democratic political leaders and the officers and soldiers of the underground armies which, during the Second World War, had fought against the occupations of Nazism and fascism.

The façade of People's Democracy did most service to the Communists by masking both the imposed regimes of Communist dictatorship and the lack of popular support. In not one of these countries, however, did the Communist parties give evidence of any extensive influence upon the people. All over Eastern Europe the land hunger of the peasants, the low wages of the workers, the great disproportion between the prices of industrial and agricultural products, the periods of unemployment, the practices of totalitarian regimes, the remnants of feudalism, tension between national groups, and intolerance played an important role. Knowing the skill with which the Communists usually exploit economic difficulties, social injustice, and national differences, it would seem that in these countries they would have found much greater support. However, despite conditions favorable to Communist propaganda, both in the countries that had always known Russia as an imperialistic conqueror and in Southeastern Europe where Russia had been considered an ally since the struggle for liberation from Turkey and where religious factors aroused no antagonism, the Communist parties did not attract a very large following before the war.

Various circumstances explain this fact. Countries at a distance from Russia could not contrast Communist propaganda to Communist reality; they learned of Russia from tours organized by the Intourist or from the study of Communist writings. The peoples of Eastern Europe, on the other hand, caught glimpses of their neighbor even through a tightly closed frontier and observed the immensity of the misery, oppression, and terror that existed in the U.S.S.R. The sudden tactical maneuvers of Lenin and Stalin which often obliged the Communist parties to act against the vital interests of their respective countries further disillusioned Russia's immediate neighbors.

It is difficult to cite exact figures concerning the Communist parties in Eastern Europe, because they operated under different names at different times and because they sometimes existed legally and sometimes illegally. Let us take for example the Communist Party of Poland. Before the First World War the Communists acted through the Social Democratic Party of the Kingdom of Poland and Lithuania, which party opposed the idea of an independent Poland. During the Bolshevik invasion of Poland in 1920, a Communist government of Poland was created at the rear of the Red Army at a time when the whole Polish nation, united under the leadership of Premier Witos of the Peasant Party and Vice-Premier Daszynski of the Socialist Party, was fighting against the Bolsheviks. In independent Poland after 1921 the Communist Party declared itself in opposition to the independence of Poland and advocated the incorporation of the Republic of Poland into the Soviet Union.

In 1926 the Communists supported Pilsudski's *coup d'état* against the democratic president and government. Only later did they announce that this had been a "mistake of the leadership of the party." When the Comintern attempted to provoke a Communist revolution in Germany in 1932, the Polish Communist Party declared that they favored granting to Germany both Silesia, which had been ceded to Poland after the First World War, and complete control over the Free City of Gdansk (Danzig).

The weakness of the Communist Party of Poland on the eve of the Second World War is proved by the fact that in 1938 it was dissolved by the Comintern on the pretext that it was completely infiltrated by the secret police of the Polish government. After the conclusion of the Molotov-Ribbentrop pact the Polish and German Communists considered the line of division between the German and Soviet spheres of influence to be the future frontier between the Communist Republic of Germany and the Soviet Union. Under these circumstances, Poland, of course, would be completely erased from the map.

The Soviet invasion of Poland, undertaken in agreement with Nazi Germany, the incorporation into the Soviet Union of almost half of the eastern territory of Poland, and the deportation of a million and half Poles to Russia were presented by the Communists as the liberation of the Ukrainian, Byelorussian, and Lithuanian peoples from the yoke of the Polish landlords; Hitler's war against France and England were presented as a battle against Anglo-Saxon imperialism. After the fall of France the Polish Communists, together with those sent from France, assumed a neutral attitude toward the Nazi occupation and terror in Poland. They did not take part in the underground struggle of the Polish nation. They were tolerated by the Gestapo and moved about freely. Only after Hitler's attack on Russia in 1941 did they regain the "spirit of patriotism" and join the Polish underground struggle against Hitler.

Various events greatly discredited the reputation of the Polish Workers' Party (one of the guises under which the Polish Communists masqueraded during the war years). Such events were the massacre of the Polish war prisoners at Katyn, the death of hundreds of thousands of people deported to Soviet forced labor camps in the years 1939-1941, the deportation in 1944 of over 40,000 members of the underground Home Army who had been fighting against the Germans and aiding the entering Red Army, and the return to Poland of a number of Poles who had experienced the Soviet reality. Further discredit was brought to the Polish Workers' Party by the presence of the Communist Lublin Committee. The Committee seized power in Poland with the aid of the Soviet army and the NKVD and nominated as ministers of the government persons who had been in the German concentration camps and had served the Gestapo faithfully.

According to its reports in 1937, the Communist Party of Poland had 6,000 regular members and 12,000 members in the Communist Association of Polish Youth. Experts are of the opinion, however, that these figures were exaggerated by the leadership of the party which was afraid of presenting to Moscow a true report of the extent of its influence. *New*

Roads, the Communist organ published after the war in Warsaw, reported that before the Second World War the Communist Party of Poland never had more than 20,000 members. In the elections for the Seym (the Polish parliament) in 1922, the Communists netted 130,000 votes or 1 per cent of the votes cast. In 1926 the Communists together with their various affiliates had 23 deputies. At the peak of the economic crisis in 1928 the Communists received 829,000 out of 11,758,000 votes, or about 7 per cent of the total number of votes cast. The Communist bloc, by 1946, consisted of the Polish Workers' Party (Communists), the Polish Socialist Party, the Democratic Party, and the Labor Party. This bloc, it was secretly reported to Stalin, did not receive more than 16 per cent of the votes either in the referendum of 1946 or in the elections of 1947, despite the presence of the Red Army in Poland and the use of terror and violence. These few samplings from the history of the Communist Party of Poland show how Communist tactics which required actions against the interests of the country and its various social classes and which contradicted the ideological theories of communism prevented a wider development of the Communist Party.

Czechoslovakia had a genuine democratic system before the war and gave the Communist Party full freedom of action. In the parliamentary election of 1925 the Communists gained 41 seats and in the elections of 1934 and 1935 they received only 30 seats out of the total number of 300 in the parliament. After the war, in May 1946, the Czech Communist Party won 31 per cent of the total Czechoslovakian vote and elected 93 deputies out of the total number of 300. In the same election the Slovak Communist Party, in a region that had already experienced the "blessing" of liberation by the Red Army, won a much smaller percentage of the total vote in proportion to the population.

In Bulgaria, before the Second World War, the number of

Communist deputies ranged from 15 to 48 out of a total number of 274 members of parliament. The highest Communist representation was gained directly after the First World War and the lowest, consisting of only 15 deputies, occurred under Stambolisky; in 1927 the Communists had 33 deputies. The phenomenon of the political opportunism of all Communist parties during the war, that is, their sudden switch to the support of Hitler, was particularly pronounced in Bulgaria. The political report of the Fifth Congress of the Bulgarian Communist Party of December 1948 shows that in August of 1944, that is, at the moment of the change of government toward the end of the Second World War, the Communist Party had only 25,000 members.

In Hungary, since the experience with Béla Kun in 1919, the influence of communism has been very weak. It is significant that after the Second World War in the elections of 1945 the Hungarian Communists received only 17 per cent of the vote, despite the Russian methods of persuasion. Even in the elections of 1947 the Communists won only 18 per cent of the vote for their own party.

According to the reports of Anna Pauker and other Communist leaders, the Rumanian Communist Party had less than 2,000 members in the years 1944-45.

The Communists could never expect to assume power in any of the above mentioned countries by parliamentary and democratic methods because the Communist parties, even in the most favorable periods, had the support of only 5 to 15 per cent of the people. Neither were the Communists able to establish police systems in these countries in the period immediately following the Second World War. Therefore, they promulgated "People's Democracies." They organized within the individual countries by stealing the traditional names of prewar political parties, by filling the top posts in these parties with their own agents, and by creating fictitious coalitions of parties. The Communists had in their actions a triple objective: to mislead the people, to prevent the postwar restoration of political parties by their original leaders and members or to break them up if they had been restored already, and to beguile foreign opinion into believing that multiparty systems still existed in the Eastern European countries.

The lack of popular support of the Communist parties is visible even today in the countries behind the Iron Curtain. For this reason, in the last elections in Poland and in Rumania in 1952, and in Hungary in 1953, the lists of candidates, made out completely by the Communists, were presented to the people under the disguise of a "National Front." The National Front is represented as a coalition of political parties, trade unions, youth organizations, scientific societies and so forth, and is highlighted by the names of "patriot-priests" and "progressive Catholics." The Communist press in Poland admits that the institution of the National Front was necessary in the elections of 1952 because in 60 per cent of the voting localities, especially in the villages, there were "white spots," that is, areas where there did not exist a single cell of the Communist Party.

In summary, it can be said that the Communist dictatorship was imposed upon the countries behind the Iron Curtain under the name of People's Democracy through the following means: Moscow's strategic and political machinations during the war; the direct intervention of the Red Army and the NKVD in the internal affairs of these countries both at the end of and after the war; either the falsification of the will of these nations in the elections or the *coup d'état,* as in Hungary in 1947, and in Czechoslovakia in 1948.

An analysis of Communist strength clearly shows that the Communists could not have expected in a single case to assume power in a democratic and parliamentary manner. And, it must be added, the peoples of the Eastern European countries have declared themselves in overwhelming majority to be opposed to the Communist system despite the pressure of the Red Army and of the NKVD. Violence and fraud were the only means by which the Communists were able to seize power in these countries.

III

In the Soviet Union strict ideological discipline became the order of the day after the wave of patriotic feeling that arose and was encouraged during the Second World War. It was during the period of the revival of this communist ideology that the Communist dictatorships in the captive countries were given the name of People's Democracy. The relation of this new doctrine to the theoretical foundations of the Soviet state should therefore be examined.

In the Constitution of 1936 the U.S.S.R. is clearly defined as a "socialist state based on the dictatorship of the proletariat" (Articles 1 and 2), and the exclusive role of the Communist Party is explicitly stressed (Articles 3 and 126). Moreover, Stalin himself wrote that "The proletariat needs the Party for the purpose of achieving and maintaining the dictatorship. The Party is an instrument of the dictatorship of the proletariat." [1] Speaking on the draft of the new constitution in November 1936, he further said: "I must admit that the draft of the new Constitution does preserve the regime of the dictatorship of the working class, just as it also preserves unchanged the present leading position of the Communist Party of the U.S.S.R." [2]

Soviet political theory assumes that socialist states must evolve from a phase in which the state continues to be used as an instrument of the dictatorship of the proletariat to a

[1] Joseph Stalin, *Problems of Leninism*, 11th ed. (Moscow, Foreign Languages Publishing House, 1940), p. 80.
[2] *Ibid.*, p. 578.

higher phase. In this higher phase of communism the state will wither away, and with the increase in production the law of society will be "from each according to his ability, to each according to his needs." That the Soviet Union still has some way to go before reaching this stage was emphasized by Stalin in October 1952, in his widely publicized treatise issued on the eve of the Nineteenth Congress of the Communist Party. Stalin described the complexity of this process of transition to the higher phase and asserted that before it could be accomplished it would be necessary, among other things, to ensure "a continuous expansion of all social production" and "to raise collective farm property to the level of public property, and . . . to replace commodity circulation by a system of products exchange." [3]

It is important to keep in mind the framework of Soviet political theory in examining the constitutional documents and legislation of the captive countries because the latter are now being cast in the Soviet mold. The term "Communist dictatorship" is used here to describe both systems— the Soviet system and the so-called People's Democracy —because in actuality there does not exist any basic difference between them. Certain differences which have existed or which still exist either concern only the name and not the substance or are dependent upon the conditions and time needed by the Soviets for establishment and consolidation of communism in these countries.

Can it be said, therefore, that from the point of view of communist theory People's Democracy, so strongly emphasized in the propaganda and in the constitutions of the captive countries, represents the first phase of communism as it existed during the period of the New Economic Policy in Soviet Russia? No, this would not be accurate. Such a comparison might apply in some measure to the years 1945-

---

[3] *Economic Problems of Socialism in the U.S.S.R.* (New York, International Publishers, 1952), pp. 51-52.

1947 but not to the years following. The period of the New Economic Policy in Russia was called "the period of a certain revival of capitalism"; in reality, it was a kind of retreat of communism from economic difficulties.

In the captive countries there was no "period of revival of capitalism." Since the very inception of communism, there has been a systematic liquidation of all private property, carried out in premeditated fashion within the limits of existing conditions and possibilities. In the beginning, the question of private property arose only in regard to small trade, dwelling houses, building, crafts, and, in a larger degree to peasant farming. Hence, the Communists advocated the principle of a three-sector economy, composed of state economy—after an immediate nationalization of medium and heavy industries, landlords' estates, and forests—of co-operative economy, and of private economy.

The fact that this period, the traces of which we still find in the constitutions of the captive countries, was planned from above as no more than a transitional period, is best proved by the accusation leveled against the former Communist Vice-Premier of Poland, Gomulka, at the meeting of the Central Committee of the Communist Party in Warsaw, in 1948. Gomulka was told then that his main guilt was not that he agreed to the principles of the three-sector economy but that he acted according to these principles. It was explained to him then that he had proceeded as though he wanted to keep the system although he knew that it was transitional.

In 1947, after the falsification of the elections and the destruction of the opposition of the independent peasant parties in Bulgaria, Rumania, Hungary, Yugoslavia, and Poland, the Cominform was established and Communist policy abandoned its nationalist line and adopted the line of internationalism. A special declaration of the differences between Communist internationalism and the "cosmopolitanism" of the West was introduced, and the Communists vigorously went about the destruction of the remaining private property, the collectivization of agriculture, and the transformation of the remaining independent cooperatives into a sector of the Communist state economy. It was therefore, in theory and practice a period of the establishment of socialist states, ruled by the dictatorship of the proletariat and disguised by the name of People's Democracy. This period was marked by the accelerated tempo of the communization of all spheres of national life, by the integration of the economies of the People's Democracy into the Soviet economy, and by political and legislative preparations for the incorporation of these countries into the Soviet Union.

Analysis of the constitutions imposed upon the captive countries shows that the People's Democracies are dictatorships of the proletariat different in form but not in substance from the Soviet system. No matter when the constitutions of the People's Democracies were imposed or whether there were differences in their wording, the most important provisions are the same in each constitution. More light can be cast on these constitutions by the political circumstances in which they were imposed and by their preambles than by a dry analysis of their provisions.

In Bulgaria in 1946 the Communists falsified the elections, and in 1947 they introduced in the Parliament the draft of a new constitution. According to this draft, the president was still to be the head of the state and not the Chairman of the Presidium of the Parliament as in Soviet Russia. On September 23, 1947, the leader of the opposition, Petkov, was hanged by the Communists, and on December 4, 1947, a revised constitution was imposed upon Bulgaria. This new constitution went further in its provisions than the constitutions imposed several years later in the other captive countries. The office of the president was abolished and the office of the President of the National Assembly was established. Article 1 does not speak of a "socialist state governed by the dictatorship of the proletariat" but neither does it mention "People's Democracy." It only proclaims that Bulgaria is a "People's Republic with a representative Government . . . where all power derives from the people and belongs to the people."

The Albanian Constitution of March 15, 1946, also proclaims that "Albania is a People's Republic in which all powers are derived from and belong to the people." It provides also that the "President of the Presidium of the People's Convention is the head of the State." The constitutions of both countries faithfully reflect the Soviet system and, in the event of the incorporation of these countries into the U.S.S.R., no significant constitutional changes would be necessary.

In Hungary on August 31, 1947, after the *coup d'état* of May 1947 against the government of Premier Nagy, new elections were held, and in August 1949 a new constitution was introduced. One section of the preamble to this constitution states the following:

> Our people under the leadership of the working class, steeled in the battles during the last decades, enriched by the experience of the revolution of 1919, and relying on the USSR laid the foundation of socialism and our country now is going forward by means of the people's democracy, toward socialism.

Hungary became a People's Republic (Article 1) and was proclaimed "a state of the workers and of the working peasantry" (Article 2). The constitution further stated that "The close union of the workers and working peasantry shall be accomplished in the Hungarian People's Republic under the leadership of the workers" (Article 3), and that "The working people shall gradually oust the capitalist elements and consistently build the socialist economic order" (Article 4). The Presidium of the People's Republic with its President was established and the post of the President abolished.

In Czechoslovakia on May 9, 1948, following the *coup d'état* of February 1948, a new constitution was enacted. The preamble reads: "We, the Czechoslovakian People, declare that we are firmly resolved to build up our liberated State as a People's democracy which will ensure to us a peaceful road to socialism." Article 1 states that "The Czechoslovakian State is a People's democratic Republic. The people are the sole source of all power in the State." According to this constitution, the President of the Republic remained the head of the state and Czechoslovakia still differs from the other captive countries in this respect.

In Yugoslavia, Tito introduced at the very beginning the most advanced form of a Soviet-style system; he recently reassumed the title of President of the Republic in place of the title of President of the National Assembly.

In Poland, after the falsification of the elections in 1947, a so-called Little Constitution, based on the Soviet system of councils, was introduced. It established a Council of State whose "chairman" was also the President of the Republic. On July 22, 1952, a new constitution was imposed upon Poland. The preamble to this constitution states:

> The Polish People's Republic is a republic of the working people. . . .
> As a result of the revolutionary struggles and changes, the power of the capitalists and landlords has been overthrown and the state of People's democracy has been established. The basis of the present people's power constitutes the alliance of the working class with the working peasantry. In this alliance the leading role belongs to the working class, the leading class of the society, basing itself on the revolutionary achievements of the Polish and international working movement, on the historical experiences of the victorious building of socialism in the USSR, the first state of workers and peasants. . . .

> The Polish People's Republic is a state of People's democracy. In the Polish People's Republic power belongs to the working people of town and country. (Article 1)

The office of the President of the Republic was abolished and the office of the Chairman of the Council of State became the highest post in the state. Poland is no longer the Republic of Poland. It is now called the Polish People's Republic.

In Rumania, the constitution of 1948 was replaced by a new constitution forced upon Rumania on July 18, 1952. The preamble to the new constitution declares that "The Rumanian People's Republic is a state of working people of town and countryside," and that "The present Constitution of the Rumanian People's Republic embodies the results so far obtained by the working people headed by the working class, in building a socialist society in our country." The highest organ of state power is the General National Assembly and its Presidium, while the highest executive and administrative organ of state power is the Council of Ministers. The organs of state power in regions, districts, towns, and rural localities are the people's councils of the working people of town and country.

The examples cited from the texts and preambles of the constitutions of the captive countries show clearly that, although the Communist dictatorship in the Soviet Union has achieved the first phase in the development of communism —"the socialist state based on the dictatorship of the proletariat"—and is now on the way to the higher phase, the People's Democracies, according to communist theory, are still on the road to the first phase. This theoretical distinction made by the Communists has no great importance in practice particularly inasmuch as constitutional changes in all these People's Republics have made complete political and legal preparations for incorporation into the U.S.S.R.

As far as Yugoslavia is concerned, in the period of friendly

Stalin-Tito relations her communist system was much further advanced than that of any other Iron Curtain country, and since the break with Stalin only insignificant changes have been made in the structure of the highest organs of government. Tito still declares clearly and without any reservation that he intends to maintain the communist system in that country at any price.

IV

When communist propaganda speaks of the liberation of the oppressed masses from the slavery of the privileged and the rich, it stresses the term, People's Democracy. But does this term really signify freedom? Does it respect human dignity? Does it recognize equality among the people? Does it abolish undue privileges and the exploitation of the working people? It does not. In practice, it does not even provide personal freedom or personal security.

The overcrowded prisons and the many thousands of people in the forced labor camps bear witness to this. The Soviet Union and all the countries occupied by it are a large prison from which the majority of the people would escape if they only could. They would flee from the "Communist paradise" partly because of the difficult economic conditions, but mostly because of the unbearable atmosphere created by the insecurity and complete lack of freedom which are part of this system.

The majority of the people escaping today are average people—workers, peasants, craftsmen, small merchants, and others who have never belonged to any privileged or exploiting class. I have read a number of books on the living conditions in the Soviet forced labor camps; I have studied thousands of reports of Poles who have passed through Soviet camps and prisons; I have had hundreds of talks with the victims of the Soviet regime. And I have come to the belief that human language is unable to express the whole truth about the greatest disgrace to mankind that the twentieth century will know—the Soviet forced labor camps.

A sentence to a forced labor camp amounts to a sentence of death because the enormous majority of the inmates in these camps cannot exist under the conditions prevailing there and die before they are released. The inmate of such a camp works beyond his strength, knowing that if his productivity falls his starvation-level food ration will be cut. The instinct for self-preservation urges him to defend himself from death, and his reactions become those of a hungry animal. All his human feelings disappear, even his attitude toward his fellow inmates. Degraded and humiliated as a human being, the prisoner works like an animal for his enemies only to prolong his life by a year or two and then inevitably to perish.

Political freedom does not exist in the Communist countries either under law or in practice. Let us take for example Article 72 of the Polish constitution of July 1952. Similar provisions will be found in all other Communist constitutions. The first lines of Article 72 say that the citizens have the right of political organization, but the third paragraph of the same article says that organization of assemblies and participation in an organization which opposes the political and social system of People's Poland are forbidden. In other words, any party which does not recognize the Communist political system is forbidden, and membership in it is punishable.

Since membership in a political party presupposes some right to influence that party, the question arises whether the Communists find it advisable to allow every citizen to belong to his country's Communist Party. The answer is no. The official statistics of the Communist parties in the occupied countries as well as in the Soviet Union show that the number of members of these parties ranges from 5 to 10 per cent of the population of the given country. Finally, even the internal structure of the Communist Party is dictatorial. The delegates of the local organizations accept only the projects and decisions of the party elite or of the chief dictator.

The Rumanian constitution, just like the others, appears to guarantee freedom of speech, freedom of the press, freedom of assembly, freedom of public processions and manifestations. Article 85 states that "These rights are ensured by placing at the disposal of the working masses and their organizations printing presses, stocks of paper, public buildings, the streets, communications facilities and other material requisites." In practice, the printing presses, paper mills, public buildings, radio, and so forth are owned by the state and are completely controlled by the leadership of the Communist Party. Even religious processions and manifestations require the consent of the state.

In theory, under the Communist system, every citizen over eighteen years of age has the right to vote. In practice, the elections are a tragic farce. They do not mean the right to select a candidate, to participate in the adoption of a party program, or even to defend social or national interests. They signify a compulsion to vote for one's hated enemies. The elector is forced to march to the polls to the accompaniment of music played by his foes while pain wrenches his heart and his fists clench in hatred and anger. The official results of the elections always show that the candidates of the Communist Party have received 99 per cent of the votes.

Does the administration of justice stand guard over civil liberties? No, it definitely does not, either in practice or in theory. The constitutions of the People's Republics have clear provisions in this respect. Article 41 of the Hungarian constitution states: "The courts shall punish the enemies of the people, defend and secure the political, economic and social order of the People's Democracy . . . they shall educate the workers to respect the rule of socialist communal life." The Polish and Rumanian constitutions of 1952 provide that "The courts defend the system of People's Democracy and the gains of the working people, and ensure the people's law, social property and citizens' rights."

In practice it is always the duty of the judge and the prosecutor to take the side of the Communist State—that is, of the Communist Party. It is always the duty of the defense to help the state prosecute the accused and to help him to accuse himself. The defendant's duty is to prove his guilt. The courts are a tool of the Communist regimes and are not independent institutions for the administration of justice. Communism introduces not only the judicial murder of innocent people but a debasement of man unparalleled in the history of mankind. The innocent defendant is forced to accuse himself of crimes which he has never committed, to accuse other innocent people, to trample upon his own dignity, to humiliate himself in the eyes of his friends and family, to spit upon the ideals in which he has believed, and to praise the loathsome practices of his enemy and prosecutor as he awaits death by the hands of his oppressor or by slow agony in a prison or forced labor camp.

V

Although it proclaims the liberation of the masses, the communist system has created unprecedented privilege for the ruling Communist elite. Everyone who has seen the living conditions of the highest Communist dignitaries in Russia as well as in the captive countries knows that these men enjoy a very high standard of living. They have privileges in all spheres of life—political, economic, social, and cultural. The life of the Communist elite is, however, not to be envied. Generally, the members of this group are hated. They are constantly threatened, even by the members of their own party. They live a life of fear in a golden cage, from which they cannot withdraw, even if they wish to do so.

In a democratic state a president elected to office lives like any free and private citizen. Under the Communist system this is unthinkable. The system of privileges finds support even in Communist theory. "It is time it was understood that Marxism is an enemy of equalization," Stalin stated in his report to the Seventeenth Communist Congress in January of 1934. "By equality Marxism means, not equalization of individual requirements and individual life, but abolition of classes. . . ." In the same connection he quoted Lenin's statement that "the claim that we want to make all men equal to one another is an empty phrase and a stupid invention of intellectuals." [4]

Freedom of religion and of faith under the Communist system does not exist, either in theory or in practice. The first articles of Communist constitutions always proclaim many civil liberties. But, when we analyze more closely the following passages of these articles, we see that as a rule they contradict and abolish the provisions contained in the first lines. Let us take for example, Article 70 of the constitution of the Polish People's Republic, which appears to guarantee the citizens freedom of conscience and of faith. It also says, however, that abuse of freedom of faith for purposes detrimental to the interest of the Polish People's Republic is punishable. In practice, of course, this means that every pronouncement against the atheistic and materialistic principles of the Communist system is detrimental to the People's Republic and is therefore punishable.

But that is not all. The Communists who proclaim the division between the church and the state do not intend to leave any freedom to the church. They demand the clergy's help in the building of socialism and consider any refusal to be detrimental to the interests of the People's State. In

[4] Joseph Stalin, *Problems of Leninism,* pp. 521-522.

practice, church organizations and the clergy are meant to have no function but that of a helpful tool in the communization of the nation.

The function of education is the same. The Communists do not even pretend to support freedom of knowledge and bluntly state in their legislation that the duty of higher schools is to educate the younger generation in the spirit of socialist dialectics and materialistic doctrines. Theoretically, the Communist system assures the youth of education. In practice, an individual's right to education is not determined by intellectual ability and progress but by membership in the Young Communist League (Komsomol), by informing on "unorthodox" professors, and by success in examinations on Communist politics and doctrines.

The articles of the Communist constitutions that deal with the rights of the citizens stress above all the rights to work, rest, and medical treatment. The Communist attitude toward the individual is like that of the horse-owner when he thinks that the main duty of his animal is to work and believes that it must be assured of rest and medical treatment only to insure the fulfillment of this duty. Actually, most farmers in the free countries treat their animals better than the Communists treat the people. Out of hatred, the Communists destroy whole social groups and even perpetrate the genocide of whole nations.

The Communists claimed that when they had freed the working man from capitalist exploitation they would not allow the exploitation of one man by another. Is this claim realized in practice? Again, the answer is no. The Communist state created the worst kind of exploitation by giving the rule of the people to the Communist elite and by providing this elite with the formidable weapons of both police and army. In a democratic state, even where large industries and sources of raw materials are nationalized, the interests of the people are guarded by trade unions, political parties, legislation, courts, and the police who protect the security of the citizens. The state authority is the mediator in the last resort in disagreements between labor and business.

The Moloch, which is the Communist state, has on its side the party, the police, and the courts. Special laws constantly increase the penalties for the plunder and destruction of the nationalized public property. Because the state is a "people's state" and "does not do injustice to the people," the trade unions act as a tool of the state in raising the productivity and quality of production and fixing the norms of work. The Stakhanovite work system, based on high norms of production and granting starvation-level wages with no means of protection against these, destroys the strength and health of the worker. Strikes are punishable because they are crimes against the interests of the state, and special laws provide discipline of work, penalties for failure to fulfill norms, and forced labor camps for "idlers" and "loafers."

Communism deprives the peasant of his beloved land, turns him into a Communist serf, and chains him to the state or collective farm in which the Communist bureaucracy demands of him ever-increasing physical efforts to produce for the insatiable state. After the liquidation of the remnants of private initiative in small business and crafts, the *kulak* peasant, the biggest "capitalist blood-sucker," is dealt with. He is destroyed by tax levies and forced deliveries of agricultural products and is finally evicted from his own farm.

Thus, behind the façade of People's Democracy, Communism practices dictatorship in every sphere of life—personal, political, economic, religious, and social. The Communist system creates privileges for the party and makes the citizen economically dependent upon the state. It debases human dignity, wrests faith out of human hearts, kills one's father, mother, brother, and sister in prisons and in forced labor camps, poisons the hearts of the young, and prepares them for participation in an imperialistic war against the interests of their own countries.

Moscow-controlled Communism also serves Soviet imperialism. It is the Soviets that occupied and imposed the Communist dictatorships upon the countries of Eastern Europe. If there had been no Soviet aggression or interference, not one of these countries would have a Communist dictatorship today. The basis for the exploitation of these countries and their systematic economic integration into the framework of the Soviet Union consists of secret trade agreements, so-called technical advisers, and economic plans for each country carefully adjusted to the plans for the Soviet economy. These Moscow-directed devices also determine the quantity of production and trade exchange in accordance with the political and economic objectives of the dictators in the Kremlin. In these countries Soviet generals and lower-ranking officers hold the posts of commanders, and prepare the younger generation for the betrayal of their own national interests and for service to their enemies.

For these reasons Communism, manifested as a dictatorship of the proletariat or as People's Democracy, constitutes, in theory and practice, a mortal danger to the existence of freedom, democracy, and peace in the world.

PART TWO

THE DEVELOPMENT OF AN
AGRARIAN SOCIETY

5 Land Reform and Agricultural Improvement

LADISLAV FEIERABEND

I

Eastern Europe was overwhelmingly peasant between the two world wars. The peasantry, for whom land was not merely a means of production or of income, but the established basis of family life, formed the majority of the population. The main problem of this region was rural overpopulation. In the period before the First World War, the surplus young people emigrated in considerable numbers to the United States and to other overseas countries. After 1918 this outlet was closed, and everybody had to remain on his home soil. There was too little land for too many people: roughly twice as many people were living off the land as was the case in Western Europe.

Everybody wanted land and therefore the price was enormously high. After money was spent to buy the land, there was not enough left to buy the numbers of cattle that the holding could support or to improve farming techniques. Lack of capital was responsible for the fact that farming methods remained the same as they had been for fifty or more years. The yields were very low, and there was no possibility of increasing them. In fact, yields decreased because the land was becoming exhausted. This was due to a lack of manure and fertilizer and to the peasants' ignorance of land preservation techniques.

Labor remained so cheap that the introduction of labor-saving devices did not pay. Overpopulation meant that there were more people living on holdings than were needed for the farm work. This situation caused underemployment. Since overpopulation decreased the output per man and with it the earnings per man, a very low standard of living resulted.

The size of the farms, which on the average was barely ten acres, was a problem in itself, and the custom of dividing land after the death of a peasant made the situation even more acute. The holdings consisted of many small and scattered strips so that it was impossible for the peasant to use machines, even when they were available. However, the land reforms, carried out after the First World War by the different governments, did have some success in equalizing the amounts of land held by the different peasants.

The land reforms grew out of political and national considerations rather than out of social and economic policy. The first and main objective of the agrarian parties was to expropriate the big landowners and to transfer their land to the peasants. The usual procedure was to fix a maximum acreage, usually about five hundred acres, and to decree that all land in excess of this amount should be sold to peasants, either to create new farms or to add to the area of peasant farms already in existence. Under these reforms, about twenty-five million acres were distributed, for the most part in quite small plots, averaging one hectare, or 2.4 acres. The smaller farms were given more land than the large, so that there was some leveling of the incomes derived from farming.

These reforms did not remedy the unhappy condition of the peasantry, since they were unable to remove the main causes for distress. If all the agricultural land of this region had been distributed equally among the peasants, the main result would have been the equalization of poverty. It was obvious that redistribution of the national income and wealth could not, by itself, greatly improve the condition of the people. The surplus agricultural population which was estimated, on the basis of the system of cultivation prevailing in that area, to be about fifteen million persons had to be absorbed, and that was an insoluble problem. This problem was heightened by the fact that between 1919 and 1939 the natural increase of population in this area remained almost three times as high as that in the West.

Some alleviation of the situation was sought in the development of industries. However, industrialization was a long-term measure, and the expense only added to the peasants' burden. The fiscal policy of the Eastern European states was to accumulate the national capital necessary for industrialization by taxes, tariffs, and prices. No money, or very little, was left for the peasants.

II

It would be unjust, however, to say that nothing was done to improve the lot of the peasantry. The governments were well aware that the land reforms should be supplemented by economic measures such as agrarian credits, modern cooperatives, development of transport, cheaper farm machinery, technical education and training. A great deal was accomplished by these measures.

The supply of credit was particularly important to the peasants. The need for capital to begin operations and to finance certain family needs, especially the weddings of daughters, made borrowing necessary. As banks would not make advances, money had to come from moneylenders who charged very high rates of interest. Often, the moneylender was the middleman who bought the peasant's produce and supplied him with goods. Frequently he had a strong and pernicious hold on the peasant.

Therefore, the cooperative movement began with the foundation of credit societies which formed a very large proportion of all cooperatives. Besides these, there were cooperative societies which supplied agricultural needs such as tools and seeds, traded agricultural products, and processed all sorts of produce. In Bulgaria, Hungary, and Rumania the cooperative movements were state-controlled. In Czechoslovakia the movement was independent but favored by the state; in Poland, beginning with the economic depression of the 1930's it was state-supported and therefore dependent.

The cooperative problem was a difficult one. On the one hand, cooperation among economically weak peasants could not succeed unless there was some collaboration with, or help from, the central authorities. On the other hand, such a relationship between strong and weak tended to develop into state domination of the cooperative movement.

The administrators of the cooperatives sometimes abused their prerogatives. They would occasionally grant government loans, not in response to genuine needs or because of commercial considerations, but with a view to the substantial number of votes which one cooperative society could guarantee at election time. In some instances, cooperatives served only well-to-do peasants because some governments were opposed to the social revolutionary ideology of the smaller peasants. In Rumania the cooperative societies were forced to assume the function of the tax collector. In Hungary the cooperatives belonged to the peasants in appearance only. In reality, they were capitalist enterprises and were not in peasant hands.

Except in Czechoslovakia, agricultural cooperation did not play any decisive role in the economic life of the peasantry, nor was it able to alleviate the existing adverse conditions. Credit was no real help unless the peasant had a reasonable expectation of being able to pay back what he had borrowed. In many cases this hope was negligible. A large proportion of the money which the peasants, particularly the small peasants, borrowed went to buy consumer goods. Thus, greater indebtedness did not point to a higher degree of investment, but to the extreme poverty of the small farm.

There was some state help for this situation, especially during the world-wide depression of the 1930's. In Bulgaria and Rumania agricultural debts were converted by government action. In 1934 some two hundred thousand Bulgarian peasants benefited by reductions in their debts and in the rate of interest and by a prolongation of the time allowed for settlement. In Rumania some two and one-half million peasants were assisted by similar legislation. Other measures, although not so far-reaching, were put into practice elsewhere in Eastern Europe to alleviate peasant indebtedness. But the credit problem was only mitigated, and not solved. The peasants' need for cash remained, and the lack of capital still prevented them from improving their farming techniques or increasing their earning capacity.

The governments promoted intensive cultivation of noncereals. Grain production was not appropriate to an overpopulated region, and a change to the production of livestock, livestock products, fruit, and vegetables was necessary. In Bulgaria and in some parts of Yugoslavia, intensive cultivation of garden crops, such as tobacco, tomatoes, wine, fruit, and roses was introduced. In Rumania, the cultivation of soya and other oil plants was introduced. These measures were, of course, just a beginning, and could not bring any substantial remedy.

Agriculture played the most important role of any single factor in all the Eastern European countries except Czechoslovakia. The largest part of the national incomes was derived from agriculture. National prosperity was dependent on the outcome of harvests and on the possibility of agricultural exports.

In the interwar period, these countries were victims of the fluctuations of the world market and of the policy of autarky which resulted from them. The countries of Western Europe from 1930 to 1932 imposed high tariffs on food imports in order to ward off the effects of the international slump in agriculture. In doing so, they ruined the Eastern European peasant. Export of agricultural products from all Eastern European countries was reduced to a minimum and prevented these countries from balancing their trade. Thus, it was impossible for them to buy the industrial goods and manufactures on which they depended to maintain industrial employment and the standard of living of the peasants themselves.

This crisis further reduced the possibilities of export because the Eastern European states were unable to compete in prices with the overseas agricultural exporting countries that had technical aid at their disposal and because they could not afford the enormous sums necessary for subsidizing exports of agricultural products. Many attempts were made by agrarian conferences to alleviate the distress by asking a preferential tariff system for this region, which would have meant the almost complete abolition of the most-favored-nation clause in bilateral commercial agreements. Another remedy was seen in the creation of an interstate grain purchasing commission that would buy up the chief surpluses from the Eastern European countries and distribute them among the different European importing countries. These proposed methods arose from the primary need of Eastern Europe, which was to acquire some form of economic security in the world market in order to provide a stable basis for peasant society.

Everything was in vain. It was impossible to achieve

stable, fair prices for agricultural products and to secure them a market. The Czechoslovakian Grain State Monopoly, established in 1934, was the only institution to bring any real benefit to the farming population. In other Eastern European countries, the situation reduced even further both the internal market and the income per head of the rural population. Less money than ever was available for improvements or for educating the peasants in new methods and techniques.

The alleviation of this situation came from Nazi Germany. Since 1935 Germany had been buying the greatest proportion of this region's agricultural surpluses and, in return, had been sending its own industrial goods into that area. Eastern Europe, and the Balkan states especially, became so dependent upon Germany's buying that the term "economic conquest" became a reality. This conquest, which was later political and military, of course did not bring any remedy to the agricultural problem of this region.

III

The Second World War devastated whole countries. Nowhere did the four horsemen of the Apocalypse reap a greater harvest than in Poland and Yugoslavia. In their wake came a troubled period which brought with it all the miseries and hardships that have always attended political and social revolutions. Vast numbers of the population were killed during the war. In Poland alone these numbered six million. The unbalance which this caused was greatly aggravated by enormous shifts of population in many of the Eastern European countries. The Germans were expelled from Poland and Czechoslovakia in millions, and from Hungary, Yugoslavia, and Rumania in hundreds of thousands. The total number of Germans expelled from this region was estimated at over eleven million. Changes in state

frontiers were another cause for great migrations. Four million Poles moved from the territory which was incorporated
into the U.S.S.R., and millions of Poles, Czechs, and Slovaks
moved into districts formerly inhabited by the Germans.
Although these changes alleviated the problem of rural overpopulation in Eastern Europe, there was still, at the end of
the Second World War, a surplus population estimated at
nine million.

The Communist parties in various Eastern European
states knew very well how to exploit this situation. They
knew that it was vital to the success of revolution that the
peasantry should not be opposed to it. They knew that the
Russian Revolution had been achieved only because Lenin
was fully aware of the desire of the peasant for more
land.

Orthodox Marxist theory required that the land be nationalized and that it be administered by the state. Land was
considered the most important means of production, and it
had to be treated as such. This dogma was abandoned by
Lenin for tactical reasons. He nationalized land in the Soviet
Union during the revolution of 1917, but distributed it under
ninety-nine-year leases to small and medium peasants for
private exploitation. It was the political pressure of the peasants which forced Lenin to change his political doctrine and
implement the agrarian program of the Populists, his political opponents. Lenin and his followers did not approve of
the peasant who, according to them, was a relic of the pre-
capitalistic society. It was Lenin's view that "small, individual farming gives birth to capitalism and the bourgeoisie
daily, hourly, spontaneously and on a mass scale," and that
in the future classless society the peasant was to assume the
status of a worker on the land as his fellow in town was a
worker in industry.

Political expediency determined Lenin's change in tactics.
He supported small agrarian property holders only because

he regarded the peasant as indispensable to the success of his revolution and to the consolidation of his dictatorship. This policy was reversed by Stalin after 1928 when forced collectivization of land in the form of pseudo-cooperatives (collective farms) was introduced in the Soviet Union.

Lenin's agricultural policy was adopted by all Eastern European Communist parties after the end of the Second World War. Being minorities in power, they knew that this was the only attitude they could take to the peasantry, the largest social group in this region. Therefore, they supported small agrarian property holders in the first stage of the development of their agricultural policy. There was only one difference between the Communist agricultural policies of Eastern Europe and Russia. Nationalization of land was not a part of the Eastern European policy, as it had not proved expedient in the Soviet Union and therefore was not contained in the agrarian policy of the Comintern for Eastern Europe in the inter-war period.

The Comintern had taken much interest in the Eastern European agrarian question. In 1923 a Red Peasants International was formed in Moscow as an effort to rally the peasantry to the Communist ideal and to combat the influence of the peasant parties united in the Green International in Prague. The Soviet move to collectivization within the U.S.S.R. in 1929 was not followed by any shift in the agrarian policy of the Comintern. Any mention of collective farming was frowned upon and the whole emphasis was upon attracting or neutralizing the middle peasant by assisting the individual and by supporting with new land reforms the peasant's struggle for more land. This policy was not changed when the Cominform took over the role of the Comintern after the Second World War.

"The land to those who till it personally," was the slogan of all Eastern European Communist parties, and land reforms were carried out in all countries. In Hungary, Albania, and in parts of Poland, land reforms were overdue, while in other Eastern European states expropriation and expulsion of the Germans formed the main basis of land reforms. Some forty-eight million acres, including forest land, were expropriated by the governments of which thirty million acres were distributed to some three million peasant families. The remainder was retained by the state.

To dispel any doubts as to the ultimate outcome of these reforms, the distributed land was declared the private property of the new owners, and in most countries it was laid down in the constitutions that "the land belongs to those who till it." The price to be paid by the beneficiaries was low, usually the equivalent of one year's harvest payable in ten to twenty installments. No compensation was paid to the old owners for the expropriated land.

The attitude toward the church and its landed property was less uniform than toward the secular owners. However, after some hesitation, most of the church estates exceeding the maximum size laid down in the land reform laws were also expropriated. In this way the church was deprived of its financial independence and of its economic influence on the rural population.

Even in the Baltic States which were incorporated into the Soviet Union, Stalin's methods were not followed. All the land and its resources, as in Russia, were declared public property and nationalized, and all the land in excess of seventy-five acres was expropriated for distribution, but no collectives were formed. However, through a system of differential delivery and farm taxes, the way was paved for ultimate collectivization.

All these land reforms had done nothing to solve the old agricultural problem of Eastern Europe. On the contrary, they aggravated the situation. The land became more split up than ever, as larger farms were abolished. The reforms did not solve the problem of technical progress, and made the reorganization of agriculture even more necessary than it had been before.

Land reform was a political measure. Its aim was not the reorganization of production, but the redistribution of income. Its aim was to win the small peasant for the Communists, and to weaken the political influence of the agrarian parties. Therefore, the Communists stole the programs of the agrarian parties and publicized them as their own. Beside private ownership, these programs called for mechanization, consolidation of scattered strips, good and guaranteed prices for agricultural products, expansion of credit, reduction of taxes, and social insurance for all peasants.

The smallholders felt quite happy, generally speaking, on their new land. It may have produced less than it had in the hands of its former owners, but the smallholders' income was larger than it had been when they were employed as agricultural laborers. Many of them started believing the Communists and joined the Communist parties. One of the Communist aims was fulfilled.

IV

It should have been obvious to all that the Communists were preparing a program of land collectivization, and that the second stage of their agricultural policy would be similar to what it had been in the Soviet Union. But sufficient attention was not paid to these trends. Practically all forests and large stretches of arable land and pastures became state property and were organized as Communist state farms. District cooperative or state stations were established and equipped with heavy agricultural machinery, which was not practical for use on small fields. The Communists favored the allocation of equipment to cooperatives rather than to private persons. The cooperatives, which performed many public functions such as bulk purchasing of food and supplies, began to be controlled by the state machine and not by their members, the peasants. At the same time, the independence of the church and its economic influence on the rural population was broken.

Once the Communists were established safely in power, they shifted their agricultural policy. Except in the Baltic States where the Communists resorted to deportations and in Rumania where they evicted some seventeen thousand Rumanian families from their homes, collectivization was started smoothly and was not recognized as such. The Communists did not speak about collectivization, but about transforming uneconomical small-scale enterprise to large-scale cooperative farming. They are still making great efforts to convince the small peasants that as members of production cooperatives they till their own land and manage their own affairs.

Collectivization is being instituted by a clever transformation of the cooperatives. This process begins with a number of peasants being instructed to form some such organization as a communal laundry, a chick hatchery, or a calf station. Then, usually before sowing or harvest time, the members are persuaded to share their labor, teams, and farm machinery, which sounds like nothing more than neighborly cooperation. The farms continue to be made up of separate private parcels. The next type of cooperative eliminates boundaries and plows out border strips. The expanded fields are worked by the cooperative, with systematic planning for crops, fodder, and hay. Thus, collective mass production is introduced, but the land still belongs to the members.

Collective management is a function of the third type of cooperative. In this type the crops belong to the cooperative, not to its members. The owners of the land give up all their rights of disposal and of management. The members contribute their livestock and most of their agricultural equipment to the organization. Cattle are kept in common barns, but a member may retain one cow and a calf, some pigs, sheep, goats, and poultry. He also retains a garden plot of one and one-fourth acres which he can cultivate according to his own wishes. Ten to 20 per cent of a season's profit is deducted from the whole profit and distributed as separate compensation to those members who contributed land for the use of the cooperative.

In the fourth type, no percentage is paid for use of land although the fields still belong to the farmers in the title registers. All profits are divided according to the labor units of the members. This is the real Soviet collective farm, in which private property has become a fiction. Members receive advances in money or supplies during the year for their work. At the end of the year their accounts are balanced on the basis of production and sales.

Collectivization is proceeding at a rapid pace in all the countries of this region. According to the latest news, over 40 per cent of the agricultural land has been collectivized or, in other words, is in the hands either of state farms or of production cooperatives.

Production cooperatives are not genuine cooperatives according to the Western definition of the term. The communist philosophy of subservience rather than freedom, class hatred rather than understanding, aggression rather than tolerance, coercion rather than mutuality, is against all genuine, fundamental cooperative principles. True cooperatives can be founded only on the initiative of their members. Those instigated by authority cannot be considered true cooperatives, nor can those which are under the domination of outside influences. There can be no true cooperatives in Communist countries, because the will of the members cannot be expressed.

Production cooperatives are excellent examples of the Communist pseudo-cooperative. They are created by the government and are dependent upon it. They must accept a government-dictated constitution. Cooperative members, instead of being the masters of their cooperatives, are their servants. They have to perform tasks which have been fixed without their knowledge or consent. In higher type Communist cooperatives, the members assume the status of landless laborers.

If the complete dependency of the cooperatives on the State Tractor and Machine Stations and on the Communist Party is taken into consideration, it is clear that production cooperatives are no more than state enterprises under the disguise of cooperatives. There is only one difference between a state farm and a production cooperative: the members of a cooperative have to bear all production risks. It is true that *de jure* they remain owners of their land, but *de facto* they cease to be owners as they cannot be sure of getting their fields back when they leave the cooperative. According to the constitution of these cooperatives, a member must accept other fields, if return of his own fields would disrupt the cooperative.

The Communists declare they prefer that peasants join cooperatives voluntarily. However, they are not above persuading private farmers to join by such methods as higher taxes and higher delivery quotas, less fertilizers and other production means at higher prices, and charges for all services higher than those paid by cooperative members. At the same time, they give private farmers no credit, no field hands, and no opportunity to use agricultural machines, while collectives enjoy almost unlimited credit and other facilities. Members of production cooperatives are rewarded by the government with free vacations in the best hotels at winter resorts and with free group travel to the Soviet Union; they are a privileged class in every respect.

In contrast, well-to-do peasants who used hired labor in free times are denounced as being "village rich," a term which is used in Eastern Europe to describe the equivalent of the

Russian *kulak*. The village rich are not allowed to enter a collective or are expelled if they become members. A merciless battle is being waged to ruin them. They are being liquidated as peasants, removed from villages, and sent to mines or to industry or concentration camps. There are roughly thirteen million peasant families in Eastern Europe, more than one million of which are *kulaks*. The children of all these families must lose the individualistic traits of their peasant heritage: that is the Communist aim.

Large-scale industrialization plans, for military purposes rather than for consumer production, are being pushed forward with great vigor in all Eastern European states and new labor is required in great numbers. *Kulaks* and other class enemies are an obvious source for this labor. By tapping this source, the surplus agricultural population will be disposed of and the people with individualist outlook gradually destroyed. If there is a shortage of workers in agriculture, as for instance in Czechoslovakia now, industrial workers already persuaded to the collective way of thinking can be utilized.

The term *kulak* has come to mean anyone who is against collectivization, and all *kulaks* are to be destroyed. The process of destruction is quickly changing the status of the agrarian population in this region. The agricultural population is decreasing and, according to estimate, does not amount today to more than 45 per cent of the total population. This decrease is the political consequence of collectivization and not its economic or social result. The collectivization policy itself cannot solve the old problem of rural overpopulation but can only aggravate it. The real aim of Communist collectivization is not to solve this problem but rather to destroy the peasantry.

Agriculture, like the other divisions of economic life, has been dictated by state plans which prescribe to the peasant what crops are to be grown and what animals are to be bred.

The peasants do not like regimentation and therefore the Communist economic plans have not brought about any increase in agricultural production.

The collectivization policy has further aggravated the situation. The peasants hate even the word "collective." They go about their work with indifference or with fear and hatred. Their aversion to coercion, dictatorship, and controls, their attachment to their land, and their pride in independence, have neutralized all the advantages of large-scale production with its mechanization and its use of modern agricultural methods. The Communist belief that large-scale operation would bring about efficient agricultural production has not materialized.

Agricultural production is decreasing. Eastern Europe used to be a very large exporter of all agricultural products, but it is suffering from shortages today. Food is scarce in these agricultural countries. Before the Second World War, nine out of ten residents of Czechoslovakia were nourished by the produce of Czechoslovakian agriculture. There were no rations. Everybody could buy what he wanted, and the standard of living in Czechoslovakia was the highest in Eastern Europe. Today, according to official Communist pronouncements, every second man in Czechoslovakia, despite strict rationing, has to be supplied from abroad. Milk, butter, and eggs are not distributed to adults at all, and even sugar is in short supply. Czechoslovakia, once the largest exporter of beet sugar in Europe, today cannot provide its diminished population with sugar although it has nearly 15 per cent fewer inhabitants than before 1938 due to the expulsion of the Germans. Bulgaria and Hungary, which had great surpluses of all agricultural products before the last war, must now import foodstuffs for their starving populations. Agricultural production in Eastern Europe has not yet attained the prewar level, although the free farms of Western Europe have surpassed it considerably.

Peasantism: Its Ideology and Achievements

BRANKO M. PEŠELJ

I

That part of Europe which lies east of the Danzig-Trieste line is often referred to as "peasant Europe." This term indicates a twofold concept: Economically, "peasant Europe" stands for that part of the continent which is devoted primarily to agrarian production under the system of small and medium holdings and in which farming represents a tradition, a civilization, and a way of life. Sociologically and culturally, the term "peasant Europe" denotes an area in which by far the greatest portion of the population is peasant and forms a group whose economic, social, and cultural aspects have been genuinely preserved.

The differences between Eastern and Western Europe were less noticeable a hundred years ago than they were at the end of the Second World War. The industrial revolution which swept Western Europe in the second half of the nineteenth century generated profound economic and social changes over the continent as a whole, and contributed to its division into two distinct sectors. A consequence of this partition was the creation of unique social and economic conditions in Eastern Europe. These conditions, in turn, provoked political and social movements, such as had never been known in the West, and which expressed the distinctive socio-economic programs and political and social philosophies of the area.

Before any analysis of these peasant movements can be undertaken, it will be necessary to examine their human element, the peasantry. There are three points which are of most significance to this discussion: first, what is a peasantry; second, what are the differences between a peasantry and the rural population of the West, usually known as farmers; and third, what are the special characteristics of the Eastern European peasantry which have justified and made possible its separate political organization.

Despite the fact that the peasantry still represents a considerable majority of the world's population, a uniform definition for it cannot be found. The reason for this is the different approach of various social and economic schools to the peasant problem. While the Marxists consider the peasantry from a purely economic point of view, evaluating this group only in the system of socialist production, liberals believe that there are aspects to the peasantry besides the economic which should be considered. The liberals point out the importance of the peasant's relationship to his land and the influence of his environment upon him. They realize that there are two elements, the sociological and the cultural, which are of great and equal significance in appraising the peasant society. The sociological element includes the individual's family life, the customs, traits, and trends of neighborhood and village communities, and the peasant's attachment to religious and other traditions. These traditions are upheld by a special type of "progressive conservatism." The cultural element includes all such features as folk songs, folk customs and habits, and so forth, which have developed independent of the cosmopolitan civilization.

In view of the foregoing, the peasantry may be defined

tentatively as a group settled on a determined territory, having its principal source of livelihood in a cultivation of the soil that is based on the system of the small farm, and possessing its own way of life and its own indigenous culture.

This definition will help us answer our second question; namely, what are the differences between the peasants and the farmers. For a long time the rural sociologists of the West made no distinction between these two groups, and it is only recently that adequate attention has been given to this problem. Today it is generally recognized that between these two rural societies there exist essential dissimilarities which result from a permanent infiltration by the cosmopolitan civilization into the rural orbit. This process has been far more intense in the European and American rural groups, the farmers, than in the genuine peasant population.

With this distinction in mind, the farmers and the genuine peasantry may be contrasted. Economically speaking, the farmers produce primarily for the market, abiding by the established norms of offer and demand. Although they are attached to the land, they consider it almost impersonally and from an economic point of view. Therefore, they are willing to move from one area to another when there are economic reasons. The peasants, on the other hand, produce primarily for home consumption. Because their land is a part of their heritage, they consider it personally, as a part of their life and of their family tradition.

Socially, life in the rural communities of the West has become increasingly urbanized. The peasant society of Eastern Europe has been infiltrated by urban ideas to a far lesser degree and has preserved, generally speaking, many of its original aspects.

Culturally, the indigenous traditions of the farmer population, if not completely vanished, are disappearing rapidly. In the genuine peasant society, cultural traits are still clearly visible and constitute an outstanding characteristic of this group.

The third point in this discussion of the peasantry concerns the special characteristics of the Eastern European peasantry which have enabled it to maintain a separate political organization. It can be said safely that nowhere in Europe have the characteristics peculiar to peasant society been so well preserved as in this region. Although numerical supremacy has been a factor in the preservation of peasant society, more important is the fact that the peasants of Eastern Europe have manifested in recent history a tremendous self-consciousness, political maturity, and determined will to create political and social organizations of their own, which, so far, have not been emulated by the peasantry in other parts of the globe. The peasantry of Western European countries, such as Spain, Portugal, or Italy, often comprises over 50 per cent of the rural population. However, this Western peasantry has never been able to generate powerful and influential peasant political organizations, nor has it been able to play an outstanding role in national life as has the peasantry of Eastern Europe.

II

The greater part of the peasantry in Eastern Europe was liberated from the bondages of serfdom in the year of revolutions, 1848. In that part of Poland which was included in the Russian Empire, the abolition of serfdom was proclaimed in 1861, and in Old Rumania, in 1864. The peasants of the Balkans, subjected to a special type of land tenure relations and vassalage as practiced in the Ottoman empire, were freed gradually with the withdrawal of the Turkish political power, especially after the arrangements made at the Congress of Berlin in 1878.

The liberation of the peasantry was a consequence of

the demands of the new liberal movement and was one of the achievements of the liberal regimes which gained momentum on the Continent after the Napoleonic era. This European liberalism had been a result of the struggle of the bourgeoisie against the old political and economic order upheld previously by the aristocracy. It originated in the theory of natural rights, as interpreted by French political philosophers of the eighteenth century, and included in its doctrine the postulate of political, economic, and social freedom and equality for all individuals.

However, it would be wrong to assume that the formal liberation of the peasantry was an immediate result of its emulation of other classes of society, in particular, of the bourgeoisie. On the contrary, the struggle for the realization of peasant rights had still to be fought.

The ruling regimes imposed political restrictions that were usually based on the tax census system and barred large masses of the peasant population from their right to vote in parliamentary elections. In many of the countries, it was not until the end of the First World War that complete franchise was granted to the peasantry.

Economic freedom, as advocated and practiced by liberalism, soon began to undermine the foundations of the peasant economy. The peasantry, which under feudalism had paid most of its rents and other fees to the landlord in natural produce, was placed suddenly in the midst of a complicated money-economy in which the autarkic arrangements of the peasant familistic economy were no longer valid. Peasant land, which throughout centuries had changed little in price or in value, was suddenly submitted to wide fluctuations in value as a consequence of the rapid development of the communication system and the erection of industrial plants. The appearance of a money-economy created the necessity of establishing an appropriate credit system which heretofore had been lacking completely in the peasant orbit. The state, however, following its policy of economic freedom, did not deem it necessary to intervene in this problem, and left the peasants open to the merciless exploitation of private banks and usurers. Economic individualism, accentuated by liberalism, induced individual members of the large peasant family groups, known among the Southern Slavs as *zadrugas,* to seek their economic independence. This process provoked a hasty and uncontrolled parcellation of the peasant land and contributed further to the economic weakness and inefficiency of the peasant system of farming.

The solemnly proclaimed social equality of the peasant was a farce. The ruling groups, derived from the bourgeoisie, the newly created bureaucracy, and the remnants of the aristocratic elements, looked upon the peasants with contempt and mistrust, considering them, although necessary to agrarian production, neither fitted nor qualified to take part in politics or public affairs. Social inequality was expressed both by the attitude of dominant ethnical groups to the "peoples of lower categories" and by the division within these groups between intelligentsia and the common people, or peasants.

Obviously, remedies were sought to correct the adverse conditions created in the liberal era, but before these are discussed, it is necessary to credit liberalism for those ideas and measures which, in principle, were universally accepted by the masses and which made possible their political organization. Generally speaking, the ideas of political freedom and of general education and a belief in the individual's capabilities were the stimulating forces behind the organization of the people. However, these ideas did not save liberalism, but prepared the road for its destruction.

The first reaction to the flaws in liberalism was the appearance of the "scientific socialism" of Karl Marx. It is important to note that this philosophy was conceived exclusively for the newly created industrial proletariat. The peasants, if considered at all, were reviewed and evaluated only from the point of view of production with no attention paid to the human side of their problems. Moreover, the contempt of Marx for the peasantry is well known. He called them a "class of barbarians," and proclaimed his desire to save humanity from the "idiocy of rural life."

The reaction to scientific socialism and a simultaneous opposition to liberalism brought about the birth of Christian democracy which attempted to formulate a middle-road policy between the economic freedom of liberalism and the socialist doctrine of the total negation of the absolute truth, of private property, and of human dignity. Being primarily a reaction to the liberal-socialist dispute on capital-labor relations, this new doctrine was concerned very little, if at all, with the peasant problem which "remained the stepchild of public opinion and of the social policy."

The first attempt to use the contemporary social and economic ideas for the organization of the peasant masses was partly accountable for the appearance of Populism in Russia in the 1870's. More specifically, Populism was an endeavor to create an ideal agrarian peasant community by applying the theories of scientific socialism. This very fact converted the effort into a unique social and economic movement sharply in conflict with the orthodox Marxism. It became clear very soon to the promoters of Populism that the formulas conceived by Marx were inefficient in a rural society and that diversified methods must be sought if the needs and hopes of the peasants were to be satisfied. This new movement, although peasant, was of revolutionary character, not only demanding the land for the peasants but also advocating its collective ownership under a particular form of Russian organization known as the *mir*. It pointed out that the essence of the Populist program must be the institutions and desires inherent in the people and that it must not represent scientific formulas imported from abroad.

Although Populism exerted some influence on the establishment of the Rumanian peasant movement, it had very little influence upon the other peasant movements in Eastern Europe. At the time when Populism was already an organized political force in Russia, the peasantry in Eastern Europe was still politically inactive. When the peasant mobilization began, more than two decades later, it was influenced little, if at all, by the Populist ideas.

The main reason for the relatively late organization of the peasantry in Eastern Europe was the presence of political and economic conditions essentially different from those prevailing in Tsarist Russia. Whereas regular political life was unknown in Russia, European liberalism favored the formation of political parties which would try to win the sympathies of the peasants by promising them the realization of their desires. Collective ownership of land was not a common institution in Eastern Europe. However, the prediction of Marx relating to the accumulation of capital and further expansion of large estates proved to be incorrect. On the contrary, many large land holdings, unable to accommodate themselves to modern capitalist management, commenced to disintegrate. The land was usually bought, in spite of heavy material sacrifices, by land-hungry neighboring peasants, and thus many new independent peasant holdings were created, which contributed considerably to the strengthening of the peasantry.

Hence, the establishment of a revolutionary peasant movement was checked by existing political conditions: the traditions of the Eastern European peasantry were opposed to collective forms of land ownership and to the socialist tenets of Populism. However, none of the existing political groups was fit to meet the increased desire of the peasantry for an organized action of their own, and, at the turn of the century, on an independent basis and in opposition to the contemporary political and social groups, peasant organization began.

The common source of the peasant movements resided in the political, social, and economic evils of the liberal regimes, but immediate motives varied slightly in the different countries. In some countries, the emphasis on the necessity for peasant organization was a reaction to the adverse economic conditions to which the peasantry was exposed. In other countries, this move was a political and economic reaction to political and national oppression, economic exploitation, and the contempt of the ruling ethnical groups for the peasantry of subordinated nations. Finally, the Croatian peasants had special motives. Their peasant movement was organized chiefly to struggle for the social and political equality of the peasants against the dominating bourgeoisie and the bureaucracy. The latter, although it represented an insignificant minority in the nation, had monopolized Croatian political life.

The first to outline the philosophical principles of a peasant movement was Ante Radić in Croatia. Influenced by French Romantic philosophers, especially Michelet, Radić published, in 1896, his work, *Osnova,* in which he set forth his concept of the people (in peasant countries this meant the peasantry), and indicated their significance in the political and economic life of the nation.

The first coherent peasant organizations were those of the Bulgarians and the Czechs who both founded their first peasant political organizations in 1896. They were followed shortly by the Croatians in 1904, and by the Serbians and the Poles in 1905. The first steps for a peasant movement in Rumania were initiated in 1907, while in Hungary the appearance of a genuine peasant movement was retarded by political and socio-economic conditions until 1908. In the Baltic States, true political life started only with the independence gained after the First World War. Subsequently, powerful peasant political organizations were founded in Estonia and Latvia. In Albania the initiative for a peasant political organization did not exist until the Second World War; the organization itself was established after the war by exiled political leaders.

In Slovenia, Slovakia, and Lithuania, on the other hand, truly peasant political organizations have never developed fully. In these Catholic countries the peasantry was influenced from the beginning by the Catholic political thought and subsequently organized on the principles of Christian democracy.

Although the immediate motives for peasant organization in different countries were varied, its demands were everywhere identical because of its common general source—its ideological basis. The programs made the following demands for the peasants: full political rights, proportional participation in public affairs, agrarian reform and distribution of the land to the peasants, social justice, and rights for the peasants in educational facilities equal to the rights of other classes in the state.

To understand better the peasant movements and their aims, three elements of their ideological and organizational structure must be discussed: first, their ideological basis; second, the dogmatic differences between these and other contemporary political and socio-economic trends; and third, the effective points of their practical programs.

The peasant ideology, or peasantism, is the outlook of the peasantry on the complex of political and socio-economic issues in which the peasants are interested and for whose solution they are fighting. The organizational forms of peasantism, established for the purposes of current political struggle, are the various peasant political parties. Unlike scientific socialism or Christian democracy, peasantism is not the artificial creation of an individual or group of individuals; it contains only those ideas which are inherent in the peasant soul and character. Consequently, the peasant leaders do not conceive the political soul of peasantism but merely interpret and articulate its principles. Hence, considerable differences must exist between peasantism and other contemporary movements.

Between peasantism and scientific socialism, there are irreconcilable differences, reflected in philosophical, economic, social, and political concepts. Philosophically, scientific socialism advocates economic determinism, dialectic materialism, and the materialistic interpretation of history. Consequently, it repudiates the existence of a superior being, rejects religion and spiritual values as detrimental to human development, and minimizes the significance of tradition. Peasantism, on the contrary, relies on the idealistic principles of philosophical reasoning, stresses the existence of God, points out the necessity for religious beliefs, and indicates the importance of spiritual values. It emphasizes as of equal importance the significance of tradition in human development and reaffirms its position in the peasant society.

Economically, scientific socialism demands the collectivization of the means of production, including land, and the introduction of a planned socialist economy. It evaluates individuals and collective groups exclusively on the basis of their role in socialist production and repudiates economic individualism in any form. Peasantism, on the contrary, defends firmly the principle of private ownership of the means of production, especially of the peasant land, and teaches that the right to dispose of the fruits of one's own labor is sacred and inviolable. It rejects the planned economy of socialism and favors private initiative and the system of free cooperation.

Socially, scientific socialism teaches the necessity of a permanent class struggle and considers as inevitable the revolutionary overthrow of the existing social and economic order by the proletariat. Peasantism, on the contrary, rejects the idea of class struggle and believes in the possibility of a peaceful coexistence of all classes of society. It also rejects

the revolutionary methods advocated by scientific socialism, believing that the necessary changes in society can be
achieved by peaceful means and evolutionary methods.

Politically, scientific socialism is totalitarian in its concept.
It does not tolerate the existence of other political and social
systems, nor is it willing to share power with other political
groups. Peasantism, on the contrary, is genuinely democratic
and ready to collaborate with other political and social forces
provided they are democratically disposed and have their
roots in the will of the people.

The differences between peasantism and other current ideologies, although existent, are less emphatic. Peasantism dis-
tinguishes itself from liberalism mainly in its economic ideas.
While it agrees with liberalism on the concepts of political
freedom and social equality, it rejects the ideas of the latter
on uncontrolled economic liberties. Past experience has
proved to the followers of peasantism that in peasant countries unrestricted economic liberties are detrimental to peasant farming and to national economies.

Ideological differences between peasantism and Christian
democracy are more subtle. Both ideologies cherish the fundamental principles of human dignity and of individual freedom; both teach the existence of God, reject the materialistic
interpretation of the world, and seek to establish a middle
road between total economic freedom and complete submis-
sion of the individual to the community. Yet, there is an important structural element which has contributed essentially
to a separate organization of the peasantry in Eastern Europe. Since 1891 when the papal encyclical, *Rerum Novarum,* was issued, and especially since 1931 with the appearance of the encyclical, *Quadragesimo Anno,* Christian
democracy has been an eminently Catholic doctrine and,
consequently, not best fitted to attract the peasantry which
is made up of different religious denominations. Peasantism,
on the contrary, while pointing out the necessity of religion,

has no preference for any particular religious denomination and is for this reason better adapted to the peasantry.

Finally, peasantism rejects definitely the political and social concepts of modern totalitarianism. Totalitarian and undemocratic regimes in Eastern Europe during the interwar period were always upheld by military cliques, aristocratic and bureaucratic groups, or by the ruling dynasties whose aims were to keep the power at all costs and whose political methods and social views were diametrically opposed to the fundamental principles of peasantism.

Politically, peasantism advocates a system of parliamentarianism with two additional features: accentuation of local self-government and direct participation in the government of the greatest number of people. Economically, peasantism favors free cooperatives because it believes that cooperation preserves the principles of private property and permits the exercise of private initiative. The latter is favored when cooperative arrangements are not adequate to meet economic requirements.

III

Although the peasant movements and parties were initiated before the First World War, they achieved their full strength and political significance only after the war was over. There were three causes for this postwar rise of peasant political organizations: the formation of the national states, the universal franchise, and the agrarian reforms.

The formation of national states in Eastern Europe contributed enormously to the development of political life. While the people of this area had heretofore directed most of their political endeavors against the oppression of the ruling nations, in the new era they directed their efforts toward the solution of vital economic and social issues.

Universal franchise enabled the peasant population to

participate in national elections and thus intensified the activities of the peasant political organizations. Only a decade earlier, because of the tax census system, none but a limited number of the peasants were entitled to vote, but in the national democratic states this right was granted to every male citizen over twenty-one years of age.

In Bulgaria, Rumania, Yugoslavia, Czechoslovakia, and Poland, a considerable number of agrarian reforms were accomplished which distributed large surfaces of arable land to individual peasants. They thus became economically independent and from then on were valiant champions of the peasant program. No substantial land reform was carried out in Hungary until 1945.

Unfortunately, the initial success of the peasant parties was not given political effect everywhere and, where peasant regimes were established, they were not of long duration. The advances of the peasant parties were neutralized soon by the counter actions of totalitarian elements which were opposed to democratic principles in general, and to peasant political and social concepts in particular. The peasant parties, faithful to their programs, favored and supported genuinely democratic systems and cooperated with other democratic groups but, with the disappearance of the democratic order, their own position became precarious. It must be admitted that the complicated machinery of a democratic regime was unable to run smoothly at all times in the newly established national states, except in Czechoslovakia. However, this deficiency should not be interpreted as a lack of interest in democratic institutions nor as a disapproving attitude toward the principles of freedom which symbolize Western political thought. The democratic regimes came up against a complex of problems whose complete, satisfactory, and early settlement was somewhat unreasonably expected by the newly created national states. Profiting from these adverse and interrelated domestic conditions, the totalitarian elements found intervention possible. They usually claimed that this intervention was necessary "to save the country from the total chaos in which it was driven by the unsatisfactory operating of democratic institutions." What was even worse, new regimes were supported often by the Western democracies who used the unjustifiable excuse that "no other solutions were possible."

Despite the mistakes and failures of the democratic regimes, today even the most bitter opponents of peasantism must admit that the peasant parties, as political organizations, were stalwart champions of democratic government and did not, in general, support the established dictatorships or their undemocratic methods.

The greatest achievement of all the peasant groups was that of the Bulgarian Agrarian Union. From its modest beginnings in 1896, the Union grew steadily. In the first postwar elections it received a strong relative majority in the National Assembly, and in the elections of April 1923, 212 deputies out of 245 were allotted to the Agrarian Union. At the relatively early date of October 1919, the first Bulgarian peasant government of Aleksander Stambolisky was formed. The most significant of its numerous political and economic achievements was the agrarian reform based on the principles that the land should be the property of those who till it and that every peasant is entitled to only as much land as he and his family are able to cultivate. In spite of the certain weaknesses and deficiencies of this peasant government which contributed to its downfall, its democratic basis cannot be denied. Its reforms converted Bulgaria into a country of small and medium peasant holdings which, despite the forcible overthrow of the peasant regime in June 1923, remained unchanged until the end of the Second World War.

In Czechoslovakia, the Republican Agrarian Party was the strongest party in the Parliament and the most important pillar of the Czechoslovakian democracy. After the political liberation of the Czechs and the Slovaks in 1918, the party's main goal was to secure economic and social prosperity for the Czech and Slovak peasants, chiefly by promoting cooperative organizations and by defending the interests of the peasant populations. The party averaged forty-five deputies on all national elections and cooperated with other democratic parties in the governments of the Republic. The President of the Party, Antonin Švehla and his successor, Milan Hodža, were for many years Prime Ministers of the Czechoslovakian governments.

The Croatian Peasant Party, established in 1904 by the brothers Ante and Stjepan Radić, reached its full political importance in the first postwar elections in Yugoslavia. This was in November 1920, and at that time the party became the undisputed choice of the Croatian people. In all free parliamentary elections since then, the Croatians, and especially the Croatian peasantry, have cast their votes in overwhelming majority for this political group. The principal aims of the party's program were Croatian national independence and social and economic justice. When the president of the party, Stjepan Radić, was assassinated in June 1928, Vladko Maček, who heads the party today, was elected president. In its political struggle, the party has opposed violently the Yugoslav centralism favored by the majority of Serbian political groups, and has been outlawed twice as "dangerous for the interests of the state." In August 1939, a compromise that opened the door for a just settlement of the Serbo-Croatian dispute was reached with the Regency of the Kingdom of Yugoslavia and with certain of the Serbian political parties.

The beginnings of the Polish peasant movements date back to 1905, when the first Polish peasant associations were organized in Galicia under the leadership of Wincenty Witos. With this as an initiative, the Polish peasant party, *Piast*, was founded in Cracow in 1913. During the First World War, in the Russian part of Poland, another peasant party, *Liberation*, was born. Its leader was Stanislaw Thugutt. This party emphasized the solution of social and economic problems, demanding primarily an extensive land reform and distribution of the land to the peasants. In liberated and united Poland, these two peasant groups united in 1920 to become the strongest individual Polish political group, but later, in May 1923, one faction dissented. Witos was repeatedly elected Prime Minister and was holding this position in 1926 when the military *coup d'état*, executed by Pilsudski, put an end to democratic government in Poland. In 1928, during the dictatorship, all peasant political groups fused in a united peasant party under the leadership of Witos and Mikolajczyk, but, because of the undemocratic regime, this group was never permitted to take part in Poland's political life.

Although it may be argued that the embryonic stage of peasant organization in Serbia started in 1882 under the influence of the socialist ideas of Svetozar Marković, it is more correct to say that the first truly peasant movement in Serbia began in 1905 with the actions of Milislav Kurtović. In 1920, in the new state, Yugoslavia, the Agrarian Union of the Serbians, Croatians, and Slovenes was established, under the leadership of Joca Jovanović. The Union had little success among the Croatian and Slovenian peasantry, and was later known as the Serbian Agrarian Party. It recruited its followers mainly from the Serbian peasants in Serbia, Bosnia, and northern Dalmatia. The party was in the difficult position of being obliged to compete politically with two well-established Serbian parties, the Radicals and the Democrats. The provisions of the electoral law were unfavorable to the smaller political formations and, for this reason, the party was hindered from obtaining a proportional number of deputies in national elections. In June 1938, after the death of Joca Jovanović, Milan Gavrilović was elected the new president of the party.

The initiative for a peasant organization in Rumania was given in 1907, in Jassy, Bessarabia, by Constantine Stere, who was influenced by Russian Populism. The Rumanian Peasant Party was formally founded in 1919, and Ion Mihalache was elected its President. In 1926, the Rumanian National Party from Transylvania, led by Iuliu Maniu, and the Peasant Party of the Old Kingdom fused into one political group known as the Rumanian National Peasant Party, which became the strongest political organization of the country. In the elections of 1928, the overwhelming majority of votes were cast for this united peasant front, and a peasant government was formed with Maniu as Prime Minister. This party brought about some administrative, economic, and social reforms which aimed at the assurance of the progress of the Rumanian state. Unfortunately, the peasant rule was definitely handicapped by the international agrarian crisis which was at its peak during the period of the peasant government. The party's position was further aggravated by its continuous struggle with the liberals and by numerous intrigues of the Crown calculated to destroy the unity and vigor of the peasant group.

Because of specific conditions which existed in Hungary, the organization of the peasantry commenced relatively late. Sandor Czismadia made the first attempt to organize the landless peasants on the principles of agrarian socialism in 1896, but the genuine peasant movement was initiated by István Nagyatádi-Szabó in 1908. The movement grew in strength after the collapse of the first Communist regime of Béla Kun, but its original success and its hopes for the future were skilfully suppressed by the Hungarian ruling class. It was not until 1930 that Zoltan Tildy and Ferenc Nagy undertook the revival of a truly peasant political organization. As a consequence, the Hungarian Smallholders Party was founded. This party fought valiantly against all the odds of the authoritarian Hungarian regime, but was not able to attain its full strength until after the First World War in the November elections of 1945.

The first international agreement among various peasant groups was reached in 1921, subsequent to the visit of the Bulgarian Premier Stambolisky to Prague. This agreement was between the Bulgarian Agrarian Union and the Czechoslovak Republican Agrarian Party, and was later joined by the Polish Peasant Party. The agreement was, however, of a short duration and of little significance in international relations. In 1923 Stambolisky was overthrown and assassinated, and in 1926 the Prime Minister, Witos, was ousted following the military putsch of Pilsudski.

In 1928 efforts were renewed to achieve an international peasant understanding, and in 1929 the International Agrarian Bureau in Prague was established. The Bureau was presided over by Švehla, and nineteen different peasant organizations from all parts of Europe participated in its work. The Bureau stood for the principles of cooperation, mutual aid, friendship, democracy, and peace. Unfortunately, international conditions did not favor such an association. Except in Czechoslovakia, democratic political movements throughout Eastern Europe were either already outlawed or under heavy pressure of the authoritarian regimes. Moreover, the international agrarian crisis and other unsolved international problems were considerable hindrances to the good will and honest endeavors of the peasant leaders. Nevertheless, the International Agrarian Bureau has contributed considerably to the presentation and defense of the peasant cause in the world. Its activities were discontinued only with the total occupation of Czechoslovakia in March 1939.

IV

As might have been expected, the main efforts of the Communists, when they formed the People's Democracies in Eastern Europe, were directed against the peasant political groups. Besides the unbridgeable ideological differences between peasantism and communism, and the proverbial intolerance of the latter, there were specific reasons why the violence of the Communist regimes reached its climax during the suppression of the peasant political opposition.

First, the peasantry forms a substantial majority in the greater part of the area. The Communists are unscrupulous in their methods, but they are not brainless when considering the accomplishment of their targets. They know that the peasantry can be temporarily intimidated but never permanently quashed if it maintains political organizations of its own. Hence, these organizations had to be crushed before the Communists could expect any success.

Second, the peasant parties constituted the strongest democratic force in the area. The totalitarian elements had been destroyed for the most part by the Second World War, but the peasants, who could not be reproached with either collaboration or totalitarianism and could not be labeled as "fascist reactionaries," remained the greatest danger to the Communists—the self-imposed "liberators and people's friends." Hence, these groups had to be liquidated before the Communist power could be effective and its program carried out.

Third, the peasant parties possessed a vigorous program, and nothing infuriates the Communists more than a challenge to their alleged monopoly on the solution of current issues. It is obvious that those who advocate outgrown ideas in a peasant country have little chance for success, but the political platforms of the peasant parties had far more to offer the peasant population than the forcibly implemented, nebulous formulas and strange institutions imported by the Communists. However, in Communist controlled countries no alternatives are permitted, and hence, the peasant leaders had to be eliminated.

In view of the foregoing, it is not surprising that the formal disappearance of genuine peasant political organizations in this region is today an accomplished fact. Various procedures were used to achieve this. In Yugoslavia, the Croatian Peasant Party and the Serbian Agrarian Union were banned, together with all other democratic parties, at the very beginning of the Communist era. Several fake peasant groups were established whose tasks were to support the proletarization of the country and to demonstrate to the outside world that the "progressive and thinking peasantry" greeted the new reforms enthusiastically.

In Czechoslovakia, some political parties were active in the postwar period preceding the Communist coup in February 1948, but the Czechoslovakian Agrarian Party was deliberately banned at the close of the war, and its leaders arrested and tried for alleged collaboration with the Germans. Today it is obvious that these collaboration charges were a skillful maneuver of the Communists to eliminate their most dangerous opponents.

The Agrarian Union in Bulgaria was at first in the coalition government with the Communists, who held the key positions in the army and in the administration. Through direct Soviet intervention and the political violence of the Communists, the Agrarians were first reduced to one third of their actual strength, and subsequently liquidated with the trial of their leader, Petkov, in September 1947.

In Rumania the situation was similar. Hopes for the promised free elections were not realized and, in August 1947, the peasant leaders, Maniu and Mihalache, were sentenced to life imprisonment as "foreign agents and enemies of the people." This meant the end of organized peasant opposition in Rumania. In Poland Mikolajczyk attempted in vain to secure the rights of the Peasant Party, but in the controlled elections of January 1947, the party was reduced to twenty-seven deputies which completely paralyzed it in its further political struggle.

The situation was different in Hungary. In the elections of November 1945, the Hungarian Smallholders Party polled 59 per cent of all the votes and subsequently formed the government under the premiership of Ferenc Nagy. However, only eighteen months later, after numerous Communist plots, the party was crushed, and in subsequent developments it was politically liquidated.

When it became impossible for the peasantry to continue its struggle within the respective countries, the exiled peasant leaders founded the International Peasant Union in Washington, D.C., on July 4th, 1947. The Union, in which all peasant groups are represented, issued a program founded on the basic principles of peasant ideology. Its primary purpose is to interest the democratic West in the peasant struggle and to offer hope to the enslaved peasantry for its eventual liberation.

V

This brief analysis of peasantism in Eastern Europe is not intended to be a glorification of the peasantry and its movement. The peasants are not a God-chosen group, neither are their leaders without faults and errors. Mistakes have been committed by the peasant parties in the past, and many more may be committed in the future. But who does not err in politics and public affairs? Surely these imperfections are not sufficient reason for disfavoring the peasantry or for rejecting the idea of an active support of peasant political organizations. The purpose of this essay has been to indicate the importance of the peasantry in the struggle of the free world with the Communists.

It is clear that the peasants, as a group, represent the greatest obstacle to Communist victory. The immediate goal of the Communists is to crush the peasant resistance, to destroy their political power, and to convert them into an amorphous, subservient mass. Hence, the free world must aim to preserve the peasantry as a separate and dynamic group, and to strengthen its political formations.

7 Industrial and Social Policies Between the Wars

GEZA TELEKI

Eastern Europe, from the Baltic to the Aegean, is a security zone both for the states of Western Europe and for Russia. Besides acting as a safety valve for neighboring powers, this region is a passageway between them. Military and population movements fan out from here into the East or converge into the West.

Both West and East have accused this part of Europe of being unstable and backward. Both have wanted to influence it and have not wanted to admit that the backwardness, confusion, and instability of this area are in large measure due to power politics. Tribes, peoples, and states have changed and have been changed in this region throughout the centuries. As a result, there is no stability of boundaries, or of peoples and governments. The evolution of the region can be viewed as a mirror which reflects the history of Europe with all its quirks and irregularities.

Although both world wars began in Eastern Europe, it would be absurd to claim that they were caused solely by these nations and their problems. The social, economic, and political interests of the great powers which clashed in this area and influenced its peoples played an important role in the course of events in Eastern Europe.

Because of this situation, the different peoples of this region turn three different masks to the world. One is always turned toward the West, one toward the East, and one is used for the stage show that these peoples put on for each other. If a nation of Eastern Europe takes off its mask, it may disappear from the stage forever. This is an important point to keep in mind in trying to understand the evolution of these countries.

Another important factor in the history of this region is that all the important ideologies and social revolutions have moved from West to East. Nationalism and the abolition of serfdom reached Eastern Europe in the nineteenth century. Industrialization advanced eastward at the end of the nineteenth century and during the first half of the twentieth. The closer a state was connected with the West, the sooner its transformation took place, while the other states were forced to develop in a comparatively short time in order to maintain their status as equals.

I

As a result of the Treaty of Versailles, everything changed in this area of constant change—boundaries, minorities, administrations, politics, and economics. In spite of these changes, and this is most important, the Eastern European countries remained predominantly agricultural.

The proportions of populations dependent upon agriculture in the several states within a decade after gaining full independence were as follows: Albania, 80 per cent; Bulgaria, 75 per cent; Rumania, 72 per cent; Yugoslavia, 76 per cent; Poland, 60 per cent; Hungary, 51 per cent; and Czechoslovakia 33 per cent. In contrast to these figures, the percentages of gainfully occupied males in industry in the same period were: Bulgaria, 13 per cent; Rumania, 11 per cent; Yugoslavia, 14 per cent; Poland, 22 per cent; Hungary, 26 per cent; and Czechoslovakia, 41 per cent. Thus it can be easily seen that, with the exception of Czechoslovakia whose industry was the most developed in the region, the countries of Eastern Europe were predominantly agricultural and peasant in nature. Yet despite the predominantly peasant character of these countries, the peasants as such had relatively little political influence.

Although there was an increase in the output of agricultural goods in all these countries between 1918 and 1945, the competition offered by overseas cereals strongly affected the agriculture of Eastern Europe. Cereals, one of the major products of the region, had to be undersold to Germany. Added to this unfortunate situation, the world depression of 1929 came as a terrible blow to the economy of Eastern Europe, the most disastrous years lasting from 1931 until 1934. Industry, with its frequent cartels, was better able to defend itself than was agriculture, and thus the "price scissors," or the disparity between agricultural and industrial prices, cut mostly into the income of the agricultural population. This resulted in a general lowering of both the purchasing power and the standard of living. Loans at high rates of interest were frequent and taxation increased the poverty of the peasants. These, as the major element of the population, pressed heavily for reforms and spread malcontent in their respective countries.

Soon after the First World War, some states realized that the solution to this situation was industrialization. Emigration, as a possible solution, was not favored in any of the Eastern European states as it would have decreased manpower. Since war was considered more or less imminent after 1933, military and industrial groups were especially opposed to any large-scale loss of population, although emigration was never prohibited by actual government order.

Bohemia, which had been in a highly advantageous position in the industrialization program of Austria before the

First World War, was the only well-developed industrial region and provided the foundations of the industrial economy of Czechoslovakia. Poland and Hungary had some valuable industries which aided their development considerably. In the other states, industrialization made slow progress and often operated on an unsound basis. Many plants were erected, the products of which were not related to the needs of the respective countries. National welfare was often neglected and industries were built for the enrichment of a few individuals. Not even mining was efficient. Mines were exhausted or were reopened mainly on the basis of sudden export needs and with no thought that the industries might convert the mineral raw materials into consumer goods. Hungary, where bauxite was sold to Germany and aluminum was repurchased at a high price, offers an excellent example.

Mining, metallurgy, heavy industry, and textiles were favored but they were not related to the purchasing power of the masses or to the production of raw materials. Because of the low production of textile raw material, large textile plants were run on imports. Cereals, livestock, and other agricultural goods were exported to balance the budget. Thus, much of the capital had to be spent on transportation expenses. The attention paid to agricultural industry was insufficient despite the fact that mineral raw materials, agricultural products, and timber were assets upon which a satisfactory program of industrialization could have been based.

The causes for this situation are to be found in the political instability of Eastern Europe and in the lack of sufficient skills and resources. It was a region of wars and insecurity where little nations faced each other with mistrust and fought each other as fiercely as they did the outside powers. Industrial policy between the two world wars was dependent on power politics. The policy of economic self-sufficiency, or autarky, was engendered by nationalistic aspirations mostly in order to develop a modern industry capable of meeting war needs.

The assumption that work invested in industrial development would improve economic conditions was a decisive factor in influencing states to industrialize. This assumption was particularly valid in regions with climatic extremities and little arable land. Some of the means used to foster industrialization were technical education, customs, embargoes, tax exemptions, monopolies, favorable credit policies, and provisions protecting the joint interests of domestic industries. The assembly line system, as influenced by the United States, was started in the industrial sector in the '30's.

Branches of industry requiring specialized skill were developed mainly in Czechoslovakia and Hungary, but they did not attract many from the surplus peasant population which still preferred unskilled jobs. The competition, such as it was, for unskilled jobs resulted in a low wage level. Therefore, the increase in purchasing power was gradual. Peasant poverty and the lack of skill and capital were the fundamental problems facing industrialization programs and the new governmental economic policies.

The general poverty was further increased by the fact that the small Eastern European countries were debtor states. The solvency of Czechoslovakia was dependent on the export of industrial goods, while other states depended upon agricultural exports or, as in Rumania, upon mineral raw materials and lumber as well as on agricultural goods. Foreign debts, incurred before and after the First World War, weighed heavily on the budgets of the individual countries. Only one half of the debts were repaid during the interwar period. Foreign loans were given too often on the basis of political considerations. The boundaries erected by the 1920 peace treaties had already broken up natural economic and geographic areas, and the disproportionate lending policies of foreign powers hindered the uniform economic development of Eastern Europe. The individual states became more and more antagonistic and trade within the Eastern European area often took a course contrary to the requirements of reasonable economic policies. Free trade, cherished in the first postwar years, was soon abandoned for the sake of a policy of protective tariffs. Customs, duties, and foreign exchange restrictions to prevent speculation, were introduced to protect economic development and strength.

Both "economic nationalism" and "small power imperialism" were features characteristic of this area in the period between the wars. When the economic position of the new states in the '20's is compared with the situation prior to the First World War, the problems of these states emerge clearly. The economic well-being of the old Austro-Hungarian empire lay in the regional character of its economic organization, which depended mostly on a coordinated internal market and a natural division of labor between the component parts of the empire. Although it was a social and cultural mosaic, the empire was organized in such a manner as to take advantage of the regional distribution of natural resources and the differing skills of the various populations.

The peace treaties ending the First World War, while meeting the political aspirations of various nationalities, did not provide a satisfactory solution to the economic problems of the region, and the newly created states were divided by serious political and economic differences. Political animosity soon led to economic warfare, and self-sufficiency, the driving motivation of the new states, precluded any real possibility of economic cooperation. The world depression of the early '30's led to the final economic and psychological collapse of Eastern European stability and opened the door wide to German economic penetration and the eventual conquest of the region.

The foreign trade of the Eastern European countries in the years 1919-1944 was far smaller than it should have been, considering the size and population of these countries. Although they comprised roughly 25 per cent of Europe's area and population, excluding the European part of the Soviet Union, they handled no more than 10 or 11 per cent of Europe's exports and imports. About one third of the trade of the Eastern European area was purely regional. With the exception of Albania which traded mainly with Italy, Eastern Europe's trade list was headed by Germany, followed by the competing states of Austria, Great Britain, and the United States. The predominance of Germany became even greater during the war years. Trade was one of Germany's most important means of influencing the political, social, and cultural life of this region.

II

By 1918 the countries of Eastern Europe had reached different stages of social evolution. In Poland and Hungary the aristocracy had preserved considerable power in spite of a rising intellectual bourgeoisie. In Rumania and Croatia the power of the aristocracy had been wiped out by the land reforms and leadership had been taken over by a commercial middle class. In Czechoslovakia a strong bureaucratic and commercial element had risen to leadership. In the Baltic states, also, it was mainly the commercial class which had ascended to leading positions. Yugoslavia, Bulgaria, and Albania had no aristocracy and only a small intellectual bourgeoisie and commercial class.

It was generally from the rural stratum of village teachers, priests, station masters, and notaries that the new bourgeoisie and the ruling class arose. The children of an educated father, who was able to secure a better place in society, had a better chance of entering a university—the sanctuary as much of social position and status as of knowledge. However, those who succeeded in obtaining graduate and other degrees in fields such as law, medicine, engineering, or economics often renounced their humble origin and were happy to be absorbed into the urban population. Even the newly formed commercial class preferred to stay in the cities. As a result, the urban population increased steadily and towns grew rapidly.

Urbanization advanced with the growth of industry. An illustration of this is offered by the growth in population of six industrial cities in each of the following countries: Poland, Czechoslovakia, Hungary, Rumania, Yugoslavia, and Bulgaria. The total population of these cities rose from six and one-half million to ten million between the two world wars. The pace of industrialization was most rapid in Bulgaria, Yugoslavia, and Poland, where the aforementioned cities almost doubled their urban population. In the other three countries (Czechoslovakia, Hungary, Rumania), the population in these cities increased by approximately 30 per cent. Striking examples of how industrialization and transportation attracted people to cities are given by Katowice, a coal and heavy industry center in Silesia, whose population rose from forty-five to one hundred and thirty-three thousand, and by Gdynia, Poland's Baltic port, whose population rose from three to one hundred and fourteen thousand between the wars.

The regional distribution of industrial population was not uniform. Around 1930, 90 per cent of Czechoslovakia's industrial population lived in the Czecho-Moravian district. Poland's industrial population concentrated around Warsaw, Lodz, and the Silesian coal basin. In Hungary, 41 per cent of the people earning their livings in industrial occupations were concentrated in Budapest. In Yugoslavia, 63 per cent of the industrial wage earners lived in Croatia and in the regions that had previously been Hungarian. In Rumania, 25 per cent of the industrial population lived in Transylvania and 28 per cent in Muntenia. Only Bulgaria's industrial population showed any tendency toward decentralization, with 30 per cent of her total industrial population living in the district of Sofia.

The industrial population of these countries was occupied as follows: 25 to 30 per cent in the textile and clothing industries; 18 to 21 per cent in heavy and metallurgy industries; 11 to 22 per cent in the food industry; and 7 to 17 per cent in the lumber industry. A variation in industrial goods and in producing plants was found only in Czechoslovakia and Hungary, in southern Poland and Transylvania, and in the areas of the former Austro-Hungarian Empire.

One of the major problems facing the new governments in their industrialization programs was to equate the growth of the industrial working populations with improvement in industrial working and social conditions. Social legislation in the interwar period attained considerable progress in this direction. Prior to 1914 there already existed in Eastern Europe various social insurance and pension plans, and these were expanded between 1919 and 1939. Compulsory workers' accident and health insurance plans were introduced whereby both employers and wage earners contributed to a central fund to provide coverage for accident, illness, maternity, disability, old age, death, and unemployment. Generally speaking, the working day was reduced to eight hours, with a maximum forty-eight hour week, and the age minimum for child and woman labor was fixed at fourteen years or, in the case of heavy and dangerous work, such as mining, at sixteen to eighteen years. However, rigid application of these measures was far from universal.

A notable innovation was the establishment by the agrarian regime in Bulgaria of a compulsory labor service for the development of public works in place of the traditional military service which had been prohibited by the peace treaty. Expenditures in 1937 for social services for the entire region averaged 3 per cent of the estimated national income. Once again, Czechoslovakia headed the list with 5.5 per cent while the Balkan countries devoted only 1.5 per cent of their national income to social services. In the same year the number of persons registered as unemployed in the various countries was as follows: Czechoslovakia, 408,000; Poland, 347,000; Hungary, 47,000; Yugoslavia, 21,600; and Rumania, 10,800.

A major consequence of industrialization and urbanization was the rapid growth both of an urban proletariat and of the bureaucracy. Those people who had been separated from their ancestral rural surroundings and traditions and often from the influence of their families became increasingly detached from spiritual matters and turned more and more towards materialistic and technical spheres. The number of bureaucrats grew rapidly and this resulted in political favoritism and in desk-level programs which very seldom touched the people of the countryside.

It cannot be said, however, that no progress was made or that standards of living were consistently low. It must be remembered that it was not until the First World War that many of these countries attained independence. A part of Poland had just emerged from Russian domination and certain areas of the Balkan states had just freed themselves from Ottoman rule. Even Hungary, Czechoslovakia, Croatia, and parts of Poland had been freed only recently from Austro-German political and economic controls. Under these circumstances, the progress made by these countries, notwithstanding failures and mistakes, was considerable indeed.

III

The states that had dominated this region before the First World War—Germany, Austria-Hungary, Russia, and the Ottoman empire—showed little interest in improving the educational standards of the large masses in Eastern Europe.

Illiteracy in the prewar era was extremely prevalent except in Bohemia, Slovenia, a part of Hungary, and the formerly German-ruled section of Poland. Following the various educational reforms and the expansion of facilities during the '20's, the illiteracy rates were: 31.4 per cent (1934) for Bulgaria, 4.1 per cent (1930) for Czechoslovakia, 6.0 per cent (1941) for Hungary, 23.1 per cent (1931) for Poland, 23.1 per cent (1948) for Rumania, and 45.2 per cent (1931) for Yugoslavia. In spite of the notable progress attained within a decade and a half of liberation, the problem of achieving literacy and education for the masses remained a considerable one.

In the interwar period, a vast number of schools were built and many universities were founded or enlarged. National statistics show that on the average 3 per cent of the estimated national incomes was devoted to education for the region as a whole. Czechoslovakia, with 3.5 per cent, had the largest budgetary provision for education, spending in 1937 the equivalent of eighty-four million dollars. Universal compulsory elementary education was introduced widely in this area. However, the number and quality of teachers did not increase as rapidly as did the buildings. Therefore, especially in the eastern and southern regions, semieducated or semiskilled individuals were numerous, and anyone who had been exposed to education considered himself an "intellectual." Under such circumstances, this term very often stood for mere prestige, and the "intellectuals" exerted influence out of proportion to their training. A poor system of communication, a dispersed settlement pattern, mediocre teachers and, last but not least, the rather uncooperative behavior of the peasants impeded the possibilities of an adequate education for the peasant class, which represented the majority of Eastern Europe's population.

Due to the prevalence of a liberalism linked with nationalism, studies concentrated on history, which was generally given a romantic interpretation. The study of geography was heavily larded with political convictions and misinterpretations of ethnography. Although the universities of Czechoslovakia and Hungary were on a high academic level at a time when other universities were just becoming active, their students spent too much time in petty politics. Most of the student organizations supported some political person or party and, as a consequence, were strongly influenced by demagogues. The Polish and Rumanian universities especially were exploited by politicians, and often even by the police, for political purposes. Frequent political meetings aroused a discontented idealism and produced only too often regrettable chauvinistic or antisemitic behavior.

Anti-Semitism became a common denominator with which Hitler was able to unite the rising youth and the politicians of Eastern Europe. The responsibility for this state of affairs lay with the governments and the ruling groups.

Although the new boundaries had been drawn on the principle of national self-determination, the mixture of nationalities in many areas, as well as historical and geographical factors, had resulted in the inclusion of important minorities within the new states. These minorities were fragments of peoples rather than whole nations as had been the case before the war and, since they were in many cases unwilling citizens of the new states, their presence constituted a grave problem. The eight million inhabitants of Poland, Rumania, and Czechoslovakia that spoke Russian, Ukrainian (Ruthenian), and White Russian as their mother tongue, the almost six million German-speaking citizens of Czechoslovakia, Poland, Rumania, Yugoslavia, and Hungary, and the almost three million Hungarian-speaking inhabitants of neighboring Rumania, Czechoslovakia and Yugoslavia—these represented the most important, but by no means all, the minority peoples. The accompanying table shows the distribution of languages in Eastern Europe in the interwar period as established by the League of Nations.

Distribution of Principal Languages in Eastern Europe about 1930 *

(APPROXIMATE FIGURES IN THOUSANDS)

Language	Al- bania	Bul- garia	Czecho- slovakia	Hun- gary	Poland	Ru- mania	Yugo- slavia **
Russian	—	12	—	—	139	451	25
Ukrainian	—	—	569	1	4,442	641	31
White Russian	—	—	—	—	1,697	—	—
Polish	—	—	100	—	21,993	38	18
Czecho- slovakian	—	—	9,757	108	38	43	138
Serbo- Croatian	—	—	6	55	—	48	10,257
Slovene	—	—	—	5	—	—	1,159
Bulgarian	—	5,275	—	3	—	364	73
German	—	4	3,318	479	741	761	602
Rumanian	13	16	14	16	—	13,181	276
Greek	37	10	—	—	—	21	—
Albanian	984	—	—	—	—	4	524
Gypsy	—	81	33	8	—	101	54
Hungarian	—	—	720	8,001	—	1,555	557
Turkish	30	622	—	—	—	288	180
Others	—	58	213	12	2,866	561	41
Totals	1,064	6,078	14,730	8,688	31,916	18,057	13,935

* Based on Dudley Kirk, *Europe's Population in the Interwar Years* (Geneva: League of Nations), Table 17, pp. 228-29.
** A. Meillet, *Les Langues dans l'Europe nouvelle* (Paris, 1928), p. 426, estimated that Macedonian was spoken by 628,000 in Yugoslavia in 1926, but in the official census this group was not distinguished from those speaking Serbo-Croatian.

The peacemakers were conscious of the problem that had been created, and in order to make certain that the different linguistic groups would receive fair treatment it was required of these states that they subscribe to carefully worded provisions for the protection of their minorities. These provisions were included in the peace treaties with Hungary and Bulgaria, and the states that had been created or enlarged as a result of the war assumed similar obligations. The provisions for the protection of minorities were concerned with the use of language in schools and courts, the practice of religion, and the equitable administration of social security. Their implementation by the respective governments was supervised by a Minorities Commission in the League of Nations, and a system of petitions was established for bringing injustices to the attention of the League. Although the principles underlying this system represented a great advance over pre-war practice, the efforts at implementation failed to meet the needs of the situation. In many cases the minorities continued to be discriminated against, and even when they were not, nationalist movements sponsored by neighboring countries often proved irresistible. As a result, the problem of minorities became one of the fundamental sources of political instability in Eastern Europe.

Another unfavorable factor was that richer families sent their children to foreign universities, especially to France, Germany, and Great Britain, while there was little student exchange among the Eastern European countries themselves. Educated people knew a great deal about Western Europe, but much less about neighboring states and peoples. Naturally, this was even more so among nations which had been enemies in the First World War and which now fiercely condemned their citizens if they praised the culture or progress of a former enemy. However, this situation was not unique to this region. It was characteristic of Europe as a whole and, like the development of nationalism and industry, moved from West to East.

Many of Eastern Europe's difficulties stemmed from the instability of its political life. Governments changed constantly and political parties fought each other to the last breath. Due to the many changes of government, an unwholesomely large proportion of state funds was used for political competition. Taxes were high and the entire taxation system was geared to make the poor people pay for the political and economic program of the government or of the ruling classes. Planning was poor and administration far from efficient. Bohemia-Moravia had inherited from Austria a relatively competent administrative machinery, and Hungary's was organized along nineteenth-century lines. Administrative systems in former Russian and Turkish areas were a continuation of the previous imperial regimes, and were considered definitely the worst in Eastern Europe. Inefficiency and corruption mitigated somewhat the dictatorial character of these administrations. Bribery was customary and necessary on every level and affected the poor and the minorities. The problem of corruption was most serious in high official circles. Often the biggest fortunes were made in politics through embezzling discretionary funds that were left at the disposal of government members. Selling protective tariffs to industrialists in order to receive shares from foreign companies for concessions was a prevalent practice. Administrative officials were endowed with the nickname "bicyclists," which carried the implication that these officials trampled upon their subordinates and bowed before their bosses.

This attitude and the belief that the masses should support all projects of the ruling circles produced a harsh conflict of interests between the bourgeoisie, the mixed aristocratic and middle class, and the industrial workers and peasants. The fundamental conflict, however, was between the bureaucracy and the peasantry. The great differences in the cultural levels in many of the Eastern European countries made things worse. Different religious and ethnic groups and contrasting social standards contributed to regional hostilities and did nothing to facilitate the task of the administrators. The fault lay not alone with the rulers and administrators as is so often supposed by Western authors and statesmen. The people in general were slow to learn and to develop their abilities. They did not cooperate with regulations and laws even when such were to their own benefit, an attitude that stems from many centuries of oppression.

IV

It is difficult to say what turn the development of Eastern Europe might have taken if, after gaining full freedom and independence in the twentieth century, the countries of this region had been given the chance to progress in a peaceful era. The countries of Eastern Europe, immediately after recovering from the traumatic depression of the 1930's, were confronted with German and Russian imperialism without even a chance to settle down for a period of healthy evolution. Unhappily, the Western European powers, after their unfortunate appeasement policy towards Hitler which completely confused the Eastern European nations, joined hands too tightly with communist Russia. The Eastern European states, semidemocratic, semidictatorial, balancing between bankruptcy and future recovery, between socialism and aristocratic-bourgeois traditions, were a brutally realistic mirror of Europe's modern revolution.

Germany used all means possible to influence and to dominate the area. Basing its actions upon meticulous studies of the history, geography, politics, economics, social life, and cultural habits of the respective countries, Germany gained influence through the use of economic penetration, antisemitism, social-revolutionary propaganda, antibolshevism, and diplomacy. The Eastern European states could not very well defend themselves against such brilliantly conducted infiltration. Nor could their economics develop satisfactorily when American, British, French, and Swiss businessmen were completely disinterested in trade and investment in Eastern Europe since the prospects for profit were not great in that area. It is unjust to accuse the Eastern European states of favoring Germany when this country alone was willing to trade with them and did not demand hard currency payments. Germany bought large quantities of Eastern European products and forced the sellers to buy from her various articles, including gadgets, luxury goods, and many other products, the prices of which were beyond the purchasing power of the buyers.

Antisemitic movements in Eastern Europe often received aid in the form of money from Nazi Germany which practice increased dependence upon that country. Through the various Nazi-supported parties in almost every country and through fifth column organizations, the Germans instigated conflicts between the ruling classes and the dissatisfied social elements. At the same time antibolshevik propaganda was strongly and successfully supported by German diplomacy.

Czechoslovakia, in 1938, was the first to lose her independence. Poland fell in 1939, and Yugoslavia followed in 1941. The years 1939 through 1944 were truly critical for Eastern Europe. The German-Russian imperialistic pincers tightened steadily. Nazi Germany won easy diplomatic victories over the Western European powers whose conciliatory policies were astounding. Even more astounding was their sudden turn to anti-German propaganda and war. Squeezed between the arbitrary policy of the Western powers and the expanding German and Soviet giants, the Eastern European nations had no other choice than to muddle through. Apprehensively watching an alliance of giants and often impressed by the achievements of these powers, they tried to appease them, aid them, or fight them.

Peace economy was turned into war economy. This decreased unemployment, and war losses decreased it even further. The most active age group, already reduced by the slump in birth rate after the First World War, was thinned even more. Youth, accustomed to tackling problems in terms of romantic politics, opposed everything that represented the traditions and experience of the older generation. The potential balancing factor, which was the activity of the middle-aged group, was already weak due to the small numbers of this group. The West did not offer any stable philosophy and the East had only a negative one—that of destroying the West. In the midst of this confusion stood Eastern Europe, a region of mixed peoples and small countries inimical to one another and not fully understanding the rights and responsibilities that they had so recently acquired. Although they foresaw the dangers ahead, they could not resist the pressure of their larger neighbors. The traditional society and the new institutions of these countries disintegrated, and once again they became an area of military conflict between the great powers.

Industrial and Social Policies of the Communist Regimes

JAN H. WSZELAKI

I

More than thirty years ago, Lenin defined Communism in Russia as Soviet power plus electrification. In our time, the essence of the situation in the countries of Eastern Europe is the Communist police state plus industrial revolution. Local or imported Communists, under the supervision of the Kremlin, have been for years in full control of all levers of power in these countries. Their basic aim in social and economic fields, just as it is in Soviet Russia, is a complete transformation of society through industrial revolution. To this supreme aim and supreme method, all other issues have been subordinated. The process of this industrial revolution with its many ramifications extends into all fields of human activity behind the Iron Curtain, influences the lives of all ninety million inhabitants of the captive countries proper, and will have profound consequences of moral, political, economic, social, and strategic character not only for these countries but for the world as a whole. From the European point of view, the industrial revolution of Eastern Europe is an outstanding historical event, comparable in its implications to the great wars of the present century. We are witnessing the gradual decline of the traditional rural and mainly peasant structure of this part of Europe and the emergence of an industrial urbanized society. This transformation is now in full swing and will continue until it runs its course—no one can say when or how—or until external factors end the Russian control of Eastern Europe and its nations rid themselves of their own Communists. Even then, the industrial development of that area will presumably continue, though for different reasons and with vastly different methods. The Communist regimes may go, but the results of the industrial revolution will remain.

This essay is concerned with the effects of these revolutionary events on the social and economic development of the countries of Eastern Europe. To cover this involved subject adequately, much time and space would be necessary. The writer must limit himself here to the discussion of the few selected aspects of the problem that he regards as fundamental. Discussion of the industrial targets as established by the single countries in their long-range plans, half or more of which have already been achieved, cannot be included in this study.

Suffice it to say here that all over Eastern Europe the Communist regimes are modernizing the existing mines and industrial plants and are building scores of new mines and thousands of large new plants, mostly supposed to produce capital goods as a basis for further industrial production. The anticipated result of the present first series of long-range plans, expected to terminate in less than two years, will be a large increase in the extraction of fuel and the doubling, in some cases tripling and quadrupling, of the heavy industrial potential of the individual nations of this region, some of which had a large industrial output before the last war. This vast operation requires that great numbers of peasants be transferred from agriculture to industry, mining, and construction. Once carried out, the first series of plans is to be followed by a second, with the targets again much increased. The preparation of these second five year plans has already begun. Their nature can be inferred from the electoral program of the National Front in Poland, published in the fall of 1952. The Warsaw regime proposes to raise the per capita industrial output of Poland by 1960 to ten times the by no means negligible standard of 1938. In other words, it intends that the Polish per capita industrial output shall surpass the present per capita industrial output of France. Other satellite governments probably have similar plans. Whatever may be thought about the feasibility of such grandiose plans, it should not be forgotten that under the Soviet regime Russia has evolved from a backward agricultural country, which it still was in 1928 when the first Five Year Plan was launched, into the second industrial power of the world, surpassing in total production Japan, France, Britain, and Germany.

The aims of enforced industrialization are several. The first is the numerical increase of factory workers who, as proletarians, are supposed to be not only the cream of society but convinced Communists as well. This early theory of the Soviet revolution, together with the term 'proletariat,' is falling into disuse. It has never been proven by facts: at other times and in other places, men entering the industrial process have not been inclined necessarily to become Communists, and there is no evidence that they are so inclined in the captive countries today. The second aim was defined on many occasions by Stalin. According to him, the Socialist transformation of society can be achieved and kept secure only by a steady growth in heavy industrial production, which at any given time must exceed the increase of light customer-serving industries and of agriculture. This rather abstract formula means, among other things, that in order to survive foreign aggression a Communist state or states must possess enough heavy industry to produce the necessary weapons at any given moment. Stalin's judgment was correct, though not necessarily Communist, since it applies to all states exposed to dangers from their neighbors. Another meaning of this formula is that Communist states cannot afford to depend on the non-Communist world for essential raw materials or machinery, since such imports might be stopped at the moment when they are most urgently needed. Consequently, a Communist state should produce these goods on its own. Here again, a distant echo of Russia's defeat during the First World War can be heard. Stalin seems to be saying that Communist Russia must never again be incapacitated or even hindered by industrial weakness. Indeed, his industrial Russia of 1941 withstood the German onslaught far better than had the imperial Russia of 1914.

The realization of this aim demands that all hitherto unused resources of manpower and dormant material wealth be utilized as rapidly as possible. At some future time these resources may well bring rich life to the people. But so long as the Soviet Union is encircled by potential enemies such resources must remain at the disposal of the state which defends "the social conquests of the revolution." The systematic realization of all these aims is assured through the consecutive five year plans for the development of the Soviet economy.

A year or two after the end of the Second World War, the Soviet Union felt certain that the West no longer had the means or desire to interfere with Soviet control of the so-called liberated nations of Eastern Europe. The countries of this region could be regarded henceforth as an extension of the Soviet Union proper, and their resources could be used for the achievements of the same aims as those of the Soviet Union. Under the transitory semi-Communist governments of that time, the captive nations showed enormous vitality in reconstructing their war-damaged economies. Since 1948-50 this vitality has been canalized into long-range industrial plans which have been synchronized with one another and with the Soviet master plans. The captive nations were allowed to preserve the external attributes of sovereignty and their governments were granted an advisory voice in the preparation of these national plans. But the supreme control of the plans remained in the hands of Moscow, and their primary goal was, and is, rapid industrialization.

II

The possibilities of industrialization in Eastern Europe are considerable, but obviously not unlimited. They depend on the availability of manpower and its technical know-how, on industrial raw materials and machinery, on capital needed for investments, and on markets capable of absorbing the products of the new industries.

Before the last war, five million persons were employed in the mining and in the medium and large manufacturing industries of the six major countries of the area. Today this number exceeds nine million. There is a shortage of labor, both skilled and unskilled, in Eastern Germany and in the Czech part of Czechoslovakia. The reserves of manpower—land laborers, dwarf-farm owners, and married women—are limited in Hungary and the Slovak part of Czechoslovakia, large in Poland, and even larger in Rumania and in the three Balkan countries. The areas where labor is short coincide to a large degree with those of low natural increase of population, and vice versa. In the first period of reconstruction after the war, there was in many parts of the area a movement of the population from the villages to the towns in search of urban, not necessarily industrial, employment. For instance, in Poland alone, two and one-half million persons moved into towns during the first seven postwar years. This movement is now over, as well as the postwar enthusiasm for reconstruction, and the governments have to recruit new workers by propaganda and sometimes by half-coercion. Unless living conditions improve considerably in the cities, the governments will have difficulty in procuring the hundreds of thousands of new industrial workers they require annually. However, manpower is still one of the principal assets of the captive countries.

The quality of this manpower is, generally speaking, better than is assumed in the West. First, there is a considerable industrial tradition, which goes back to the Middle Ages, in Saxony, Bohemia, and southern Poland. Second, the average intelligence of the people is fairly high; given time and education an average village boy or girl can become a skilled worker and, in many cases, a qualified technician, although of course such students lack the always evident association of American youth with motor vehicles and other machinery.

It might be interesting to quote here a relevant passage from the report of the mission of the U.N. Food and Agricultural Organization, which was composed mostly of American experts, after its return from Poland in 1948:

> It is the opinion of the Mission that if the Polish nation had an opportunity to be educated according to the standards of western Europe and to carry out a peaceful economic development, the world would be amazed by the result. Imperfectly developed resources of intelligence constitute the greatest potential wealth of the Polish people. It is a raw material of far greater value than [Polish] coal . . .[1]

Assuming that this is a sound judgment, there is no reason to doubt that it applies also to the other countries of this region.

The number of graduate engineers, chemists, and scientists in Eastern Europe declined greatly during the last war and during the postwar flight to the West, but is now increasing rapidly. The joint know-how of such technicians should not be underestimated, especially when Russian technical experience is added to it. Technical inventions and improve-

[1] *Report of the FAO Mission for Poland* (Washington, 1948), p. 18.

ments made by single countries of the area are systematically exchanged with Russia and other captive countries, and many thousands of Soviet, Czech, Eastern German, and Hungarian experts, technical advisers, and skilled specialists are employed by the less advanced countries of the area. It is difficult, if at all feasible, to compare the sum of technical knowledge behind the Iron Curtain to that in the free world. Undoubtedly, the countries of Eastern Europe lag behind the free world in all technical respects, but it would be imprudent to believe that they are not making much technical progress.

The area as a whole and the single countries within it, except for Eastern Germany and Czechoslovakia, are, generally speaking, self-sufficient in foodstuffs. It also has sufficient reserves of solid and liquid fuel. Using both these reserves and their hydroelectric power, it can produce an increasing amount of electric power. On the other hand, the area is poor in metallic ores. There is much bauxite in Hungary, and supplies of lead and zinc in Poland. Yugoslavia and Bulgaria are rich in many ores. However, there is not enough iron or manganese ore in Eastern Europe, far from enough copper, no tin, and a lack of many supplementary metals of significance to modern metallurgy. Chemical raw materials are abundant, especially in Poland and Rumania, but the area lacks phosphate rock and is poor in sulphur compounds. It has no jute, very little cotton, not enough wool, and no rubber. The resulting limitations to industrial expansion are obvious. They are offset to some extent by the existence of dormant resources and by the fact that the southern Balkan area has not yet been properly explored. It is possible that the Balkan mountains contain more mineral wealth than has been assumed hitherto. Soviet geologists are certain that this is so. Some deficiencies in raw materials can be met, as was the practice under Hitler, by using substitutes such as synthetic oil, rubber, yarn, and plastics. This area can produce many substitutes. Today, shortages of raw materials are covered by imports from abroad, most of these from the Soviet Union. Economic autarky is not possible in Eastern Europe alone, but the Soviet bloc, including Russia and China, is almost self-sufficient in raw materials.

Under the unrelenting pressure of Moscow, the output of machinery and plant equipment in this area is making steady and rapid progress. The period when most of these countries must depend on importation of machinery from the West is almost over. Were all Western sources of industrial machinery to be completely closed to the captive area, its industrialization would be slowed and delayed but not halted. As things stand now, much industrial equipment is still imported from Western Europe, legally or illegally, and the Soviet Union can take care of the other shortages. Czechoslovakia, Eastern Germany, and, to a lesser degree, Hungary produce machinery above their home requirements, and part of the surplus goes to other captive countries, to the Soviet Union, and to China.

According to United Nations data,[2] the 1951 indices of industrial production in the single countries of this area in comparison to 1938 were as follows: Eastern Germany, 115 per cent; Czechoslovakia, 168; Rumania, 206; Hungary, 267; Poland, 270; and Bulgaria, 345 per cent. In considering these figures, it is necessary to bear in mind that 1938 was not the peak production year in Eastern Europe. Between 1938 and 1943-44, the industrial output of Czechoslovakia and Hungary rose noticeably owing to the erection of many new industrial plants, so that only a part of their industrial expansion since 1938 can be attributed to the efforts of their present governments. Poland's industrial potential increased in 1945 by at least one third, due to the acquisition of ex-German Silesia. Bulgaria's industrial po-

[2] *Economic Survey of Europe Since the War* (Geneva: United Nations, 1953), p. 239, Table 1.

tential in 1938 was, and still is, insignificant. It is claimed that in 1952 the industrial output of the area rose again by about one fifth.

An estimate of the relative industrial strength of the individual captive countries was made recently in a United Nations publication.[3] If the total industrial output of the area at the end of 1952 is taken as 100, the output of Eastern Germany constitutes 34 per cent of this total, that of Poland 27, of Czechoslovakia 21, of Hungary 9, of Rumania 6, and of Bulgaria 3 per cent. The total industrial output of the entire captive area is equivalent, roughly speaking, to nearly 40 per cent of the total industrial output of the Soviet Union.

All this rapid, even violent, industrial expansion cannot be smooth and is, in more ways than one, terribly expensive. There are no miracles in economics, and wealth can be created at different rates of speed, but not at will. The tremendous increase of the state-owned industrial plant in this area is only feasible because the citizens have been deprived of their individual capital, because the consumer demand is being systematically curtailed, and because more and more of the national income, siphoned off by taxation, inflation, and other methods, is being reinvested in industry. This reinvestment is being done at great cost to agriculture. Quantitative industrial progress is also speeded up by the fact that the police state has the means to make everyone work. The prewar urban unemployment and, to some extent, the huge peasant underemployment, caused by the extreme subdivision of rural property, are things of the past. Billions of man-hours which were wasted before the war in enforced idleness are now used for production or, at least, are on tap for production purposes. On the other hand, a large proportion of the men and women kept in concentration and labor camps

[3] *Economic Bulletin for Europe* (Geneva: United Nations, 1952), Vol. V, no. 2 (July, 1953), p. 84, Table 1.

produce little, if anything, and the vast apparatus of standing armed forces, of police and political supervision, of party machinery and propaganda, does not create wealth but consumes it. The onetime waste of unemployment has been partly supplanted by the waste of the immense state machinery of control and compulsion inherent in all totalitarian systems and particularly odious under Communism.

In addition to this costly political overhead, there are three other burdens to the national economies of these countries. One is the cost of planning both on a national scale and in minute detail, an economically unlikely proposition, resulting in duplication of work, omissions, bottlenecks, and other forms of economic confusion. This has been one of the main reasons why the Yugoslav Five Year Plan has never been fully realized. This type of waste can only be eliminated very gradually, if at all. The second type of waste is directly due to Communism. In the free world, private property is fairly generally respected and cared for by its owners and by the public at large. Public property, being the exception rather than the rule, also enjoys respect and cases of vandalism are few. In Eastern Europe, state property is the rule, and very few people give it proper respect. The Communists are aware of this general neglect and the ensuing injury to the economy but believe that in time society will be taught to take care of what is defined as people's wealth. However, during thirty-five years of Communism in Russia, there has been little progress in this direction. The third burden on the state economy is a specific feature of the countries of Eastern Europe. All of them have to pay heavy tribute to the Russian big brother. Russia exploits the captive nations in many ways: by reparations in kind, mixed companies, trade agreements, high prices for imports from Russia and low prices for exports to Russia, maintenance costs for Soviet troops, high salaries for Russian experts and advisers, and the like. These nations cannot express themselves on this topic, but there is overwhelming evidence that they are aware of being fleeced by the Russians to the extent of hundreds of millions of dollars annually.

III

One of the main results of the existence of the Iron Curtain is the gradual integration of Eastern Europe into the Soviet economy. Under the present circumstances, Soviet Russia lays hands on many of the raw materials and industrial goods, both capital and consumer, that are put out by the captive countries. The realization of its economic plans depends in no small way upon these goods. The industrialization of this area also depends on imports and could not proceed at its present rapid rate without the importation of machinery and, more important, of raw materials from the Soviet Union, in particular from the Ukraine. These countries are meeting with restrictions on the importation of so-called strategic goods from the United States and from some other Western countries. However, even if there were no such restrictions, these countries would have difficulty in paying for imported goods, since they do not produce sufficient surpluses of goods that interest several of the most important Western markets, for instance, the United States, the British dominions, France, and possibly Western Germany. On the other hand, the capacity of the Soviet Union and China to consume goods produced by the states of Eastern Europe is practically limitless.

For all these reasons, in addition to political expediency, trade between this area and the Soviet Union has been increasing rapidly from year to year. Were it not for Soviet iron and manganese ore, colored metals, phosphate rock and sulphur, cotton, wool, and, in certain parts of the area, coke and pig iron, many metallurgical, chemical, and textile plants in the area would have to close down. Indeed, they will do so if for some reason, general mobilization in Russia, for example, freight traffic with Russia is interrupted. To sum up, links have been created between these states and Russia which, because of the self-isolation of the latter, did not exist before the war and which would be difficult to sever in the future.

At the same time that economic links are being established between Eastern Europe and Russia, the individual states, in particular Eastern Germany, Czechoslovakia, Poland, and Hungary, are being economically integrated with each other. This is an inevitable result of the present process of the industrialization of these countries. Trade among them is also expanding constantly, and many plants are being erected by the technically more advanced states of the area on the territory of the less advanced. To quote but one example, the Czechs are building many electric and chemical plants in Poland, Hungary, Rumania, and Bulgaria. There are other forms of this interregional economic collaboration which is, for the most part, better justified economically and more natural than collaboration with the Soviet Union.

The two movements toward integration, one with Russia and the other interregional, are developing in a parallel way. It is difficult to say which of the two trends is more intensive, although possibly that with Russia is. They can be judged by the data, published several months ago in Moscow, on this area's foreign trade for 1951. When checked with United Nations information on the same subject, the following table appears to be substantially correct.

The table shows that the northern part of the area conducts more trade with other states than with the Soviet Union, while the contrary is true of the south of the area. Soviet Russia does as much trade with Rumania and Bulgaria as Nazi Germany used to do around 1940. Because of their geographical position and the rural structure of their economies, these two countries are on their way toward being drawn into

Foreign Trade of Poland, Czechoslovakia, Hungary, Rumania, Bulgaria, and Albania—1951 [4]

(IN PERCENTAGE OF TRADE WITH)

	USSR	Other Communist Countries (including Eastern Germany and China)	Free World
Poland	25	33	42
Czechoslovakia	28	32	40
Hungary	29	38	33
Rumania	51	28	21
Bulgaria	58	34	8
Albania	57	43	0

the economic system of the Soviet Union. The remaining four countries are less economically dependent on Russia. The place of Eastern Germany in interregional trade is very important. It is able to supply the rest of this area with much heavy and precision machinery, as well as potash and other fertilizers, in exchange for fuel, foodstuffs, and raw materials.

IV

The social policies of the satellite governments follow in their general outlines those practiced by the Soviet Union but may be described as somewhat more moderate, if only because the respect for human values has been more deeply ingrained in the westernized societies of Eastern Europe than they have in Russia.

The principle dominating these policies is that the Soviet-type revolution was made in the Eastern European countries in the interest of the people and that it continues to serve their interests. There is no speech made or publication issued be-

[4] P. Suslin, "The Consolidation of the Democratic World Market," *New Times* (Moscow), No. 5 (January 28, 1953), p. 10.

hind the Iron Curtain that does not emphasize the eternal dedication of the People's Democracies to this fundamental concept. It is likely that some members in the lower echelons of the party are sincerely persuaded that this indeed is the case. Not so the ruthless social engineers among the top Communists. These experienced pupils of Moscow realize, of course, that in the Communist system there is a very definite hierarchy of goals, that first things have to come first, and that the expansion of industry comes before the welfare of the people. The two cannot be sought at the same time with the same intensity since the Communist state has not the means to proceed in both directions at once. There is reliable evidence that the four northern satellite governments opposed, insofar as they were able, the imposition on their countries of the immense goals and back-breaking burdens of industrial expansion. They regarded the enormously revised targets of 1950 and 1951 as burdens too heavy on their economies. Nevertheless, they had to yield to Moscow's pressure, which was probably connected with the outbreak of the Korean war. The relatively poor nations of Eastern Europe cannot afford both guns and butter. Since it had to be guns, butter has had to be delayed to a more or less distant future. If this is the case in the Soviet Union, it must be even more so in Eastern Europe. The result is a gradual, though uneven, lowering or at least stagnation of standards of living in Eastern Europe as compared to what they were during the first years after the recent war.

Such a generalization would, of course, be vehemently denied by the satellite governments. They publish statistical data to the effect that much new housing is being built, that more food is being produced and therefore consumed, and that the population is better clad with every passing year. A trained researcher will not accept these claims at their face value. The extremely generalized social statistics from this area are even less reliable than statistics on agricultural output and are without value unless properly interpreted. These statistics should not be rejected outright, but should be juxtaposed with the mass of evidence available from other sources, and then interpreted. It would be misleading to accept blindly every report on life behind the Iron Curtain, whether brought by refugees, published in the exile press, or found in letters coming from that area. The Communist press tries to suppress most adverse information but there are limits to such a policy. If the Iron Curtain papers complain about any material shortage or attack any given material situation, it is a sure sign that the situation has become unbearable for the citizens.

On the basis of joint interpretation of the press, private information, and statistical data, the following picture of the economic and social conditions of the captive nations may be formed. The housing situation is bad and probably getting worse because, however large the current building project may be, it cannot provide homes for all those living in the existing deteriorating dwellings and because the building cannot keep up with the rapid increase of urban populations. New apartment houses are jerry-built and in need of constant repair, and the family of a privileged worker or technician will be happy if his services are recompensed by a flat of two rooms with kitchenette and shower. The great urban masses are housed much below this level. The housing problem has not been solved in Russia outside of Moscow. There is no reason to believe it has been solved in Eastern Europe. It will take a dozen or more years to rebuild the war-destroyed cities of East Berlin, Dresden, Budapest, Warsaw, Danzig, Stettin, and Breslau, to mention only a few, and, even when these cities are restored, the quality of the new construction will almost certainly be inferior to that of the prewar years. According to the United Nations, the rate of new construction behind the Iron Curtain is several times slower than it is in Scandinavia, Britain, and Western Germany. Domestic commodities, such as kitchen equipment and furniture, are rare and expensive, above the means of an average family, and modern house appliances are hardly known at all. A private car is an extreme rarity and will remain so within the foreseeable future since few passenger cars are being manufactured and almost none imported.

As far as food is concerned, there is much truth in the Communist assertion that with the rapid increase of city populations the production of foodstuffs lags behind the growing demand. Figures for food production in this area do not indicate the amount of consumption, since much of the food produced is stocked as army and war reserve or exported to Russia and China. The true situation is that while there is no actual hunger most of the population is fed at standards far below those of Western Europe. The diet is monotonous, consisting largely of bread, noodles, cereals, potatoes, common vegetables, and puddings, to judge from advice given to housewives by women's publications. Protective foods are fewer than before the war though probably more evenly distributed. Before the war, in the poorer parts of the area, the urban unemployed and millions of so-called dwarf-sized farm holders were as a rule underfed. Today the unemployed have disappeared, but the inmates of the labor camps are starving, and the poor peasants are no better off than before. The families living on middle-sized farms consume more food than before the war, because an incentive for selling produce is lacking.

The caloric value of foodstuffs consumed by the working population in the cities has, if anything, decreased. At home, families eat what the British used to eat a few years ago, but they have less of it. The quality of food consumed in the public eating places maintained by factories and the like is described as extremely bad, and so is the service. Standing in food lines, often in vain, consumes a large part of the housewife's time. This, added to the difficulty of cooking because of the fuel shortage, makes a bitter joke of the Communist pledge to liberate the housewife from drudgery. There are a few brighter spots in this picture. The soldiers and policemen are well fed and so are the privileged classes of senior government and party workers, and of artists and writers. The numerical strength of these new, privileged strata of society is less than that of the pre-war middle class, and their standard of living is undoubtedly lower.

Data have been published lately that illustrate the low level of consumption of food behind the Iron Curtain. These data concern the increase of sales of certain staples in Czechoslovakia in 1952 over those in 1951, and, for once, they are disclosed not in meaningless percentages, as is the rule behind the Iron Curtain, but in absolute figures. An analysis of these figures shows the increase in sales of sugar and butter to the extent, respectively, of two ounces and less than half an ounce per capita per month. The alleged increase in sales of coffee actually lags behind the increase in the population. Only the amount of tea sold has really increased. However, the Czechoslovakians are not tea but coffee drinkers. They used to produce more sugar than they could consume before the war. Yet the text in question continues: "The above figures show that the standard of living of the Czechoslovak people is irresistibly on the upward trend." Another example is a long letter from a coal miner in Poland, whose only subject was a detailed description of how he tried in vain for weeks in the fall of 1952 to buy a piece of sausage. In his fury with the regime and "the Russkis" behind it, the humble writer rose to the rhetoric of a Patrick Henry and declared that since there was no sausage life was not worth living. "And to think that I actually used to grumble against the pre-war government!" was his final confession. It should be noted that pre-war Poland had a large surplus of pork.

In the summer of 1953, the Soviet government announced that it would take many measures to relieve the all too obvious shortages of consumer goods and to increase substantially the standard of living of the Soviet population. This announcement was followed by similar declarations in the captive countries. Their governments bound themselves to increase investments in agriculture, housing and light industries producing consumer goods. In Eastern Germany, Hungary, Czechoslovakia and Rumania, and somewhat later in Poland, qualified promises were made to the effect that the hitherto very rapid rate of heavy industrial expansion would be slowed down. At the same time two of the greatest works under construction in the area have been interrupted if not abandoned: the Danube-Black Sea canal in Rumania and, to all appearances, the huge HUKO iron and steel 'combinat' in Eastern Slovakia. These public statements were in themselves equivalent to an official admission that the condition of the population was miserable.

Time alone will show whether, and to what extent, these new policies will be realized. The bumper 1953 harvest in most of the key provinces of the area would undoubtedly relieve its food scarcity if it were not for the fact that a great deal of this harvest has been earmarked for export. The Soviet government stated recently that it would import food and consumer goods from Eastern Europe to the extent of some 660 million dollars, and Eastern Germany expects to import similar goods from this area, as well as from China which has little to export, in the amount of 125 million dollars. The captive area proper, suffering itself from an acute shortage of consumer goods, would thus be forced to contribute to the betterment of the Soviet and Eastern German economies at the rate of more than eleven dollars per capita of its population. Even if the governments of the area do their best to increase the standard of living of the working masses, much time must inevitably pass between the inauguration of the new policy and the actual increase in the production of consumer goods. For example, the present insufficient production capacity of cement plants and brick factories would have to be increased before there can be any question of more housing. This is but one example out of many of its kind. There is a manifest contradiction between the present Russian-enforced armament production in the area, which has not been curtailed, and the intended mass production of consumer goods. The two cannot be carried on simultaneously. For these reasons alone, the recent statements of the Communist governments should be regarded with much scepticism.

The situation as regards clothing and footwear is even worse. The problem of obtaining it is nearly insoluble for the average family. It is far more difficult than in Russia where millions wear Polish textiles and Czech shoes. To discuss this question in detail is beyond the scope of this essay. Suffice it is to say that, according to the present long-range plans, Eastern Germany expects to produce in 1955 only 1.3 pairs of leather shoes per capita, Rumania 1.2 pairs, Hungary 1 pair, and Poland 0.7 pairs. No one can say what proportion of this footwear will be earmarked for export to Russia and China or assigned in advance to the army and security police and what will be left for the population. It is for such reasons that behind the Iron Curtain it is illegal to photograph the people on the streets or to export abroad such documentary evidence of their poor garb.

In contrast to the situation regarding food, housing, and clothing, the number and range of social services have been considerably extended, and these state services should in all fairness be regarded as significant steps taken to offset the low standard of living. It is little known that prewar Poland and Czechoslovakia, not to speak of Germany, had state-operated systems of social insurance and public health more advanced than any existing at the time in France or the United States. These systems have been enlarged under Communism. The quality of their services is too often insufficient, but the people accept them as their due and can no longer visualize life without them. A large and, according to official claims, growing part of national income is being spent on social insurance, public health, family allowances, maternity and children care, workers' vacations, so-called physical culture, and the like. There is no comparison between the philosophy of the welfare state in Britain and that of Communism in Eastern Europe, but there are some similar functions in both systems. For much the same reasons that the Conservative government in London could never think of taking back the social reforms of the Labor government, no post-Communist government in Eastern Europe will be able to consider curtailing the privileges accorded to the working class by the present regimes.

V

The most important and politically the most decisive of the privileges granted by the State is education, understood always strictly in the Communist sense of the term. The Communist regimes are aware that they cannot seriously expect to win the minds of the majority of the adult population. Anyone who was twenty years old in 1938 in Bohemia or Moravia, in 1939 in Poland, in 1941 in Serbia, and as late as 1944 in Hungary or Rumania, can contrast his present situation as an individual and as a part of his nation to his situation under a non-Communist government, however imperfect the latter may have been. There is no way of knowing how many of these men and women regret the past and hate the present, but they undoubtedly constitute a large majority of the adult population of the area. From the Communist point of view, these men and women are incurable. The future of the Red regimes depends on the youngsters who know nothing about the past, are isolated from the freedoms of the West, and are daily taught that Russia is their shining example. The regime knows that it cannot assure a decent standard of living to the adult population and probably realizes that the coming generation will not live much better. However, it hopes that the young ones will be more pliable. Since they will not know that life can be better, they will not grumble. In the political and moral field, the desire to capture the minds of the youth is what industrialization is in the economic domain—the primary goal to which all others must be subordinated. From another angle, education, especially technical education, is the necessary counterpart and precondition of the fully industrialized, urbanized, and mechanized socialist society.

The first point of the Communist program for the young generation is to insure its numerical strength. Before the last war, the populations of Poland, Rumania, Yugoslavia, Bulgaria, and Slovakia were increasing with great though gradually diminishing rapidity. In the Czech lands proper and in Hungary, the natural increase was low with a trend towards demographic standstill. Some economists believed that the key problem of Eastern Europe, that of rural poverty due to overpopulation, could not be solved unless the population ceased to multiply so rapidly. From the strictly economic point of view, there was much truth in that assertion. The Communist regimes, including that of Yugoslavia, have taken the opposite stand. Their publications wage a war against the prewar theory which they say is born of despondency characteristic of capitalism. Communism, they claim, will solve all problems. But to prosper, People's Democracies need many children. Whether because of these social policies or because of other reasons, the prewar trend toward low natality has been reversed in most countries of the area. No demographic data on Rumania have been published for some years, which may mean that the policy of high natality has not been successful there. Elsewhere, data show that many more children are being born now than before the war and more of them survive infancy. In consequence, if rather fragmentary national statistics are to be believed, the rate of increase in population has risen to what it was a generation before. Roughly speaking, the number of Hungarians has been increasing annually by 60,000, that of Czechs and Slovaks (mainly Slovaks) by 140,000, that of Yugoslavs by 180,000, and that of Poles by over 400,000. Whether this trend will continue for a long time, no one can say.

The second point of the program in respect to youth is an all-out attack on illiteracy. Before the war, the area as such was making rapid progress in schooling, and in its western part illiteracy was no longer known. In its eastern and southeastern regions, however, there were still large residues of illiteracy in the adult population and, in spite of compulsory elementary education, there were not enough schools in some rural districts. The result was that some children never went to school. The Communist regimes claim that they have done away with a large proportion of illiteracy among adults and even elderly people, and that illiteracy as a condition is gone forever. There is no way of checking this assertion but it is likely that it is correct. The obvious comment is that the more literate people there are, the stronger a weapon Communist printed propaganda will be. Thus, the new schools behind the Iron Curtain are but the first installment of a vast campaign of propaganda and indoctrination.

The third and, in a sense, the most important point of the program is the great effort of the Communist regimes to promote professional and technical education on secondary and academic levels. The fulfillment of the long-range economic plans depends, in the last analysis, on its cadres, that is, on its trained personnel. To use a Communist simile, the new industrial army, millions strong, needs hundreds of thousands of noncommissioned and commissioned officers. These men and women are being graduated all over the captive area from technical schools of every description. The numbers both of graduates and of schools are several times larger than before the war and are still increasing. The educational level is much lower than it was either before the war or in the free West, but it tallies with the Communist conception of superior education which aims at mass production of technicians specialized in one limited field and not instructed in general culture. Here again, these countries have to follow Soviet precedents, and narrow specialization is the method and the aim of education.

The emergence before long of thousands of newly graduated engineers, chemists, and the like, will have a profound effect on the economic and social structure of the area. These young people will be the managerial class of the future. Their lives will be dependent on the industrial trend of the economy of the captive nations. Unlike the new teachers, lawyers, writers, and other intellectuals, who will have to be agents of the Communist political machine, the new technicians will be allowed to serve both their own and national interests without being associated day in and day out with the sinister doings of the police state. Technology, like medicine, is one of the very few fields of creative activity open to non-Communists. When this is taken into consideration, it will be seen that the young men and women who besiege institutes of technology and other technical schools behind the Iron Curtain are very largely those who wish to preserve some independence of spirit. In their own domain, they will be able to dedicate themselves to creating national material wealth without paying more than lip service to the political framework in which they exist. This kind of work, where there is much less political supervision, may possibly come to be considered the closest thing to individual initiative. In contrast to the 'Commissar' group of the new middle class, the new managerial stratum of these societies is, or may become, aware of the superiority of life in the free world and thus be a potential ally of the West. There seems to be, however, a condition attached to such a speculation. Were the West to deny the principle of industrial transformation of these countries and to envisage their 'return to pastoral status,' the new managerial class together with the working class would range itself automatically against the West.

VI

The economic and social revolution which these countries have undergone has been imposed on them very largely from the outside. It has been successful because it was backed by the whole strength of a great military empire but also because the material and moral ravages of war and German occupation had shattered the prewar fabric of society and exposed its structural weaknesses. The society which is emerging from this revolution will be very different from the former one. Even if a true liberation of this part of Europe were to occur, the restitution of many old forms of life would not be feasible. The greatest harm that the captive nations have suffered and will suffer through the imposed revolution are the inflictions upon the souls and the minds of the people. Gradual de-Christianization, loosening of family ties, fear and distrust of political authorities and of the neighbor, Russification and falsification of national past, coarsening of manners, and the awful deposit of lies and prejudices of propaganda and non-technical schooling: all these are weapons which are levelled upon the minds and souls of the people. The undoing of these moral effects of Communist policies could only be gradual, and it would take a long time.

In the social and economic fields, the effects of Communism have not been so uniformly somber. That goods can be produced under Communism has been learned from Russian precedents. That Communism cannot assure to the people a decent standard of living is a fact that cannot be denied by any amount of propaganda, and it is also true that never in the last century have so many people worked so hard for such meager rewards. However, in the social field, the extension of social services and of technical education can be credited to the Communist regimes. In the economic field, although the tax on the people has been almost unimaginably great, it must be admitted that the badly needed industrial development of formerly rural areas of Eastern Europe is due to the Communists.

The latter point needs clarification. The Wilsonian Eastern Europe of 1918 inherited from Austria-Hungary, imperial Russia, and the old primitive Balkans an obsolete social structure of rural overpopulation and poverty due to insufficient industrial and urban development. The Czech lands, Polish Silesia, and a few lesser industrial regions were exceptions to the general structure of the area. Left to themselves by the indifferent West, having undergone the shock of the depression as only rural states can suffer it, the free nations of the area, again with the exception of Czechoslovakia, could in the interwar period neither solve their grave social problems nor defend themselves in the hour of danger. The existence of a poor and defenseless group of nations in the heart of Europe surrounded on East and West by two highly industrialized powers was an anachronism and an indirect invitation to aggression. After the disintegration of Eastern Europe between 1938 and 1941, the causes of this disaster were examined by thinkers of many nations, and many of them came to the conclusion that the disaster was inevitable, not only because of the political disunity of this area but also because of its economic and productive inferiority. Rural societies had no chance of survival in the heavily armed world of the late '30's if only because they were unable to produce the weapons with which they could have deterred aggression effectively. The awareness of this fact has deeply influenced the political thinking of the nations concerned. It is inevitable that the Poles, to take but one example, should reflect that, had their country had a sufficient industrial basis in 1939 to equip ten armored divisions for which she had enough trained manpower, her loss of independence and many other events in modern history could have been prevented.

The present industrialization of Eastern Europe is gradually eliminating this handicap of the past. To be sure, the increase of the industrial potential of these countries lies in the interest of the Soviet Union in its own military preparations. The men in the Kremlin may dispose as they wish of this area's industrial plants together with all its human and material resources with the single exception of the spirit of its peoples. From the standpoint of both the immediate and long-range interests of the West, any addition to the wealth or the strength of Eastern Europe is unwelcome so long as the latter remains a part of the Soviet bloc. These countries are of course aware of this situation, but they have to think also about their future. They hope that one day the Iron Curtain will be lifted and they know that at that time they will need all their new industrial wealth in order to cease being an area of social unrest and a target for exploitation by powerful neighbors as well as a hotbed for world wars. Nobody has disputed the right of Russia to evolve into an industrial power. No one can expect the countries of Eastern Europe to relinquish their hopes of freedom and their rights to prosperity which, in the light of their past, are linked to the modernization of their economic structure. Wendell Willkie said during the last war that "Only the productive can be strong, and only the strong can be free." His words apply to all nations alike. The nations of Eastern Europe are potential allies of the West. Those who earnestly desire a better world should bear in mind that the lasting interests of these friendly nations transcend their temporary position as Russia's enforced associates.

PART THREE

THE SEARCH FOR
REGIONAL SECURITY

9 International Relations Between the Wars

HENRY L. ROBERTS

I

The most striking aspect of the constellation of states in Eastern Europe after 1918 was that it should have come into existence at all. It is not that these states were "artificial" creations. It is rather that the appearance at that time of a zone of independent nation-states, from the Baltic to the Aegean, was largely the consequence of the simultaneous collapse, through war and revolution, of both Germany and Russia, an eventuality not anticipated in 1914. One cannot say what would have been the picture in Eastern Europe had either Germany or Russia emerged victorious, but certainly it would have been very unlike that which actually came about.

The continued independence of the area was dependent upon preventing either of the two great powers from gaining ascendency or from working with the other to control the non-Germanic and non-Russian peoples of the area, as they had done during much of the nineteenth century. This was a common burden of all the states of Eastern Europe after 1918. Unfortunately, it was almost their only real point of unity. The other unifying factor was that they were predominantly agrarian states, rather uncomfortably situated between a highly industrialized West and a "proletarian" U.S.S.R.

In nearly all other respects the area is marked by wide diversity. The boundaries between the different linguistic and cultural groups, often not clear, were generally not congruent either with natural boundaries or with the frontiers as they emerged after the First World War. In consequence, there were a series of territorial controversies which, in keeping the region at odds with itself, were of tragic significance. To take a few of the more critical examples: Vilna was contested by Poland and Lithuania, and Teschen by Poland and Czechoslovakia. Hungary and Czechoslovakia disputed the borders of Slovakia and Carpatho-Ruthenia. Transylvania was an issue between Rumania and Hungary. The Dobrogean quadrilateral divided Rumania and Bulgaria, and the latter was in turn in conflict with Yugoslavia over Macedonia and with Greece over access to the Aegean. In addition, of course, there were the unresolved issues involving the great powers which bordered Eastern Europe: Danzig, Upper Silesia, and Bessarabia, to name only three sore points.

Accompanying and to some extent a consequence of these differences was the constant controversy over minorities. It is unjust to say that the Versailles treaties, in breaking up the old multi-national empires, merely reproduced the old nationality conflicts within the new components. On the contrary, many more people than before lived within states controlled by their own nationals. Yet the solution was far from perfect. The very establishment of the national principle as the basis for the state carried with it a strong impulse to consolidate and coordinate—with resulting pressures on the minorities. Certainly the mood of strong nationalism, often accompanied by an inner lack of self-confidence, frequently led to unfair treatment of minorities. One must admit, nevertheless, that the multi-national principle, as represented in actual fact by the Austro-Hungarian Empire and the Russian Empire, did not in the years before 1914 seem to offer any real framework for constructive development. To be sure, there were many projects for the reorganization of these states, but on close examination they reveal little basis in reality.

In addition to the frontier and minorities problems, there was also the phenomenon of economic nationalism. Insofar as the restrictive effects of economic nationalism, especially the high tariffs, added to the difficulties of the region, they were symptomatic rather than a basic cause of trouble. In most instances, economic nationalism developed as a natural, if not particularly enlightened, reaction to the fact that these new states were under strong incentive to strengthen their economies as rapidly as possible. Because of many political uncertainties, they tended to proceed along the path of economic nationalism: "By ourselves alone" as the Rumanian liberals used to say. In this, of course, the behavior of the Eastern European states was not unlike that of the larger states, but the results in this area were often preposterous. For example, the chopping up of the Danube basin into a number of different tariff areas certainly was not a rational action.

Before turning to the development of international relations in this period, one further observation should be made. In comments on the vicissitudes of this part of the world, one encounters two opposing views. One is expressed by the phrase "the Balkanization of Europe," which carries with it the implication that the stability of Europe was perennially upset by the bickering, intrigue, and petty rivalries of the small states of Eastern Europe. The other view is that the Eastern European states were behaving as well as they could under constant subjection to the machinations of the great powers who tried to use them as pawns. Both views are misleading. During the interwar period, the wisdom and stupidity of statesmen and peoples were fairly evenly distributed. It is true, of course, that the actions of the great powers inevitably had the more far-reaching effects, and in that sense their responsibility for the course of events is the greater. But one may doubt that their motives were either nobler or meaner than those of the small powers. The real trouble lay in the interplay of relations between the great and small powers, and for this all must carry a burden of responsibility.

II

It has been noted that the occasion for the independence of the Eastern European states was the collapse of both Russia and Germany in 1918. From the point of view of the new Eastern European states, the most favorable postwar situation would have been a continuation of Russian and German weakness, with these two powers at odds with one another. The worst situation would have been a strong Russia and a strong Germany working in cooperation. During the 1920's German-Russian relations were comparatively close, but both powers were weak. In the 1930's they both were much stronger, but in general hostile. In 1939 they joined forces with catastrophic results. Unfortunately, the states of Eastern Europe were not in a position to control these developments. The recovery in strength of Germany and Russia lay beyond the range of the small countries' influence as did the course of German-Soviet relations. There were two possibilities open to the Eastern European states: to gain support from other great powers, more specifically, the victors of the First World War; and to work among themselves in building up their collective strength.

They were ultimately unable to realize either possibility, but the failure to accomplish the first was of more consequence. In the last analysis, the great powers responsible for the outcome of the First World War and for the Versailles settlement were likewise responsible for the ordered evolution of the new peace. The reasons for their failure in this undertaking lie in a field of international relations beyond the scope of this essay. A few points must suffice. The United States, during the interwar period, was of little positive value in this connection. Great Britain's position, until the spring of 1939, may be summarized by Sir Austen Chamberlain's private remark in 1925 that "For the Polish corridor, no British government ever will or ever can risk the bones of a British grenadier." Time was to show that British as well as Pomeranian grenadiers were not beyond risk.

The case of France was different, and one of the anchor points of European stability appeared to be France's military and other connections with the states of Eastern Europe, especially in the 1920's. Unfortunately, the French policy, particularly evident in the 1930's, of working with the states of Eastern Europe came into conflict with two of her other policies. One was the tendency to work out relations with Germany directly, or in concert with the other great powers. This pattern is traceable from Locarno, through the Four Power Pact, to Munich, and was a trend that the Eastern European states viewed with justified alarm. The other policy was the tendency to rely upon the Soviet Union, especially after 1934, as a counterweight to Germany. This was a development unacceptable to that part of Eastern European strategy which looked for support against both Germany and Russia.

Italy, the fourth victorious power at Versailles, was also interested in Eastern Europe, but in this case the consequences were more damaging than helpful. Although Italy was a victorious power, it had strong revisionist interests, and the 1920's were marked by an intense Franco-Italian rivalry in the southern part of Eastern Europe. The Stresa Front in 1934-1935 temporarily aligned France and Italy in their opposition to German pressure on Austria, but later Italy usually sided with Germany, although not without certain uneasy doubts.

In general, then, France was the one great power really committed to support the *status quo* in Eastern Europe, and France, as it proved, was not enough.

Within the area itself, all the Eastern European states had a common interest in avoiding great power control, an interest whose object became tragically apparent when the whole area was dominated by Hitler after 1941. The First World War had brought into being several formations or groupings of the Eastern European states. However, the beneficiaries of the war must be distinguished from the losers. Some states were new creations, or had greatly added to their prewar territory. Others—Bulgaria, Hungary, and Austria—had been in the camp of the Central Powers. Bulgaria's losses date both from the First World War and from the Second Balkan War of 1913, in which it had lost territory to Rumania, Yugoslavia, Greece, and Turkey. In the case of Hungary, a strong case could be made that it, too, was a successor state, but as a defeated power it was obliged to sign the Treaty of Trianon. One can, perhaps, justify each of Hungary's territorial losses to Czechoslovakia, Rumania, and Yugoslavia, on either ethnic, economic, or strategic grounds —though not all three at once—but the cumulative effect of all these detachments was such as to make the Hungarian cry, "No, no, never," a justifiable response. This meant, of course, that in Danubian and Balkan Europe, there was a profound disunity, which served to block efforts at extended common action.

North of the Carpathians a somewhat different situation prevailed. Finland, the Baltic States, and Poland were all beneficiaries of the new settlement. Unhappily, Vilna and Teschen provided, or at least symbolized, disputes which inhibited common action in that region.

III

Despite this disunity, important efforts were made to bring greater cohesiveness and unity to Eastern Europe. Of these the most important was the Little Entente, formed through a series of treaties between Czechoslovakia, Yugoslavia, and Rumania in 1920-1921. The sponsors of these treaties had as a broader and eventual aim the establishment of a great entente extending, as expressed by Take Ionescu, the Rumanian statesman, from the Baltic to the Aegean. Nevertheless, the immediate and specific objective was more limited: the defense of the territorial settlement of the Treaty of Trianon against Hungary and opposition to any effort to bring back the Habsburgs. In the case of the Yugoslav-Rumanian treaty, provision was also made for the defense of the Treaty of Neuilly against Bulgaria.

In the course of time a fairly extensive philosophy of the meaning of the Little Entente was formulated. The Entente became active in the League of Nations, of which the Entente members were ardent supporters. By 1926, the Entente became linked with France through a series of understandings and agreements. The statutes of the Entente were gradually enlarged to include agreements for the settlement of mutual disputes by arbitration, and later, in 1933-34, for the creation of a Permanent Council, an Economic Council, and a permanent secretariat. All these steps were aimed at coordinating and unifying the foreign policies of the three members and at increasing their efficacy in the world as a whole.

Seen in retrospect, the Little Entente had certain shortcomings. It was directed against Hungary and, despite various efforts, the rift between the Entente and Hungarian revisionism was never overcome. Perhaps too great emphasis was placed on Hungary which was, after all, a very secondary power in these years, and probably weaker militarily than any single Entente power. At the same time, the treaties had nothing to say about meeting threats arising from great powers. There was no immediate community of interests in this regard, since each of the three members was potentially threatened by a different great power: Czechoslovakia by Germany, Rumania by Soviet Russia, and Yugoslavia by Italy. The Czechoslovakians had no direct conflicts with the Russians, the Rumanians had no direct conflicts with the Germans, and neither were at odds with Italy. This meant that the Entente was overprotected from internal, but underprotected from external, danger. This flaw became evident in the later half of the 1930's.

To the south of the Little Entente, a Balkan grouping also came into being. The idea of a Balkan confederation was not a new one. Programs for achieving South Slav unity had been in the air from the time the Balkan states began to emerge from Turkish control. But a series of quarrels, especially concerning Macedonia, had always blocked these efforts. In the early 1930's a number of Balkan conferences were held. While significant achievements could be listed—the creation of machinery for the settlement of disputes, projects for intellectual cooperation, and even a project for a customs union —these achievements were largely procedural and technical. They did not extend to real political innovations. The Balkan Entente, formed in 1934, comprised Greece, Turkey, Rumania, and Yugoslavia, but not Bulgaria, which was not willing to accept the premise of no territorial revision. The Bulgarian position was not as intense as the Hungarian, and in certain political groups there was a real desire for South Slav unity. But it should be noted that a reconciliation on such lines would have had a doubtful reception in such a state as Rumania which was very sensitive about being an island of Latinity in a sea of Slavs, as the phrase went. The terms of the Balkan Entente provided for defense against a Balkan aggressor only, not against a great power. The Balkan

Entente was linked by two of its members to the Little Entente, but one cannot say that this association measurably increased the unity of Eastern Europe.

An extension of the Little Entente to the north was blocked by the Polish-Czechoslovakian conflict, by Poland's unwillingness to enter a grouping directed against its traditional Hungarian friends, and by a certain Polish reluctance to become committed to the preservation of the *status quo* south of the Carpathians. The one real link here was the Polish-Rumanian joint defense agreement which, unlike the other arrangements, was directed against a great power, the Soviet Union.

As for the Baltic region, no great achievement can be recorded. Finland tended to orient itself toward the Scandinavian states. Poland and Lithuania did not even establish diplomatic relations until 1938, and then only under a Polish ultimatum. There was an alliance between Latvia and Estonia in 1923, and in 1934 a modest Baltic Entente covering the three Baltic states was signed, but it was not of great moment.

In general, looking from north to south, one sees the appearance of a number of groups aiming at the preservation of stability and independence in the area. Nevertheless, there were ominous gaps between and within the groups, and no sufficient measures for threats from without. The key connections, of course, were the Little Entente and the French ties with it and with Poland.

Apart from these alignments, which stood for the *status quo* and the Versailles system, there were certain other combinations which should be mentioned. Italy, which was in competition with France, attempted to counter the French ties with the Little Entente by the Rome Protocols of 1934 with Austria and Hungary—a clear example of the dangers of the reciprocal interplay of great and small power differences. Poland, under Colonel Beck, had some rather ambitious plans for achieving a bridge to the West via the Scandinavian states, and to create a great Baltic bloc. But the Scandinavian states, at this time, were not entering into the power combinations of Central and Eastern Europe, and the project never got beyond some goodwill tours. Finally, in 1938, Beck, with Ciano, discussed the formation of a Rome-Belgrade-Budapest-Warsaw axis, with the intent of checking German eastward expansion which was now clearly in the offing. But it was very late in the day for such a project, and it never came to any practical fulfillment.

Perhaps the most extensive, although abortive, effort to increase the security of Eastern Europe, this time in conjunction with the great powers, was the French attempt to achieve a so-called Eastern Locarno agreement. The states of Eastern Europe had been understandably disturbed by the Locarno agreements of 1925 which had seemed to settle, by international guarantee, Germany's western frontiers but which had done this at the cost of inviting German revisionism on its eastern frontiers. In 1934-35 France tried to achieve an agreement on the Eastern territorial settlement; Germany, Russia, Poland, Czechoslovakia, and the Baltic states were to be signatories with France as a guarantor of the treaty. Germany, however, refused to participate. This led to a Polish refusal to underwrite what would then have been an anti-German combination. Eventually the project was reduced to the French-Soviet-Czechoslovakian mutual assistance agreements of 1935, which were clearly something other than a regional organization.

Apart from these various diplomatic combinations, certain other efforts were made to increase the unity of Eastern Europe. Of some interest in this respect is the International Agrarian Bureau, also known as the Green International, founded by leaders of peasant or agrarian parties in a number of Eastern European states in 1921. In its heyday in the 1920's it included peasant parties from Czechoslovakia, Bulgaria, Yugoslavia, Rumania, Austria, Switzerland, Poland, France, the Baltic States, and Finland. The literature of the late 1920's concerning Eastern Europe shows that this peasantist or agrarian movement was widely regarded as the hope of the future. Here was a movement representing a basic common interest of the area and transcending national frontiers.

Unhappily the promise in this movement was never realized, and the movement eventually collapsed. The agrarian parties were not able to dominate the domestic political scene in most of these countries, and the whole position of agriculture was undermined by the advent of the depression in 1929. A governmental effort to organize some defense of agricultural interests was made in 1930 in the form of an agrarian bloc, including Bulgaria, Estonia, Hungary, Latvia, Poland, Czechoslovakia, Yugoslavia, and Rumania. At a number of international conferences and at the League of Nations, this movement attempted to coordinate economic policy and to gain preferential treatment for agricultural exports from the industrial states of Western Europe. This effort achieved nothing tangible, and under the lash of the depression, these states were driven to a policy of *sauve qui peut*.

IV

The depression and the rise of Hitler were undoubtedly the major factors in starting the breakup of whatever cohesion had been achieved in the calmer years of the 1920's. For a time, to be sure, even after Hitler came to power, the Eastern European states showed a good deal of ability to act together. The Little Entente, together with Poland, was largely effective in protesting against the Four-Power Pact of 1933. The extension of the powers of the Little Entente in 1934 and the creation of the Balkan Entente in the same year also showed a positive response to the new dangers. In the false calm of 1934 a number of voices could be heard saying that at last the Balkans had come of age and were no longer a source of European trouble. This was partly true, but somewhat irrelevant.

Unhappily, the breakdown was not far off. In 1934 Poland signed its non-aggression pact with Nazi Germany. Poland was clearly in a very difficult position and it is not hard to understand the attraction of an offer which seemed to promise an alleviation of the German revisionist campaign. The pact served, however, to increase the disunity of Eastern Europe. Although it was the basic intention of Polish policy to maintain an even balance between its two great neighbors, this agreement served in effect to bring Poland increasingly to a position paralleling that of Germany. This tendency was heightened when Czechoslovakia, by its 1935 pact with the Soviet Union, came to look eastward for support. Here again the local Polish-Czechoslovakian conflict became involved in a more extensive and dangerous diplomatic issue.

The other states whose interests lay in the preservation of the *status quo* also engaged in an increasing amount of fence-mending. The Stoyadinovíc government in Yugoslavia moved to improve its relations with Germany. In Rumania, Titulescu, who had favored a cautious *rapprochement* with the Soviet Union, was replaced in 1936, and King Carol tried with increasing difficulty to follow a policy of balance. This was a hard job since he was being pressed domestically by the growing threat of the pro-German Iron Guard.

The events that led to the disintegration of Eastern Europe are too familiar to require more than the listing of a few of the more important: The failure of France and Britain to challenge the German remilitarization of the Rhineland left Hitler relatively free to turn eastward. The formation of the Axis and Mussolini's withdrawal of support from Austria paved the way for the Anschluss. And finally, of course, the Munich crisis was followed by the breakup of Czechoslovakia, in which Hungary and Poland participated. Certainly the ultimate responsibility for the collapse of Czechoslovakia must rest with the Western powers, yet it is conceivable that had the Eastern European states, above all Poland and Czechoslovakia, stood together, it might have been possible to stiffen the French spine at this fatal juncture. From Munich the road led to the crises of 1939, and eventually to the German-Soviet pact of August, which spelt the end of independent Eastern Europe.

Germany's economic penetration of Eastern Europe after 1933 was not a primary factor in the breakup of this region. While the reality of the penetration cannot be denied, for it meant much more than foisting aspirin and cameras on the Eastern European states, its importance may be questioned. This penetration did not really impair the political independence of these states until after the diplomatic situation had deteriorated greatly, and some of the German trade agreements which really bound the economies of the area were a result rather than a cause of the shift in the balance of power.

One may ask at this point about the influence of the domestic political and social problems of Eastern Europe on international relations. A good deal has been written about the failure of parliamentary and constitutional regimes in Eastern Europe, and their replacement by authoritarian regimes. Some have concluded from this that there was a tendency on the part of these regimes to gravitate toward Hitler and to refuse to have anything to do with the Soviet Union at a time when Litvinov was loudly calling, at the League and elsewhere, for collective security against aggression.

The relationship between foreign and domestic policy is always a complex and debatable one. In the case of Eastern Europe, however, one must steer a course between two inadequate interpretations of this relationship, which may be called the Popular Frontist and the Retrospective Vindicationist. The first, which is roughly the one described above, is not tenable. Documentary evidence which has appeared since the war makes it difficult to consider the Popular Front as anything but an instrument of Communist advance. It is quite evident that the Communists were not renouncing their ultimate aims either in Eastern Europe or elsewhere. It is also clear that the U.S.S.R. was not seriously prepared to stand up for the collective security it was calling for, although admittedly it was never required to do so. At the time of Munich, the Germans were not particularly anxious about the danger from the Soviet side. Moreover, it appears from the diplomatic memoirs of the Eastern European statesmen that they tended, as a group, to view the Soviet danger in the traditional terms of the "colossus of the East" as a perennial threat, whether or not it had a Communist regime. Thus their suspicions of the U.S.S.R. cannot be reduced to a reflection of the "class conflict."

Regarding the second interpretation, it should be recognized that there was a special antipathy to the U.S.S.R. on the part of the Eastern European countries, which led to certain misjudgments of the relative dangers existing in the 1930's. Pilsudski, for example, after ordering an intelligence survey of his two powerful neighbors in 1933-34, concluded that, while both were dangerous from the Polish point of view, in the short run the Soviet Union was more likely than Germany to follow an erratic and aggressive course. This proved to be a miscalculation. One nevertheless gains the impression that a similar mood was prevalent in the diplomatic circles of Eastern Europe. This served to reduce the area of maneuverability in the final crisis and did not afford any way out of the tragic impasse of 1939.

During the war years, Eastern Europe disappeared as a region of independent states. Germany and the Soviet Union divided most of the area into spheres of influence and, with the German attack on Russia in June 1941, the whole region fell directly or indirectly under German domination. There was, nevertheless, some continuity. Among the governments-in-exile, the struggle for future independence was clear and explicit. Likewise, among the German satellites, there was a persistent attempt to maintain a degree of independence. The extent of the resistance of Hungary to Hitler has come out quite clearly since the war in the memoirs of the statesmen involved. Even such an active and cooperative Eastern European satellite leader as Marshal Antonescu seems finally to have placed his hopes on a German defeat from the West, while he continued in the effort to keep Russia at bay in the East.

It should also be noted, however, that the old frictions did not disappear. One major motive for Antonescu's entering the war, apart from the desire to recover Bessarabia, was his wish to put himself in a favorable position vis-à-vis Germany to press for the return of Northern Transylvania, which had been lost to Hungary in 1940. This old conflict continued unabated throughout the war.

It is worth noting, finally, the importance to Eastern Europe of the fact that Russia did not emerge victorious in the First World War. We do not know what such a Russian regime would have been like or how it would have treated Eastern Europe, but we do have some clues from the secret treaties and arrangements made by the Entente powers during the war. Poland, including the German and Austrian sections, would probably have been incorporated into Russia. By an agreement in 1915 Russia was to obtain Constantinople and the Turkish territory in Europe. In a Russian-French exchange of notes in February 1917, Russia was given complete freedom to determine its own western frontiers. Thus the intrusion of Russia far into Eastern Europe was a likelihood in 1914-18, and was staved off in 1919-21 only to reappear as a reality in 1945 under new and decidedly more dangerous circumstances. In this sense there had been a rather bleak continuity, of which Eastern European states-men were far more aware than were the diplomats in Western Europe or the United States.

V

From this brief survey of international relations in Eastern Europe, it is clear that the states of the region, certainly singly and perhaps even collectively, had only a marginal control over their destiny. Traditionally they have been the objects rather than subjects of history. This appeared less true in the twenty years between 1919 and 1939, but in an age of super-powers it will be more true than ever and their only hope will be to speak and act together.

It must be recognized that the mutual conflicts which divided the Eastern European states were not merely damag-ing but exorbitant in their cost. Surely Teschen was not worth the struggle either to Czechoslovakia or to Poland when it is set against the disaster which overtook both and which might possibly have been averted by their common action. However, creative steps were taken by the Little and Balkan Ententes in the 1920's and 1930's toward increasing coop-eration. One should not underestimate these achievements because of their ultimate failure. At the very least, they showed that the states of Eastern Europe could work together and devise an institution capable of growth and of assuming an increasing number of functions. Yet they arouse only moderate enthusiasm. One authority has said that "Both ententes made excellent beginnings, and they constituted steps in the right direction." This same authority had to grant, however, that Hungary and Bulgaria were never included, and that the stimulus for these Ententes lay largely in a fear of neighboring Eastern European states.

In looking ahead, one must recognize that these national conflicts represent a major hurdle to be overcome. One cannot assume that the Little Entente eventually would have reached a stage when Hungary also would have joined. It is extremely difficult for institutions to transcend the limitations inherent in the motives for their formation, and it remains to be shown that the so-called functional approach to international organization—that is, an approach by economic, technical, or intellectual cooperation—can successfully bypass the real political conflicts that stand between nations. Any future federative or entente movement that hopes to encompass all of Eastern Europe must squarely face all political problems of a divisive nature. Only by transcending rather than disregarding the national principle can harmonious order be achieved in Eastern Europe.

10 The Structure of the Soviet Orbit

JACOB B. HOPTNER

       Political satellite systems are not unknown in recorded history. Maintaining the myth of independence, satellite governments are always similar in structure and political ideology to the primary political planet around which they revolve. Thus the path or orbit in which the secondary planets travel is preordained by the major planet.

I

       The Soviet orbit was born in the winter of 1944-45, when the standards of the victorious Soviet armies were firmly implanted by their bearers into the soil of Eastern Europe. By May 1945, the flag of the Kremlin flew from Stettin in the Baltic to the frontiers of Greece and Turkey. This territorial conquest cannot be ascribed to the success of Russian diplomacy alone. The decisions reached at the diplomatic conference tables merely confirmed the advances of the Red Army divisions. The diplomatic agreements, which were derived from wartime military developments, nevertheless contributed their share to the extension of Communism over Eastern Europe. The Soviet Union successfully utilized the

196

main body of interallied agreements—particularly those of Moscow, Teheran, Yalta, and Potsdam, along with the armistice agreements and the subsequent peace treaties—as their authority to impress the Soviet system of controls over the territories newly taken from the Germans.

By the end of 1945, the Soviet Union was in a position to control the political destinies of Rumania, Hungary, and Bulgaria under the sanctions provided by the armistice terms. However, the process of coordination into the Soviet sphere was anything but smooth and gave little evidence of the much-vaunted Russian planning. Although Rumania was under the Russian thumb within twelve days after the signing of the Yalta agreement, that unhappy country remained a monarchy until December 1947. Czechoslovakia did not fall completely into the Soviet net until 1948, while Hungary fought a losing battle until 1947. Controlled elections elsewhere facilitated the extension of Communist power, so that between the period 1945 and the end of the year 1947 the process of political assimilation was completed. Local Communist parties were installed in all countries—save Yugoslavia where political control had been in the hands of the Communist Party since 1944—by the grace of the Soviet power. In this period the Soviet pattern of inculcating obedience through terror was rapidly imposed.

From the Soviet point of view this revolution was but an action on the part of sovereign states, rather than of satellite states as that term is used in the West. Not only were the states of Eastern Europe sovereign, according to Communist doctrine, but the Communist parties that controlled the political life of their respective countries held that their major function was to protect the national independence of their states against the imperialism of the West. This theory had expression in the basic document of the Communist Information Bureau—the resolution on world affairs which appeared on October 5, 1947.

The Communist Information Bureau, or the Cominform as it is generally called, was formed in September 1947, and at that time embraced the Communist parties of the Soviet Union, Bulgaria, Hungary, Rumania, Poland, Czechoslovakia, Yugoslavia, France, and Italy. The Cominform has never claimed to possess the authority of the earlier Communist International, or Comintern, through which Moscow transmitted instructions in the years between 1919 and 1943, but it seems likely that it was originally intended to be something more than a propaganda agency. Nevertheless, apart from four conferences on public record, the only evidence of the activity of the Cominform has been its journal, *For a Lasting Peace, For a People's Democracy*. As a publicity agency on the policy level the Cominform can command attention for its public statements, but there is no evidence that it exercises any authority in determining Communist policy.

It is rather to the Communist Party of the Soviet Union that one must look for the source of policy decisions in the Soviet orbit. The evidence supports the view that all decisions on policy in the satellite states are made by the central organs of the Communist Party in Moscow, and are transmitted through its instrumentalities. No one can say with certainty which Soviet deputies in the individual countries are the principal source of authority, or which leaders of the local Communist parties are the trusted agents of Moscow. Experience has nevertheless shown that, with the important exception of the Yugoslav Communists, none of the satellite parties has strayed very far from the path determined in Moscow.

In addition to the dominant influence of the Communist parties, both the revival of Pan-Slav sentiment and what may be called the Soviet myth contributed to the creation of the Soviet orbit. With the coming of the Second World War, Russia once again proclaimed itself the liberator of Eastern Europe and the ideas of Pan-Slavism were revived, but with a decided difference in emphasis. It is significant that in August 1941, shortly after the Nazi invasion of Russia, the Soviet government summoned an All-Slav Congress to Moscow. The emphasis of this meeting was on industrialization, cultural autonomy, and respect for the national culture and language of each Slav people. The message sent by the Congress to the Slav peoples was typical of its sentiments:

> Oppressed brother Slavs! A grave danger threatens us. The hour has struck for the entire Slavic world to unite and destroy fascism utterly and without loss of time.
>
> We have come together as equals among equals. Our one, burning desire is that the Slavic nations, together with all other nations, should live their lives freely and in peace within the boundaries of their countries.

In a speech later that year, on November 6, Generalissimo Stalin amplified these sentiments by declaring:

> Our aim is to aid the peoples in their liberation struggle against the Hitler tyranny and then to provide them with the opportunity freely to build their life in accordance with their desire. There must be no interference with the domestic affairs of other nations.

To this Slavic appeal was added an admiration for the Soviet war effort. Many Slavs saw the Russian sufferings as mirroring their own on a gigantic scale, so that the ordinary peasant, to whom a military account of a Red Army victory would mean nothing, carried in his mind a vivid image of the scorched earth, the devastation which Russia suffered, and the hardships and ferocity of his Slav brother's struggle. With the memory of their own unaided fight deeply rooted in their minds, the Slavs watched Russia bearing the brunt of the land war in a way they could understand because the conditions were familiar to them. In Yugoslavia, for example, the Communist Party's growing prestige as the war progressed provided the Soviet Union with a great measure of reflected glory as a communist state. Many Yugoslavs transferred their admiration for the Communist Party's role in their own liberation struggle to admiration for communism itself, and so to the Soviet Union.

Thus the Soviet myth—the supposed victories of the ideals of social reform of the Bolshevik revolution over police and bureaucratic persecutions of the Tsars—went hand in hand with the ties of race of the old Slav mystique. But by 1946, the emphasis of Pan-Slavism shifted to a position reminiscent of the "Slavophile" doctrines of the nineteenth century. Danilevski's prophecies in his *Russia and Europe* (1869) were in the process of realization. Using the language of peace and love, which seemed to him two typical Slav qualities, he had predicted a federation under Russian leadership, as the outcome of a war between Russia and Europe. The federation would consist of Russia (including Galicia, northern Bukovina and Carpatho-Ukraine), the territory of the South Slavs with Istria and Trieste, Rumania, the Czech and Slovak territories, Hungary, Bulgaria, Greece, and Constantinople, as well as sections of Turkey. Many of his prophecies, which at the time undoubtedly seemed fantastic, have come true in the last five years.

The triumph of Russia over Eastern Europe set the tone for the great Slav Congress which was held in Belgrade on December 8, 1946. That the permanent headquarters of the Pan-Slav movement was to be located in this city, as was the headquarters of the Cominform newspaper—*For a Lasting Peace, For a People's Democracy*—is hardly surprising. The speeches and the program of the Congress proclaimed that the Slav peoples lead the world both in the struggle against war, for peace and democracy, and in cultural achievements. Finally, the Congress created the usual organizational methods to further Slavic cultural cooperation. A serious blow was dealt by Tito's defection from the orbit to this attempt at empire building through the Pan-Slav idea, but nevertheless the flow of propaganda continued.

II

The reality of Soviet political control over Eastern Europe, implemented by the Communist parties in each country, has been supplemented by a network of political and economic treaties. During the period between December 12, 1943 and April 6, 1948, the Soviet Union concluded "treaties of friendship, cooperation and mutual assistance" with each of its present satellites—Czechoslovakia, Poland, Rumania, Hungary and Bulgaria—as well as with the then satellite Yugoslavia and with a neutralized Finland. Each instrument is a treaty of military alliance defining the *casus foederis* which brings it into operation and prohibits the satellite from joining in coalitions directed against the Soviet Union.

The conclusion of these treaties formalized an already existing reduction of the status of the Eastern European countries in the field of international policy to the rank of campfollowers of the Soviet Union. The treaties were only a screen behind which political control, military planning and rearmament were exercised. The Eastern European satellites are linked with each other by a network of seventeen bilateral treaties bearing the same title, concluded between March 18, 1946 and April 16, 1949. It seems that thereafter no further alliances were signed inside the Soviet bloc.

After Tito's revolt and excommunication in June 1948, the Soviet Union and its satellites unilaterally denounced their alliances with Yugoslavia during September and October 1949 in violation of the pertinent treaty provisions. Nevertheless the network of the Soviet bloc was almost completed after Yugoslavia's defection by the conclusion of four other inter-satellite alliances. The present state of the structure must naturally be evaluated in the light of the Yugoslav gap, of Tito's still precarious ties with the West, and of the recent Ankara treaty of friendship and collaboration of February 28, 1953 linking Yugoslavia with Greece and Turkey against "non-provoked aggression" from the north.

A detailed analysis and comparison of the provisions of these treaties as a method of arriving at conclusions of some political significance is obviously open to serious objections. The instruments of alliance are a symptom of complete subservience rather than a reflection of actual legal relations prevailing between the contracting parties, and must be reinterpreted in the light of the changed political situation. It must nevertheless be recalled that the first four inter-satellite treaties were concluded before the creation of the Cominform and the following nine, including all but one in the Balkan-Danube region, before Tito's revolt at a time when Soviet control was not yet absolute.

The first obvious fact that emerges from a tabulation of a total of twenty-four military alliances is that Albania is not linked officially by such a treaty to the Soviet Union, and together with East Germany remains without a formal guarantee of Soviet military assistance in case of attack. Such a situation was not unreasonable so long as Tito was the Kremlin's staunchest ally. A treaty of July 9, 1946 linked Albania to Yugoslavia, and Albania's status was one of a sub-satellite, practically under the control and supervision of the Yugoslav government and Communist Party. The ultimate transformation of Albania into a federal state of Yugoslavia or the Balkan Federation was privately discussed.

Albania is now formally linked only to Bulgaria. The alliance signed December 16, 1947 ironically and without precedent stresses Albania's ties to Yugoslavia. The Soviet Union probably was and still is reluctant to commit itself formally to defend such an isolated and exposed position, preserving complete freedom of action depending on actual circumstances. The lack of formal Soviet pledges may prove to be fallacious, but an ostensibly Bulgarian airlift and sea supply of Soviet arms is more probably envisaged.

East Germany, in the legally paradoxical position of an occupied part of an ex-enemy country and at the same time a Soviet satellite representing in Malenkov's recent words "a bulwark in the struggle for a united, peace-loving and democratic Germany," has so far concluded no alliance treaties either with the Soviet Union or with any of its satellites. Its treaty with Poland of July 6, 1950, recognizing the Oder-Neisse boundary as definitive, contains no military alliance clauses. However, the joint German-Polish, German-Czechoslovakian and German-Hungarian declarations of June 6, June 23 and June 24, 1950, respectively, represent an accession on the part of East Germany to the Soviet "peace" camp and a pledge to "use all its forces in order to foil the plans of the imperialist war incendiaries and to strengthen peace." In Soviet semantics this may create almost the same obligations as a formal alliance.

The alliances concluded by the Soviet Union with its six (now five) Eastern European satellites represent a consistent pattern. In these treaties the *casus foederis* bringing military assistance into operation does not consist in an overt act of aggression, but typically: "Should one of the . . . parties be involved in armed conflict with Germany, attempting to renew her policy of aggression, or with any other State allying itself with Germany, directly or in any other way, in her aggressive policy. . . . " (Art. 2, USSR-Rumania, and Art. 3, USSR-Czechoslovakia). The term "policy of aggression" was substituted and therefore probably means policy of "Drang nach Osten," and consequently may be applied to any official statement directed against the Oder-Neisse boundary, considered by the Soviet bloc as "the boundary of peace."

The Soviet alliances have two major characteristics: First, they are operative regardless of whether the attack originates from Germany or its allies, or from a member of the Soviet bloc. Of special importance in connection with the latter eventuality is the typical obligation preceding the *casus foederis* "to take jointly all measures in their power to remove any threat of repeated aggression on the part of Germany, or of any State allying itself with Germany directly or in any other way" (Art. I, par. 1, USSR-Rumania). The involvement may well arise from such "measures." Secondly, they are directed not only against Germany but also against any state allying itself directly or in any other way with Germany in its aggressive policy. This vague language may cover any kind of endorsement of the revision of Germany's present eastern border.

So far as Germany itself is concerned, such a *casus foederis* is based in part on the language of Article 53, paragraph 1 of the United Nations Charter which stipulates that the authorization of the Security Council is not required for "measures against any enemy state . . . provided for . . . in regional arrangements directed against renewal of aggressive policy on the part of any such state. . . ." This provision, absent from the Dumbarton Oaks proposals, was introduced in the joint amendments submitted by the Big Four to the San Francisco Conference on May 5, 1945. This formula was used by the Soviet Union even before that date. The Soviet Union has repeatedly declared that the satellite alliances are based on Article 53 of the United Nations Charter, although insofar as they are directed against the Western Powers they violate the Charter. The possibility of a pseudo-legal alibi for a unilateral Soviet military action against Germany and the North Atlantic powers after a ratification of the European Defense Community Pact should therefore be recognized.

A detailed analysis of the original sixteen (now only ten) inter-satellite alliances reveals roughly two separate types covering different though partially overlapping geographical sectors of the Soviet bloc. The links connecting countries located in different sectors belong to one or the other type apparently ... random.

The first group includes the Balkan and Danubian states (Bulgaria, Albania, Hungary, Rumania and, formerly, Yugoslavia), which are bound together by treaties manifesting a consistent pattern. They are operative only in case of formal military aggression, and not in cases of aggression by means short of war. A typical provision reads: "In the event . . . [of] attack . . . [on] one of the . . . Parties threatening its independence, or to enslave it or sever part of its territory." Moreover they are directed not only nominally against Germany but more generally against "Germany or any third power," which in practice means against any state outside the Soviet bloc. Greece was mentioned by name together with "American and British imperialists" when some of the treaties were signed. Italy is also a possibility in connection with Albania. Obviously the name of Germany is used here as a transparent camouflage and the Balkan-Danubian bloc is a military alliance clearly directed against the Western powers and their allies in the region, although it is cast in the form of a defensive alliance.

The second, or northern group embracing Poland and Czechoslovakia—to which Hungary and Rumania are separately linked—forms a bloc partially overlapping with the first. They are connected by the type of alliances linking all satellites to the Soviet Union. The familiar provisions regarding "joint measures" against any threat of aggression by Germany or her allies, the "aggressive policy" of Germany as the *casus foederis,* and the direction of the treaties against states "joining Germany's aggressive policy directly or in any other way," are also to be found here, as well as the reference to Article 53 of the United Nations Charter.

The fact that the political and military alliances within the Soviet orbit are exclusively bilateral, has more than legal significance. It represents the application of the old Russian distrust and fear of multilateral groupings formed by neighbor states along Russia's borders. This traditional attitude has been applied by the Kremlin to its satellites in the Soviet orbit to prevent federation schemes and especially closer economic and ultimately political ties between Communist Poland and Communist Czechoslovakia, that might eventually give groups of these countries bargaining power with the Soviet Union.

III

In any discussion of the Soviet orbit—particularly during the developments of the first postwar years—a clear distinction must be made by the reader between two types of states. The first includes the former enemy countries: Rumania, Hungary, and Bulgaria. In the second are the countries that were in the Allied camp: Albania, Czechoslovakia, Poland, and Yugoslavia.

The former Axis satellites were required by the peace treaties to pay reparations not only to the Soviet Union but to certain allied countries as well. Thus Hungary was to pay reparations to Yugoslavia and to Czechoslovakia while Bulgaria was to pay Yugoslavia and Greece. Since payments were made in goods, they represented a budget item rather than items in international trade. The armistice agreements further established the right of the Soviet Union to charge Bulgaria, Hungary, and Rumania with the costs of occupation. The Potsdam Agreement also recognized the right of the Soviet Union to the so-called German and Italian assets located in the territories in these three countries. In this period the orbit served as a source of raw materials and a processor of finished and semifinished goods for the Soviet Union.

As early as 1945, the Soviet Union began to negotiate

trade agreements with all the Eastern European countries. In the beginning these trade agreements were limited to the determination of goods to be mutually delivered during a specific period of time. In time these trade agreements were replaced by more elaborate documents which established definite goals to be achieved in the exchange of commodities between the countries concerned. If the new treaties and agreements indicate anything, they indicate the primacy of economics in the Soviet outlook. This was but one means by which the preponderance of the Soviet Union in the area was assured.

Although the Council on Mutual Economic Assistance (Comecon) was announced to the world in 1949, it is not yet clear that complete economic integration exists. What is clear is a trend to make the various captive countries of the orbit dependent upon the Soviet Union, since the area does not possess half the basic raw materials that it needs. Thus while there is no economic integration of the satellites as a regional bloc, there is a tendency because of their need for raw materials for them to become part of one centralized Soviet system.

This system is best evidenced by the existence of joint or mixed companies. In Rumania, the oil fields are owned by a mixed Soviet-Rumanian company. In effect this means that the Soviets control Rumanian petroleum production. The Russian representatives on the company board control the majority of votes and are in a position to decide policies and production norms. In addition, the companies operate rent free, receive the highest priorities in labor, equipment and resources.

The extent of Soviet parasitism in Eastern Europe might have remained a "state secret" had not the Yugoslavs divulged it to the world. As the Yugoslav *White Book* so well documents, one of their major criticisms of the Soviet behavior arose from the negotiations over the so-called Soviet-

Yugoslav joint companies. The Yugoslav experience is of particular interest since it reflects that of the rest of the orbit. The Soviet Union and the Federated People's Republic of Yugoslavia signed an economic agreement on April 11, 1945. The communiqué released after the negotiations stated that the Soviet government agreed to supply the Yugoslav army with arms and ammunition on long-term credits and to aid in the restoration of the Yugoslav war industry. At the same time both sides agreed on mutual deliveries of goods. The Soviet government was to meet the requirements of the Yugoslav economy as to raw materials, technical advice and other services.

The signatories have never made public the details of this agreement, but the Yugoslav-Cominform differences threw some light on Soviet trading techniques. On March 31, 1949, *Borba,* the official newspaper of the Communist Party of Yugoslavia, charged that the Soviet government had violated the agreement for the financial support of Yugoslav students attending Soviet schools by forcing the Yugoslav government to pay for their upkeep in dollars instead of dinars. It also charged that the Soviet Union unilaterally reduced the volume of trade and that the Soviet government forced the Yugoslavs to sell their raw materials at prices below world market prices.

In his description on October 7, 1949, of the operations of Soviet-Yugoslav joint companies, Dr. Vilfan, permanent Yugoslav delegate to the United Nations, branded Russia as an exploiter. Speaking before the Economic and Financial Committee of the United Nations, Dr. Vilfan described Soviet imperialist practices. As an example, he cited the Joint Yugoslav-Soviet Steamship Company (Juspad). Russia, he claimed, had among other things rigged the transportation charges, causing a loss of $19,000,000 to Yugoslavia in 1948. Vilfan further observed that "the superiority of capi-

talist monopoly has been replaced by the monopolistic position of the more developed Socialist country."

While Soviet economic policy had much to do with Yugoslavia's ultimate defection from the orbit, the causes lie deep
in Yugoslavia's historical experience and that of Tito and his
party's rise to political power. Many of the documents regarding the break have been published, yet much more has to be
made available before a definitive judgment can be made and
many questions answered.

IV

One fact that should be made clear regarding Yugoslavia
and its role in the Soviet orbit is that Tito never "broke"
with Moscow. While it is true Tito declined the invitation to
attend a Cominform meeting called to consider his case, his
action cannot be described as a break. It was Moscow that
gave Tito the *coup de main*. It was not until a year later that
the Yugoslavs attacked Stalin openly.

For centuries, the geographical position of Yugoslavia has
made the country a target for political and military pressures
from all sides. Now, to the struggle for the control of Yugoslavia's land and sea positions and her resources, the break
between Moscow and Belgrade adds a contest for the control
of the minds and unquestioned obedience of men. Since
Yugoslav Partisans based their National Liberation Movement on the principle of unconditional loyalty to the Soviet
Union, prior to the break the Soviet Union had a privileged
and controlling position in Yugoslavia's domestic and foreign
policy, resources, and manpower.

The institutional system of Yugoslavia fully indicated the
allegiance the Partisan leaders had pledged to the Kremlin,
and faithfully reflected the structure of the Soviet Union.
The People's Front, with the Communist Party of Yugoslavia

at its head, differed only slightly from Russia's one-party state. In external affairs, too, Yugoslavia supported the Soviet Union's aims in Eastern Europe by doing its part to make that area safe for Russia. It participated in the Soviet network of political alliances, it maintained close economic relations with the Soviet Union, it voted in unison with the Soviet bloc in the United Nations General Assembly and its agencies, it participated in the establishment of the Cominform, it sponsored the Pan-Slav Congresses in Eastern Europe and it acted as a supply and training base for violations of the frontiers of the Greek state.

Neither before nor since the dispute have the Yugoslavs given the Western powers opportunities similar to those afforded the Russians, despite the fact that the present regime relied heavily during the Second World War on British technical assistance and on American Lend-Lease.

During the war, the Anglo-Americans supported Tito and his followers solely on grounds of military necessity, and only the British gave some thought to the political consequences of their actions. The two Western powers based their policy on the fact that Tito's Partisans were killing Germans more effectively than their countrymen, the Royalist and anti-Communist Chetniks, who committed political suicide by confusing the main issue of fighting the Nazi invader with their secondary aim of carrying on a civil war with the Partisans and non-Serbian groups. From the start, Tito demanded Western aid not only for military reasons but also for the ultimate purpose of imposing his own political and economic system upon Yugoslavia.

It seems in retrospect that the Western powers made two mistaken assumptions in regard to the Partisans. They believed that the Soviet Union would permit a "representative" government in Yugoslavia after the termination of hostilities, and that Tito and the Partisans would repay their military obligations in acceptable political tender. Once the Communist Party in Yugoslavia seized power, at the end of the war, the thin veneer of friendship for the West disappeared. In unison with its neighbors, Yugoslavia directed its controlled press and radio to speak in diatribes and strictures against the "capitalistic and warmongering Western democracies," and, at the same time, to speak in glowing terms of their brother Slavs and comrades-in-arms, the people of the Soviet Union.

The rupture between Belgrade and Moscow has not changed this picture in its essentials. Soviet pressure on Tito has not caused him to alter the existing one-party political or economic structure of his country. Just as Tito has demanded that the socialist countries base their relationships on the principle of equality because he is aware of the Soviet Union's aims in Europe, so too he will resist Western demands for the modification of his policies in return for economic and military support.

The Soviet Union erred in trying arbitrarily to mold the Balkan area to the Kremlin pattern. It failed, in the manner of dictatorships, to take into account the long South Slav tradition of opposition to tyranny and conquest. Unfortunately for the Soviet Union's expansionist plans, the pattern did not allow for the forces of human nature, of which there seem to be more in the Balkans than elsewhere in the world. Only if one recognizes that this is a problem in power relations rather than an ideological dispute, can one grasp the full implications of this dispute.

The shift of Yugoslavia at this juncture is best described by what has been termed "integral nationalism," which expresses itself in totalitarian terms. Integral nationalism is totalitarian not only in domestic affairs, but in foreign affairs as well. The nation attempts to make itself feared or "respected" by pursuing firm and bold policies. The nature of Tito's rise to power, the geographical characteristics of Yugoslavia, and Tito's power position relative to the Balkan states have all contributed to the making of Titoism. Specifically, Titoism can be defined as a form of nationalism which conceives of Yugoslavia as an end in itself, and the rulers of that country are concerned only with the exclusive pursuit of national policies. It is thus not unique in political history nor does it contribute anything new to the diplomatic techniques available to the Western democracies. Titoism is then but a matter of lack of loyalty to a higher power center outside the national state itself.

Tito and his colleagues in the Communist Party of Yugoslavia exhibited the utmost faith and loyalty to Stalin and the Soviet Union throughout the war and in the immediate postwar years. Certainly in this period Tito was a marked Stalinist "internationalist." That is, one "who is ready to serve the Soviet Union unreservedly, unhesitatingly, unconditionally. . . ." The Communist Party of Yugoslavia was the sole Communist Party to engage in partisan warfare in the days immediately after the invasion of the Soviet Union by Germany. Up to 1948 the Yugoslav government was completely servile to the Soviet programs in the world diplomatic forums.

The Soviet Union had undoubtedly cast another role for Tito than that of a mere extra on the diplomatic stage. In May of 1946, Tito arrived in Moscow for a number of discussions regarding armament. How important this meeting was is best indicated by the rank of the individuals he took with him. Not only was he accompanied by Alexander Rankovich, who as Minister of Interior is also head of the secret police, but also the chiefs of staff of all the armed services. While it is not known what Tito promised in return for Soviet arms, one is able to speculate from the series of events which began the following month.

In July, Yugoslavia and Albania signed a military alliance, and in August two American planes were shot down in the vicinity of the Austrian-Yugoslavian border. Aid to the Greek Communists began in September; in the following month

British destroyers were struck by mines in the Corfu Channel, and at the same time the wave of imprisonment of individuals who might prove dangerous to the regime rose even higher than heretofore. By Christmas of 1947, Radio Belgrade announced the existence of the Greek Communist guerrillas as a "free and democratic" government. But this was not recognition. What the Greek Communists required was that very act, and open resistance which would go beyond that already granted by Tito and which was vigorously criticized by the United Nations Special Committee on the Balkans.

Who then was to recognize the Greek Communists first? Certainly not Stalin, but Tito who occupied the central position. Undoubtedly Tito was impressed by the counter measures issued by the Western Powers: the immediacy of American air and sea power then in the Mediterranean, and the announcement of the Truman Doctrine on aid to Greece and Turkey. It is almost mathematically certain that if Tito had recognized the Greek Communists, the war would have been fought on the streets of Belgrade and not on the bare mountains of Greece. How Stalin tried to bribe Tito into recognition is implicit in the negotiations on the Balkan federation in Moscow in February 1948. Stalin proposed that Yugoslavia and Bulgaria unite, and in so doing bring Albania into their fold. Although Tito's representatives did not accept this proposal, Kardelj signed an agreement with Molotov agreeing to mutual consultation on matters relating to foreign policy. Stalin was seemingly now in a position to control Tito and Soviet advisers were serving with the Yugoslav army. Tito's rejection of the invitation to participate in the Marshall Plan made the success of the Yugoslav Five Year Plan contingent upon Stalin's generosity, and the signing of the articles on mutual consultation on foreign affairs closed the circle.

Yet the fact remains that Tito did not recognize the Greek Communist guerrillas. For between the pressures exerted by the Kremlin on one hand and the West on the other, Tito chose to keep Yugoslavia intact by refusing to become a mere instrument of Soviet policy. He undoubtedly saw clearly that the Kremlin took no risks and would certainly get all of the benefits accruing from these political adventures. In the light of Stalin's definition of a true internationalist, this is what the Cominform communiqué meant when it denounced the Communist party of Yugoslavia as identifying "the foreign policy of the Soviet Union with the foreign policy of the imperialist powers," a policy "appropriate only to nationalists."

What effect has Tito's departure from the table of "brotherly Communist parties" had on those parties? Titoism is primarily a matter of loyalties. In Yugoslavia, there was no higher loyalty than to the state personified by Tito himself. Consequently, the party, the army, and the new bureaucracy could and did remain faithful to Tito. If Titoism is to spread, similar conditions and a similar concept of limited loyalty must exist in the people's democracies. To date there is no evidence that Titoism has taken root in the effective leadership circles of the satellite states, since both Western-minded and Moscow-trained Communists have been affected by the purges. Certainly the purges of Communist leaders in satellite Europe which have occurred since 1948 afford no index as to the extent of Titoism. The purgees had no machinery for independence of action available to Tito. Even if they had, it is not sure they would have acted as Tito did if faced with the choice.

What effect has the break had on Yugoslavia itself—on its policies and political philosophy? From the time of the break in June 1948 until November 1949, the Yugoslavs inveighed against the Communist parties of the satellites but not against the sacrosanct personage of Joseph Stalin. The second Cominform meeting held in November 1949 proved quite conclusively to Tito that there were no longer any grounds for conciliation, and he prepared a new political dialectic which would reflect the changes in his country's international position.

First, the policies of the Soviet Union and the ideas of Stalin himself were attacked as marked departures from the true path of Socialism. Second, in contradistinction to the policies of "bureaucratic state capitalism" evolved by the Kremlin and followed in slavish pattern by the satellites, Yugoslavia decentralized its machinery of economic planning, gave greater power to workers' councils, reorganized local government, and re-wrote the national constitution. An interesting feature of the recently amended constitution is the provision for a Council of Producers, as one of the two parliamentary bodies. In this council industrial workers are disproportionately represented by 135 deputies, while only 67 represent agriculture. Under this arrangement, the agricultural population has one representative for every 150,825 peasants, while the urban is represented by one deputy for every 30,239 workers.

In its organization, the Council of Producers is strikingly similar to another proposal advanced by another state that adopted the philosophy of integral nationalism, Mussolini's Corporative Italy. According to the latter, the corporations were instruments responsible for "the regulation of the productive forces, with a view to the development of the wealth, the political power and the well-being of the Italian people." This statement of purpose does not differ greatly from the ideology advanced by Kardelj on behalf of the new constitution.

In any event, the character of the power structure—that is, the structure of social power focused on the state—has not changed. Decentralized though the power may be, the Communist party still controls the councils where important decisions are made. Effective opposition to the regime is still unknown. Democrats who have opposed Tito and his policies still remain imprisoned and, while important concessions have been made to the peasants, state cooperatives are still maintained in the heavy grain producing areas by forces other than the peasants' love of the soil and its products.

If the Yugoslav government will learn the meaning of Lord Acton's axiom on the nature of power, and if the West pursues an intelligent, long-range foreign policy supporting Yugoslavia against Soviet aggression, it may be possible to revive in Yugoslavia and hence in the Balkans as a whole the elements of an independent political life.

V

The months following the death of Premier Stalin in March 1953, saw a number of internal changes in the various people's democracies. The principal means of coercion and political control nevertheless remained unchanged: the army and the police forces. These were still bound tightly to Russian controls.

The total number of men in the satellite armies available for service with the Soviet army has been estimated at a million and one-half. Since they are not only trained under Soviet commanders, but operate under the Soviet military code, it is possible to state that the Sovietization of the satellite armies has been completed. Together with the armies, the satellite police form the backbone of the Soviet instruments of coercion. Estimated at a total of 700,000 men, police units organized in military formations range in function from the well-known secret police to People's Militia, Frontier Guards, and Railway Guards. Like the satellite armies, the satellite police are governed by Soviet regulations. Together they enforce a system of order which has been designed to conform with the Soviet model.

In common with Yugoslavia, certain states in the orbit are strengthening the weakest sector of the economy: agriculture. It is not certain that the Yugoslav experience compelled the changes in agricultural policy in the people's democracies. The only causal factor common to both areas is a very practical one: agricultural production has not been in a position to supply the needs of the growing industrial population. The socialist objective of complete nationalization of agriculture has nevertheless not been retracted or withdrawn. On the contrary, the satellites are acting within the orthodox pattern of Soviet experience.

In the economic sphere, the orbit is passing through a period comparable to the Russian New Economic Policy. In the words of Stalin this is a "special policy of the proletarian state counting on the tolerations of capitalist elements, the commanding heights being in the hands of the proletarian state. . . .", in short a policy which aims "at overcoming capitalist elements and building a socialist economy by the method of a direct exchange of products. . . ." As if the Soviet experience itself did not suffice as a guide, there is the advice of Stalin on the proper agricultural policy required to prepare the transition to communism: continued development of the country's industrial resources, the gradual adjustment of collective farming to the nationalized sector of the economy, and the raising of the standards of living and culture. All these the satellite states are in the process of attempting to accomplish. There may be compromises in the short run, but there will be no compromise regarding the ultimate objective—the complete socialization of agriculture.

Changes in agricultural policy are particularly marked in those countries which have been heretofore heavily agricultural: Yugoslavia, Hungary, Albania, and Bulgaria. The restiveness of the population arising from the social and economic consequences of enforced industrialization made these changes necessary. The changes are short-run changes. While budgets for agricultural development will be increased, prices lowered for industrial goods and increased for farm products, establishment of producer cooperatives delayed, and fines for delay in delivery of agricultural products abolished, the basic policy of collectivization remains. The problem facing the satellite governments is one of tempo, not of objective.

The governments of the Soviet orbit are subject to all these strains and stresses which arise from a system of dictatorship over the minds and bodies of men. Nevertheless, the Western observer must be cautious in reading into these changes any amount of wishful thinking. It does not follow that a process of disintegration is taking place within the Soviet orbit. A more realistic attitude would be to assume that since there is no change in the rate of capital investment and armament production, the Soviet empire is anything but on a decline.

At the same time it would be a mistake to ascribe to the rulers of the Soviet orbit a monopoly of political omniscience. They are handicapped by a political dogma which prevents a clear assessment of the problems which face them day in and day out. It would also be an error, on the part of the Western democracies, to examine the problems of Europe today from the vantage point of the past alone. They must be conscious of new variations which arise from the current Eastern European experience.

11 Problems and Prospects of Federation

KARL W. DEUTSCH

I

The distribution of sovereign states in Central and in Eastern Europe has undergone some striking changes during the last one hundred years. A century ago, in 1853, there were six sovereign states between the Baltic Sea and the Aegean: the empires of Austria, Prussia, Russia, and Turkey, the kingdom of Greece, and the small principality of Montenegro. Two generations later, in 1913, there were ten states in the area, for by then Serbia, Bulgaria, Rumania, and Albania had all become sovereign states. Another ten years later, the number of states had increased to sixteen. Serbia and Montenegro had merged into Yugoslavia, but Hungary, Czechoslovakia, Poland, Latvia, Estonia, Lithuania, and Finland had all been added as sovereign states. After the convulsions of the Second World War, thirteen sovereign states remained in what was now called Eastern Europe. They were the same states which had existed there during the 1920's and 1930's, with the exception of the three small Baltic states of Latvia, Estonia and Lithuania, which had become incorporated under the Soviet dictatorships in the style of the federal republics of the Soviet Union.

By 1949, Soviet-style dictatorships had been established in seven of these thirteen sovereign states. In these "Iron Curtain" states, dictatorship was and is exercised through a native minority who could not have won power without the support of the Soviet Union and the Soviet armies, and who—with the conspicuous exception of Yugoslavia—could not retain this power if Soviet support were withdrawn. The indirect rule thus exercised by the Soviet dictatorship, with the help of native personnel, over six of the Eastern European states —Poland, Czechoslovakia, Hungary, Rumania, Bulgaria, and Albania—might remind the observer at first glance of the indirect rule exercised in past centuries by the empires of Turkey and Russia over some of the principalities then existing in the region. Upon this superficial view, it might seem that despite all the violent changes in political sovereignty and national allegiance during the last one hundred years, the fundamental dependence of the peoples of this region upon foreign powers had remained essentially unchanged.

This impression would be quite deceptive. In 1853, the government of Eastern Europe by only six powers had endured for more than two hundred years, with Sweden and Poland rather than Greece and Montenegro playing the roles of the fifth and sixth power at the side of Prussia, Russia, Austria, and Turkey. With the single exception of Poland, which by the end of the eighteenth century had become the victim of her neighbors, the administrative services of these powers were generally based upon foreign personnel drawn from peoples outside the region. Austria and Prussia depended upon the military and administrative services of Germans, Russia upon those of Great Russians, and Turkey in the last analysis had to rely upon the support of the Ottoman Turks. Natives of the different regions supplemented the personnel of these administrative services but did not dominate it. The rule of these foreign or semiforeign empires over the peoples of Eastern Europe was based upon this region's overwhelmingly peasant character, its political apathy and military weakness.

Today, in the middle of the twentieth century, most of these conditions have been transformed. All the peoples of Eastern Europe have literate majorities. They have native professional and middle classes. All of them have at least some more or less modern industries and transportation systems. All of them have had two or three generations of broad national and political development, a flourishing of national languages and literatures, and a vigorous growth in native political participation. They have memories of national independence and skills of political organization and action. They can no longer be ruled by alien rulers, and even the Russian dictatorship must deal with them by indirect methods. The peoples of Eastern Europe today can be governed stably only by native political administrations, by native civil services and school systems, and by the appeal—however distorted—to native symbols and traditions, or they cannot be governed at all.

All these changes seem to be irreversible. It would be as difficult to restore illiteracy, apathy, and fundamental ignorance to the peoples of Eastern Europe as it would be to restore the economic and social institutions of 1853. If history teaches us anything, it is at the very least that the distribution of political and military power is subject to rapid change and that every submerged people that has preserved its identity and its capacity to think and act may well expect to find again some opportunity to determine its own destiny in freedom.

II

Yet all was not well with the growth of sovereign states in Eastern Europe. Perhaps the most characteristic feature of the political institutions of the area was the widespread

discontent with them. If people had resented the oppressive-
ness of the old large empires, many now chafed under the
smallness and divisiveness of the national states that had
come to succeed them. Eastern European states, large or
small, seemed to have a way of frustrating the hopes and ambitions of significant numbers of their citizens. Where men
had complained about the lack of national freedom in the
past, many now complained about the "balkanization" of the
region. It is this underlying restlessness, this *malaise* of Eastern European politics, that gave a peculiar appeal to the
demand for Eastern European federation. If we are to understand the prospects and the problems of a federal union in
this region, we must first turn our attention to the fundamental needs and discontents that gave rise to the proposal.

Eastern Europe was a relatively backward area in terms of
economic development. Even some of its most highly developed regions, such as the countries of Austria, Hungary, and
the Russian-held parts of Poland, had lagged in economic development during the two crucial generations between 1815
and 1875, during which time most Western countries went
through decades of tremendous economic growth.[1] In 1850

[1] Cf. Paul Muller, "Osterreich seit 1848," in Hans Mayer, ed., *Hundert
Jahre Osterreichischer Wirtschaftsentwicklung,* 1848-1948, (Vienna:
Springer Verlag, 1949), pp. 1-20, esp. p. 8; and in the same volume, for
the old monopolistic traditions of business at Vienna from 1221 to 1848,
and "conditions bordering on lethargy" during the decades preceding
1848, see Otto Gruss, "Ein Jahrhundert Osterreichischer Binnenhandel
(1848-1948)," pp. 310-358, esp. pp. 311-317; for figures on the slow
introduction of steam engines, the lag in the growth of towns, the slow
relative growth of the population occupied in industry, the lack of capital, the national fragmentation of markets, etc., see Karl Heinz Werner,
"Osterreichs Industrie und Aussenhandelspolitik 1848 bis 1948," *ibid.,*
pp. 359, 479, esp. pp. 624-678, esp. p. 659. See also J. Slokar, *Geschichte
der osterreichischen Industrie* (Vienna: Tempsky, 1949), pp. 16-19,
46-54, 177-179; Richard Schuller, "Die Entstehung des osterreichisch-
ungarischen Wirtschaftsgebietes," in G. Gratz and R. Schuller, *Der wirt-
schaftliche Zusammenbruch Osterreich-Ungarns* (Vienna and New Haven: Holder-Pichler-Tempsky and Yale University Press, 1930), pp.
1-35, esp. pp. 23-24; Oscar Jaszi, *The Dissolution of the Habsburg
Monarchy* (Chicago: University of Chicago Press, 1929), pp. 185-212.

Vienna was larger than Berlin and Austria did not appear to lag conspicuously behind Prussia; but by 1866 the lag had become conspicuous and was confirmed on the battlefields of the Austro-Prussian War. There seems to have been a significant acceleration of economic growth between 1880 and 1914; and it has been estimated that between 1900 and 1910 the percentage rate of growth in the national income of Austria was even somewhat faster than it was during the same decade in Western Europe. The percentage growth of the low income of Austria-Hungary was unable, nevertheless, to keep up with the very much higher levels of national income and industrial productivity which meanwhile had been attained in the West.

Such economic growth as did occur was quite unevenly distributed. The economic position of the Germans and a few other groups was a great deal better than that of the rest of the peoples concerned, and the attempts of non-German groups to equal German economic standards often brought them into economic competition and political friction with Germans. After the economic depression of 1873, German nationalists raised the cry for the preservation of German supremacy, and the very attempts to mitigate or overcome economic inequality thus led to intensified economic competition and political conflict.

Economic development was poorly distributed between town and country, as well as between nationalities. In most Western countries, country people had come to share many of the educational and cultural standards of the city populations. In Eastern Europe, by contrast, even the German-Austrian peasants were described before the First World War by the Viennese architect, Adolph Loos, as people wearing different clothes, speaking a different language, and having an infinitely more primitive way of life than the populations of the cities.

The uneven distribution of economic opportunity was reinforced in its effect by the extreme splintering of national, linguistic, and religious affiliations. A good map of the nationalities, languages, and religions of Eastern Europe would have shown not the large patches of relatively homogeneous populations which are found in so much of Western Europe but rather a polka-dot pattern of intermixed minorities.

The relative national uniformity of the West is perhaps, at least in part, the product of a history rich in the processes of successful social learning and acculturation, which merged and melted the different ethnic groups that were left in the Western countries by accidents of migration, wars, and settlement. In Eastern Europe, such accidents of conquest or settlement may well have been even more numerous, but there is also some reason to think that the processes of assimilation were much slower and less effective.

Greater uniformity of language and culture means greater interchangeability of social roles. This is not merely a contributing cause to the growth in social mobility and in the interchange of social roles but is also to some extent their product. Where societies are rigorously stratified, where religions fail to impress upon people an awareness of their essential unity, where the obstacles to a change in occupation or in social role are great, and the rewards for mobility are uncertain and small—in these societies individuals may best succeed in gaining security by clinging tenaciously to their familiar groups, languages, customs, and traditions, and by rejecting any assimilation to other groups except the most privileged as a threat to their existence. The more privileged groups, under these conditions, can only be expected to resent and resist the assimilation or intrusion of strangers, unless these strangers come from regions of clearly greater wealth and greater prestige and seem to bring to the new group assets clearly greater than those they would demand. The lack of unity and assimilation in language and culture in Eastern Europe thus appears as one more aspect of the relative lack in fundamental economic innovation and social learning in that geographic area, if we take the extent of such learning and innovation in the Western countries as our standard.

On this view, the Western way of life—thus far the way of life of a minority of mankind—has been built upon a certain fundamental willingness to learn, and a basic acceptance of both some mobility, at least in society, and of some innovations in accustomed practices and habits. Against the background of this Western culture, large-scale markets and economic competition, as well as the impact of the modern centralized state, had a chance of functioning as accelerators of technological and social change: they tended to lure or push people away from social roles or economic occupations which were poorly rewarded and into new roles or occupations where the gains were greater. Western economic and political institutions succeeded the better in this function of accelerating social change where they impinged upon individuals who had the economic and social resources for moving, and at least a minimum of cultural and psychological willingness to do so. Where these economic and cultural preconditions did not exist, however, or where they existed only in part, the effect of the impact of Western institutions was bound to be quite different, and these differences became dramatically visible in the area of Eastern Europe.

III

Eastern Europe, seen from this aspect, was a semi-Western area. It was fully exposed to Western practices and institutions both in the field of higher education, particularly university education, and in the fields of military drill and warfare, and particularly in the use of conscripted armies, although it could operate in this field only as long as no extensive industrial facilities for the use of massed artillery were needed. Large parts of the area were exposed to Western methods of tax collecting, accounting, and fiscal policy, as well as public administration. They were exposed to the activities of modern bankers, and to a considerable extent to the practices of modern commerce, newspapers, and advertising. They were also exposed in large part to compulsory elementary public education.

As a result of these exposures in the nineteenth century, the peoples of Eastern Europe learned to accept completely the prevailing Western standards of theoretical science, as well as of intellectual and artistic life. They accepted to a considerable extent Western ideals of living standards, standards of consumption, wage levels, working conditions, and social welfare. Finally, many of them came to expect Western standards of farm prosperity, rural welfare, and peasant independence and cooperation. In sum, a large part of the populations of Eastern Europe accepted Western living standards as their goal, or at least as a pattern of their claims and expectations.

This rapid diffusion of Western-style claims and expectations was not matched by any comparable diffusion of Western-style work habits, savings and investment patterns, levels of productivity, or propensities to technological innovations. Land reforms in Eastern Europe were not only slow in coming, but they did little to increase productivity. The consolidation of separate strips of land, long accomplished in Scandinavia and Western Europe, was still not completed in Eastern Europe by the time of the Second World War. The tools and implements of artisans and peasants changed their traditional shape much more slowly in Eastern Europe than they did in Germany or England and pathetically more slowly than they did in the United States. Throughout most of the regions organized labor feared that increases in productivity would only lead to losses of employment. Employers and businessmen aspired to use the profits of their businesses for the purpose of retiring from business themselves, rather than for expanding their productive equipment.

While productivity grew slowly, public health measures were effective and birth rates remained high. Throughout most of the region, the population pressed upon the limited supply of land and on the limited productivity of existing agricultural methods. At the same time, the lagging growth of towns and industries did not absorb completely the increases in population. The results were underemployment in the towns and industrial districts, hidden unemployment in the rural areas, and a general cheapness of human labor. While labor was thus abundant, and was often wastefully used, the skills of most workers remained low, and there was little incentive to improve them. Since capital goods and capital were scarce, there were fewer opportunities for engineers and applied scientists. And since universities, public administration, and banking had become modernized, there were ample employment opportunities for civil servants, clerks, lawyers, teachers, and research scientists.

The result was a startling precocity of Eastern European intellectual life. First-rate university training was fairly widely available throughout the region. Food, land, and domestic services were relatively cheap. Civil servants, intellectuals, and members of the professions had high prestige socially, and they found no severe economic difficulty in maintaining their families and sending their children to universities. While the top-level jobs in commerce, civil service, and universities under the Austro-Hungarian monarchy were perhaps somewhat more easily accessible to persons recruited from the German or Jewish minorities, there were some opportunities for careers for men of outstanding talent from all national backgrounds. Czech scientists reminisce today about the remarkable generation of Czech and Slovak intellectuals and scientists who made their careers during the last thirty years before the First World War in the Austro-Hungarian monarchy. At the same time, there was relatively little competition for the services of men of high talent on the part of industry, applied science, or practical politics, since all of these activities remained relatively underdeveloped.

The coincidence of intellectual precocity with widespread social and economic backwardness led to widespread experiences of frustration. Intellectuals, not unlike the ancient philosopher Plato, dreamed of equalling one day the power and prestige of the aristocracy, for which they lacked the land holdings and family connections; and they dreamed of equalling the comforts and securities of the bourgeoisie—the upper middle class—without either owning a bourgeois amount of property or devoting a bourgeois proportion of their time and attention to money-making or to business matters. They resented the influence of the church and the clergy in the rural areas, without being either willing or able to devote a major part of their own time and attention to the needs of the country population. Almost all classes of society had come to desire Western standards of income, comfort, security, and power, without possessing as yet either the means or the skill necessary to produce them. And all these discontented groups and individuals, pushed forward by the fundamental incongruities in their social evolution, turned to politics and to the state as a remedy for their frustrations.

IV

Under these conditions, no type of government and no size of political unit could for long live up to the rising level of popular expectations and the increasingly pressing demands of society. Already, before the year 1914, large states as well as small, national states as well as international, became increasingly strained by social tensions.

In a supra- or multinational state, such as the Austro-

Hungarian monarchy, an obvious reaction of the population to prolonged social and political disappointment was an increasing demand for national freedom. The sovereign nation-state would give the Czechs a fuller opportunity for careers for their young people and a more worthy share in determining their own destiny. A nation-state centered on Hungary would give Hungarian industries the protection they wanted and would free Hungarians from the delays and frustrations of the imperial relationship to Austria. The national state uniting Slovenes and Croatians with Serbia would help these peoples at long last to make real headway in escaping from their backwardness. During these same years, the peoples in the small national states of the region dreamed of escaping from the compromises and frustrations of their own small-scale political existence by national expansion into some greater and victorious power in their own area. Serbians and Montenegrins came to hope that their lives would somehow improve once Bosnia, Herzegovina, Slovenia, and Croatia had been joined to their own territories in a new Yugoslavia. Bulgarians, Greeks, and Serbians all came to believe that somehow their own lives would improve significantly if all or most of the territory of Macedonia were added to their respective countries.

Throughout large parts of Eastern Europe, the burdens and demands put upon the existing governments thus exceeded the capabilities of those governments and of the states they represented. The Eastern European states, large and small, were thus becoming overcommitted politically, economically, militarily, and socially. Among their peoples this situation encouraged the belief that things would become better once the size of political units in their region was changed. Citizens of small national states such as Serbia hoped for improvement from expansion. Citizens of large states, such as some of the Hungarians or Czechs in Austria-Hungary, began to wonder whether their position could not be improved by secession. All of them thought that they could improve their position by finding that exact size of political unit in which their own language and their own national culture could be made to predominate and in which their own nationality or ethnic group could be turned into the leading class or social and political elite.

Nationalism in Eastern Europe was thus a reaction to the rapid diffusion of Western claims and to the expectations of security and opportunity throughout a group of societies that were only slowly, if at all, acquiring the productive skill and equipment to satisfy them. National secession, national expansion, and the national state appeared to almost all nationalities in the region as plausible short cuts to the prosperity, power, and prestige they all desired.

In the course of events, the experiment was actually made. The Austro-Hungarian monarchy was destroyed and a number of successor states arose from its remains. There is no doubt on the whole that the emergence of these national states represented a significant step forward toward higher levels of popular participation in public affairs, toward political democracy, toward popular education, and even, in some respects, toward greater economic opportunities. But at the same time it seems clear that the change in the size of political units did little or nothing to come to grips with the fundamental causes of the poverty and backwardness of the region, or with the fundamental sources of its peculiar psychological and political frustrations and resentments. National and regional markets and consumer preferences remained as small and as unfavorable to mass production in the new states as they had in the old. Capital remained as scarce and productive investment as uneven and erratic as before. Tools, technologies, and work habits changed slowly if at all. Poverty persisted. Purchasing power remained low and prices high. Production remained scattered over many small and inefficient factories. Innovations were accepted reluctantly or not at all. Unemployment became worse than it had ever been.

Thus social tensions persisted or grew worse. Sometimes they appeared as growing tensions between left and right, with the political middle-of-the-road parties increasingly threatened by fascists or by communists. Sometimes they appeared as tensions between different nationality groups, such as between Serbians and Croatians or between Czechs and Germans. Often the same angry and frustrated individuals could be found backing communism in one year, extreme nationalism in another, and some more or less supranational fascism in a third. Whole districts voted for right-wing radical candidates in one election and for left-wing radicals in another. Nationalism in Eastern Europe was thus the symptom of a more fundamental maladjustment, even though nationalistic policies, once adopted, often served to make this maladjustment worse. Nationalistic governments, as well as most other governments in this region, were becoming increasingly unpopular and during the 1930's showed increasing reluctance to face their own voters. By 1939, before the first German or Russian soldier stepped on their soil, every country of Eastern Europe, with the exceptions of Finland and Czechoslovakia, had succumbed to some form of dictatorship. Nationalism had thus failed to cure the fundamental maladjustments of Eastern European political and economic life. From some points of view its failure was hardly less shattering than the failure of the supranational empires that had preceded it.

It was nationalism which first undermined and in part destroyed the traditions of property and the respect for property in Eastern Europe. This attack against property began as early as the era of Prince Bismarck in Germany. The so-called Polish legislation sponsored by the German government and by the German nationalists during and after the Bismarck era showed scant respect for the property rights of the Polish minority in Germany. It was designed to prevent them from acquiring what was considered German land and to deprive them of such German land as they had managed to acquire in the past. In addition to driving the Poles from German soil, this policy was also designed to eliminate Polish minorities in Eastern Germany by assimilation or expulsion, and the German word *ausrotten*—or exterminate—leaves little doubt as to the ruthlessness of the determination behind this policy. After the First World War, when certain parts of Silesia were incorporated in Poland, former German properties in industrial corporations and other valuables had a way of coming into Polish hands. When from 1939 to 1944 German armies in turn occupied a large part, and later all, of Poland, large amounts of Polish property were again transferred to Germans.

In one shape or another, with or without benefit of legal form, this game of transferring property from the temporarily weaker to the temporarily stronger nationalities was played in large areas of Eastern Europe. When in the course of the First World War the Austro-Hungarian government collected large amounts of taxes and additional amounts of ostensibly voluntary war loans for the war efforts of Germany and Austria from the unwilling Czech, Slovakian, and Polish populations, the Austrian empire was in effect transferring important parts of the national wealth of these regions into German hands to be spent for German political and military purposes.[2] After the First World War, formerly Austrian or German mines, banks, and industrial enterprises in Czechoslovakia had a way of becoming Czechoslovakian. After 1939, when the Nazis occupied this country, Czecho-

---

[2] Cf. G. Gratz and R. Schuller, *op. cit.,* pp. 171-188; Wilhelm Winkler, *Die Einkommensverschiebungen in Osterreich während des Weltkrieges,* (Vienna and New Haven: Holder-Pichler-Tempsky and Yale University Press, 1930), pp. 74-78, 219-221; Alois Rasin, *Financial Policy of Czechoslovakia during the First Year of Its History* (Oxford: Clarendon Press, 1923), pp. 7-25.

slovakian-owned enterprises soon found their way into German hands, and the Dresdner Bank emerged as a major owner of formerly Czechoslovakian property. After Germany had lost the war in 1945, the new government of Czechoslovakia with the support of all political parties—anti-Communists as well as Communists—proceeded to expel all Sudeten Germans and to confiscate their property. Sudeten German anti-Nazis who had been loyal to the Czechoslovakian republic were nominally exempt from these provisions, but the burden of proving their loyalty was put upon their shoulders, and by 1947 the nationalistic atmosphere in the new Czechoslovakia was such that many German anti-Nazis with proven democratic records preferred to emigrate voluntarily to Germany, leaving behind the properties and savings of a lifetime. At the beginning of the year 1948, shortly before the Communists seized power in Czechoslovakia, there were perhaps 2,000,000 individuals who, in one way or another, had acquired some parts of former German property either in the Sudetenland or elsewhere in the country. These people may have found it rather difficult to resist the power and the confiscatory threats of Communism, so long as they themselves were using other people's furniture and were living in other people's houses.

Throughout the region, property rights thus became the plaything of nationalistic politics between Poles and Germans, Czechs and Austrians, Hungarians, Slovakians, and Rumanians, Serbians and Croatians. Few, if any, of the persons who participated in these confiscations considered themselves criminals. Rather they persuaded themselves that they were patriots. They had perhaps suffered themselves during the preceding periods of war or foreign occupation, and this may have seemed to them the only opportunity for getting some sort of reparation. No rationalization, however, could change the ultimate result: during the last thirty years in Eastern Europe, the ownership of property, the right to travel, and the right to work in desirable occupations, have been dependent not upon a man's diligence, honesty, or thrift, but upon the accident of his affiliations with the group temporarily in power. A man's property and freedom thus came to depend upon the official estimation of his "political reliability" or loyalty, which was defined for him by a rapidly changing sequence of politicians and political regimes. Many of the men who practiced these policies of confiscation and repression considered themselves anti-Communists, or professed themselves as such. Yet in their disregard for property rights and civil liberties they did much to pave the way for Communism.

V

Perhaps it has been memories of the stagnation under the old empires and the conflict and repressions of the following eras of nationalism that have turned many to visions of a safer, broader, and more generous life under an Eastern European federation.

In the minds of those who accepted this vision, a federation of Eastern European states would offer its peoples military security against invasion by outsiders. It would insure economic prosperity, provide a more stable distribution of economic welfare, safeguard property, provide broader opportunities for all, reward work, thrift, and enterprise, and by all these means serve to insure broad and rapid economic growth. In regard to politics, it would safeguard civil liberties. It would guarantee nondiscriminatory treatment to all peoples and minorities and free mobility to individuals throughout the region. It would assure to both individuals and peoples throughout Eastern Europe respect for their diverse habits and traditions, so that none of them would be forced to change their respective customs, work habits, and social institutions more rapidly or more radically than they might freely choose. To ease the complex and subtle problems of culture, emotions, and psychology, it was hoped that the federation would insure widespread opportunities for education. It was hoped that it would give to the inhabitants of the region both social and international prestige. It was hoped that it would bring them to a status of equality with the reference groups which they had chosen as yardsticks for comparison, or that in some way an Eastern European federation would make its citizens the equals not only of the French and German peoples but perhaps in time even of the English and American peoples, who have now become the reference groups for standards of achievement throughout the world. Finally it was hoped that such a federation would give rise to inspiring common enterprises that would unite the peoples of Eastern Europe in a new sense of their own identity, as in past centuries the monarchies of Western Europe, according to the philosopher José Ortega y Gasset, have united their own peoples into a sense of dignity and nationhood.

In striking contrast to the splendor of these visions was their relative poverty in specific detail. None of the larger projects for federation in this region were ever negotiated by governments or even by responsible political leaders from the different areas. There was a negotiated project of the Polish-Czechoslovakian federation, worked out by Czechoslovakian and Polish leaders-in-exile during the Second World War, but this project which included only two states in the region was not followed up by the established governments or by the major political organizations after the war.[3]

[3] Cf. United States Department of State, Division of Library and Reference Services, *Danubian Federation: An Annotated Bibliography* (*Bibliography No. 66*), Washington, D.C., October 28, 1952 (multigraphed); Felikas Gross, *Crossroads of Two Continents: A Democratic Federation of East-Central Europe* (New York: Columbia University Press, 1945), pp. 28-34, and for the text of the Polish-Czechoslovakian Declaration, signed in London on January 25, 1942, by representatives of the two

Projects for a Balkan union usually failed to include even the Danubian states and practically never reached out toward Poland and the Baltic. Projects for a Baltic union usually remained limited to Poland and the small Baltic states, leaving the latter faced with the prospect of becoming a minority in what would become in practice a greater Poland.

Perhaps most of the substance behind the projects for federation did not consist so much in plans for the future as in memories of the past, and in particular of the Austro-Hungarian monarchy. A reconstituted and enlarged Austria-Hungary, reaching in the North through the accession of Poland and the Baltic states to the shores of the Baltic Sea and including in the South all the Balkan states down to the border perhaps of Turkey, would sum up the many projects for uniting Eastern Europe which have been discussed so often during the last thirty years. It is the general project of a federation of the Danubian countries, enlarged by the addition of Poland to the north, and conceivably by that of Albania and Greece in the south, which needs closer examination.

It is true that such a federation would carry a certain amount of international prestige by virtue of the sheer numbers of its inhabitants, the enormous sums of productive capacities, natural resources, and miles of railroad track scattered throughout the area. Any more fundamental and lasting prestige, however, might well depend upon the effective military capabilities and the actual levels of economic prosperity and growth, and of educational progress and political democracy which the federation could maintain.

The obvious military task for such a federation would be to form a counterweight to Germany or Russia, or to both of them together. Many of these military tasks, how-

governments-in-exile, pp. 102-104; Antoni Plutynski, *We Are 115 Millions* (London: Eyre and Spottiswoode, 1944), pp. 33-36, 114-122; etc.

ever, seem well beyond the capabilities of the region. Such
a federation would have no clear-cut advantage in manpower
over either Germany or Russia and would be definitely inferior to the heavy industries and economic war potentials
of these two countries, as well as to their productive facilities
and transport systems. The military security of such a federation would depend primarily upon the military strength of
Western Europe, and perhaps even more upon that of the
United States. Given sufficient strength and determination
in the Atlantic community, an Eastern European federation
could be made secure, but its own military contribution
would hardly be necessary, and certainly not decisive. In
the absence of sufficient strength among the Western Powers,
on the other hand, no amount of military effort on the part
of these peoples could make them secure. Any situation in
which the military strength of the Western and Eastern
Powers were in such delicate balance that an Eastern
European federation could make a decisive difference in
their military prospects would be extremely rare; and if
it should occur, it would be a situation of extreme insecurity rather than security, and would be unlikely to last for
long.

A commitment to an active military policy might thus
be beyond the military as well as the economic capabilities of
the area, as commitments in the First World War proved to
be fatally beyond the capabilities of the Austro-Hungarian
monarchy. In this case, the result of overcommitment was the
dissolution of the larger political unit and its replacement by
a number of smaller ones, accompanied for decades by the
widespread unpopularity of the very idea of union.

As regards economic prospects, projects of Eastern European union are frequently based on a naïve version of the
nineteenth-century economic theory. According to that theory, economic growth would automatically result from free
competition; no severe depression or protracted unemploy-

ment could result under truly free competition, and all actual depressions would be merely the result of political interference in economic life on the part of misguided governments. Under such a *laissez faire* economy, the rates of saving and capital formation would automatically be high, capital would be invested in the most productive uses, and a continuous stream of creative innovations and technological improvements would be introduced as a matter of course.

These visions have little to do with the realities of the economic development of underdeveloped areas, as economists now know them. The propensity to save, the rate of capital formation, the tendencies to invest money in productive machinery rather than in land or liquid funds and to apply science and to accept technical innovations—all these are largely matters of society and culture and, to a significant extent, matters of public policy.[4]

None of these problems—terms of trade, capital formation, the savings rates, investment patterns, and innovation rates—are necessarily insoluble, but their solution is essential to economic growth, and none of them will be solved automatically by the effects of federation. Free trade has resulted not only in the relative wealth of England, but also in the relative poverty of Portugal. If English rather than Portuguese living standards are eventually attained in Eastern Europe, this will be due to a very considerable amount of careful

---

[4] Cf. W. W. Rostow, *The Process of Economic Growth* (New York: Norton, 1952), pp. 12-106; J. M. Clark, "Common and Disparate Elements in National Growth and Decline," in National Bureau of Economic Research, *Problems in the Study of Economic Growth* (New York, N.B.E.R.), July 1949 (multigraphed), pp. 33-37; Joseph Schumpeter, "Theoretical Problems of Economic Growth," *The Journal of Economic History,* Supplement VII, 1947, pp. 1-9; Albert Kervyn, "Approaches to the Problem of Economic Development," *World Politics* (July 1953), pp. 569-578; B. F. Roselitz, Ed., *The Progress of Underdeveloped Countries* (Chicago: University of Chicago Press, 1952); United Nations, *Measures for the Economic Development of Underdeveloped Countries* (New York, 1951).

study of the problems and conditions of economic growth in this region.

As long as major economic difficulties and frustrations persist in Eastern Europe, political democracy in that region is likely to remain in a precarious position. With the persistence of rural tensions resulting from village poverty and overpopulation, with strikes and unemployment among labor, with bitter competition for white-collar jobs, with the ever-present tendency of the wealthy to flee with its accumulations of capital (a tendency likely to become worse under government-imposed currency regulations and controls), economic stagnation or disruption will probably be a constant threat, and always with it will be the twin temptations of nationalism and dictatorship. The fatal gap between the rapid growth of popular needs and expectations and the slow growth of economic and social opportunities might continue to plague and eventually might even shatter an Eastern European federation, much as it plagued and eventually shattered both supranational empires and national states in the past.

If the plans for an Eastern European federation do not offer in themselves any answer to the general problems of economic growth and political stability, neither do they offer any answer to a number of the most burning specific problems of the area.

Just what would be the role of the Austrian and German peoples in an Eastern European federation? An increasing number of Germans is demanding rather vehemently the return to Germany of the formerly German territories which at present form the western provinces of Poland and which contain a large part of the industrial capacity of the Polish republic. There are almost 3,000,000 Sudeten German evacuees scattered through Germany and Austria, and many of these persons cherish hopes of returning some day to the

Sudetenland and to their former properties, and perhaps even hope to gain additional properties and power by way of compensation or booty at the next turn of the wheel of political fortune.

To be sure, German claims for restoration or new expansion may recede into the background as the present generation of German evacuees grows old and if the children of this generation find new roots and new prospects within the present boundaries of Germany. However, German claims on Eastern Europe, backed by the existence of some 10,000,000 displaced Germans from Eastern Europe as well as by the growing German industry and the growing prospects for the restoration of a German army, will continue for at least ten or fifteen years to be a major factor in the political universe of Central Europe.

Distinct from the issue of the East Germans is the problem of German Austria. The German city of Vienna lies east of both Zagreb and Prague. If Bohemia has been compared by German writers to a Slavic wedge thrust into Germany, so Austria could be compared to a German wedge pushed into Eastern Europe. Would the Austrians be included in an Eastern European federation and, if so, what would their position be? If they were not included in an Eastern federation, would they be permitted to resume their efforts for union with Germany, as was attempted by both the German and the Austrian Social Democrats after 1918 and again by the Bruening-Curtius government in 1930, and as was finally accomplished by the violent action of the Nazis in 1938? If Austria were to join neither Germany nor an Eastern European federation, where would it go, and how would its people make a living?

The German and Austrian problems are only two of the major nationality problems of the Eastern European area. What would be done about the Magyars and Rumanians in Transylvania? Would the former Ukrainian territories of Poland and Czechoslovakia remain outside the Eastern European federation?

Perhaps more important, where would the center of the federation be? There seems to be no first-rate rail center east of Vienna between the north and south of Eastern Europe. Are there one or more potential metropolitan regions for the entire European area, and could they be linked by an integrated transportation system? If not, could an Eastern European federation function without them?

VI

At present none of these questions can be answered easily or quickly. Necessary to their solution are many more facts than are now available. Among the first steps that can be undertaken at this time towards strengthening the prospects of a free and democratic Eastern European federation is the undertaking of some of the fundamental research which has been given insufficient attention in the past.

Such research would enable us to evaluate more correctly the extent to which political amalgamation of Eastern Europe is practicable and how likely it is that integration without amalgamation could maintain peace and security. Political amalgamation would mean the merging of political institutions and would emphasize particularly the abolition of sovereign national governments in Eastern Europe and the transfer of their powers to a single common government. Integration without amalgamation might mean the retention of national sovereignty, modified by a sense of community among all participating political units that would lead to the conviction that a war among them would be anachronistic and impossible.

Integration without amalgamation can be found between Norway and Sweden, and perhaps among all the Scandinavian countries. It can also be found between the United

States and Canada, and perhaps between the United States and Mexico. In all these cases, the nations involved have demilitarized the borders separating them from each other. They stand ready to defend their national soil against foreign invaders, but they do not expect to be invaded or to go to war with their neighbor. The United States and Canada have even entered in substance into a relationship of alliance under which they stand ready to aid each other against outside enemies. The demilitarized borders between Norway and Sweden and between the United States and Canada are visible expression of the development of the habits, practices, and institutions of mutual trust and quick responsiveness possible between neighboring nations.

Common governments, too, require such mutual habits and understanding and responsiveness, if they are to mean more than the forcible subjection of the peoples living under them. It seems significant that the Swedes and Norwegians were on the verge of open hostilities at the beginning of the twentieth century when they were still living under a common crown and that relations between these two peoples have improved continually since Norway, like Sweden, attained its sovereign freedom. It may well be that the greater the degree of common government, the greater must be the amount of effective mutual understanding and responsiveness. And it may also be true that, at a given level of mutual understanding and voluntary self-adjustment, a nonamalgamated community would be practicable where a common government would founder in mutual conflict.

Dependable habits of mutual understanding and responsiveness are indicators—though not the only indicators—of the capabilities of the political institutions which maintain a political community. Some of the many other indicators of such capabilities are the material resources at the disposal of the community and the speed with which these can be recommitted to meet new pressures or new challenges. The number of duties a government must discharge and the amount of expectations and pressures a security community has to meet represent a load upon the institutions or community; there is a balance between the political load of decision-making, responsiveness, and capacity to act on the one hand, and the actual capabilities of a government or a political community on the other hand.

It is this balance between integration loads and integration capabilities which may decide the fortunes of a political community, whether it be a unitary state or a regional federation. A better understanding of the probable loads and strains and of the probable resources and capabilities of the political communities in Eastern Europe will do much to indicate what degree of political amalgamation will prove practicable in this area, and what kind of political, economic, or military overcommitments may have to be avoided.

During the presidential campaign in the United States in 1952 both General Eisenhower and Governor Stevenson agreed that the liberation of the peoples of Eastern Europe would eventually come, not through destructive war, but through the steady pressure and the increasingly attractive example of the strong and successful development of the Western democracies. In the age of atomic energy, the chains of tyranny cannot be burst by atom bombs if men are to liberate anything more than cemeteries. Rather, the chains will have to be corroded gradually by the ever-present and relentless example of Western freedom.

This may be a slow process but it may in the end be a surer one. It will require from the Western world more and better research and a greater understanding of the needs and conditions of the Eastern European peoples. Such research may show that historical developments are not always slow and that centuries are not always necessary for the evolution of conditions necessary to a great and democratic federation. There is much to be accomplished before a free Eastern

European federation can emerge from the assembly line of history. But it is possible that preparations can be made quickly as well as slowly, once people know what they must do, and once they have gained faith that tyranny and war can be banished forever from Eastern Europe.

12 Eastern Europe and the Postwar Balance of Power

C. E. BLACK

In the Second World War as in the first, Eastern Europe was the scene of the opening hostilities and became one of the principal battlefields. Yet this region played a different role in the peace settlements following the two world wars, for after the first it remained a power vacuum for a generation and after the second it became a part of the power system of one of the victorious states. An understanding of the process by which this region came to occupy a critical position in the postwar balance is essential to a discussion of the policies that have been formulated to redress this situation.

I

During the Second World War, the three leading members of the United Nations coalition were in agreement that Eastern Europe should be liberated from the Axis, but when it came to discussing what political system should replace Axis rule it soon became apparent that their points of view conflicted. Of the three powers, the Soviet Union had the most immediate interest in this region. The policy of establishing a sphere of influence in Eastern Europe has deep roots in

Russian history and formed an important aspect of Tsarist foreign policy before the First World War.

Soviet weakness after the revolution forced this policy into the background, but the disintegration of the European political system in the decade after the world depression prepared the ground for a revival of Russian influence. It is not known for certain when this traditional Russian aim was reformulated in Soviet terms, but it was unmistakably discernible in Molotov's negotiations with the Western democracies and with Germany in the summer of 1939. The Soviet terms in each case stipulated an extension of Soviet influence, through annexation or political control, along the entire borderland from the Baltic to the Black Sea. The fact that the Germans were better able than their rivals to pay this price gave them an initial advantage in the ensuing war, but did not prevent Nazi-Soviet relations from foundering on the same issue in the winter of 1940-41.

As soon as the U.S.S.R. had recovered from the first impact of the Nazi attack, Soviet diplomacy set its sights toward confirming and extending the sphere of influence acquired during the period of the Nazi-Soviet pact. Molotov tried unsuccessfully in the spring of 1942 to have recognition of the recent Russian territorial gains made a condition to the conclusion of the Anglo-Soviet treaty of alliance. Soviet policy then turned its attention to the Eastern European governments-in-exile, and the treaty of alliance concluded with the Czechoslovakian government at the end of 1943 marked the first success in this line of action. Where this kind of diplomacy failed, as in the case of Poland and Yugoslavia, Soviet support was transferred to rival organizations.

Communist-organized partisan movements were an important instrument of Soviet policy in Yugoslavia and Albania, as well as in Greece. In Poland, Rumania, Bulgaria, and Hungary, on the other hand, no progress was made until

Soviet troops arrived on the scene in 1944. These operations took place behind a screen of propaganda that stressed the desirability of establishing independent and democratic governments in Eastern Europe after the war, and in the prevailing spirit of wartime unity only the most clear-headed students of Russian affairs grasped the nature of Soviet intentions.

From long experience, the British government sensed the danger to postwar stability inherent in the Soviet domination of Eastern Europe. At the same time, British strategy supported a plan, which arose from military necessity, to outmaneuver the Axis armies by striking at them indirectly on their southern flank. Thus, both interest and expediency inclined the British towards supplementing the cross-Channel attack by a major campaign from Italy aimed at the Danubian region, and they pressed for this strategy in Anglo-American councils once the initial success in North Africa had been assured. The American and Soviet objections that were registered at the Tehran Conference and the reluctance of the Turks to abandon their neutrality spelled the defeat of these plans.

The British now tried to gain influence in Eastern Europe by other means. Although it was clear that the extended Soviet frontiers of 1941 would have to be conceded at the end of the war, Churchill originally favored the formation of a Danubian and a Balkan federation as members of a European Regional Council. However, under the circumstances that developed after the Tehran Conference and with the growing possibility of a unilateral Russian settlement in Eastern Europe, Churchill was forced to seek a foothold for direct British influence as an alternative to the European solution for which he had found no backing from his allies. The transfer of British support from Mihailović to Tito, the attempts to restore relations between the U.S.S.R. and the

Polish government-in-exile, the encouragement of Beneš in his efforts to develop close Soviet-Czechoslovakian relations —these and other measures were now taken.

The most important of these policies, adopted initially without American participation, was the decision to negotiate directly with the U.S.S.R. for a division of the Balkans into spheres of influence. This policy led to the conclusion in October, 1944, of a formal agreement that conceded to the British a predominant interest in Greece in return for the recognition of a similar Soviet interest in Rumania and Bulgaria. In Yugoslavia and Hungary the influence of the two powers was to be shared. Although this agreement was made only for the duration of the war, it established a pattern for subsequent developments.

A number of considerations led the United States to pay less attention to Eastern Europe during the war than did the U.S.S.R. and the United Kingdom. The most immediate was the essentially military outlook of the American leaders, which led them to regard the defeat of Germany and Japan as ends in themselves and to disregard the realignment of power that might result from this policy. Underlying this approach, was the profound distrust of American public opinion for any strategy, particularly in Europe, that was not clearly directed towards the earliest possible conclusion of hostilities. The experience of President Roosevelt as a member of the Wilson administration had taught him the indecision of American opinion on issues of foreign policy, and the plan for the drafting and ratification of the Charter of the United Nations before the termination of hostilities reveals the modest view taken by the administration of the support that it could expect from the voters on these issues.

This cautious American approach was also evidenced by the handling of foreign affairs in the Presidential elections of 1940 and 1944 and by the many constitutional devices that were used to bypass Congress on delicate issues of foreign policy. Moreover, the prospect of a prolonged struggle with Japan after the defeat of Germany served only to increase this caution regarding commitments in Europe. That this assumption regarding American opinion was soundly based became evident as soon as the war was over, when the rapid demobilization of the armed forces and the abrupt termination of Lend-Lease reflected the belief of the American voter that with the military defeat of the enemy a stable peace had been established.

In addition to these considerations, it should be noted that President Roosevelt apparently left the Tehran Conference convinced that Stalin's promises and statements of policy could be taken at face value. Although the President would have been quick to recognize the fallacy of this assumption once the evidence became available, as is clear from his reaction to events in Poland during the last weeks of his life, he spoke and acted during the period in which the determining decisions were made as though the extension of Soviet and Communist influence were matters of no serious concern. In his Fourth Inaugural Address, in what was intended to be a summary of his political philosophy, President Roosevelt conveyed to the American public his views on foreign policy in a manner that was characteristic of his thinking during this period:

> We have learned to be citizens of the world, members of the human community.
> We have learned the simple truth, as Emerson said, that, 'The only way to have a friend is to be one.'
> We can gain no lasting peace if we approach it with suspicion and mistrust—or with fear. We can gain it only if we proceed with the understanding and the courage which flow from conviction.

In view of the predominant American influence in the war councils of the Western allies, the major dispositions made in the last year of the war all tended to leave Eastern Europe to the Russians. The decision to weaken the campaign in Italy—with the possibility of pressing on into the Danubian region—in order to invade southern France in the summer of 1944, followed from this attitude, as did the granting to the Soviet High Command of overriding powers in the armistice terms concluded with Rumania, Bulgaria, and Hungary. Under the circumstances, the only limitations placed on Soviet influence in Eastern Europe were those created by the advance of the allied armies in the West and by the prompt British occupation of Greece. By the time of the Yalta conference this tendency to accept a Soviet orbit in Eastern Europe was in full swing. It followed logically that the provisional postwar governments of Poland and Yugoslavia should be based on the Communist regimes already on the spot and that full confidence should be placed in the Soviet agreement to assist "the earliest possible establishment through free elections of governments responsive to the will of the people."

In the immediate postwar period, the American and British foreign ministers made some effort through diplomacy to reduce Soviet influence in Eastern Europe. By this time, however, their bargaining power had been largely dissipated, since neither their own governments nor public opinion gave them strong support, and the U.S.S.R. found it necessary to make few concessions to win the Western signatures to the peace treaties concluded with the former Axis satellites in 1947. By the end of that year the governments of Albania, Bulgaria, Hungary, Poland, and Rumania were in Soviet hands, and that of Czechoslovakia was within easy reach. Exceptional circumstances limited Soviet influence in Yugoslavia and permitted Tito to break loose in 1948, but after this incident the Soviet hold on the other countries in Eastern Europe was tightened and these countries were soon consolidated into a closely knit political and economic orbit.

II

In the bipolar system of international relations that emerged in the first postwar years, Eastern Europe played a critical role in the balance of power—defining this term as a system of political organization in which no single state is permitted to gain sufficient strength to impose its will on the other states. It is easy enough to demonstrate the increment to Soviet power represented by the Eastern European orbit in terms of strategic positions, manpower, production, raw materials, and a rich variety of skills. Yet the importance of Eastern Europe to Russia does not lie primarily in these gains. It lies rather in the advantage that it gives to Soviet policy in neutralizing and eventually absorbing the continent of Europe itself, which at this stage constitutes the key to the balance of power. Russia and Eastern Europe alone clearly do not spell world domination, but Russia and the European continent as a whole represent a sum of power that if properly organized could give the Soviet leaders a dominant position.

The alternative to a Soviet orbit in Eastern Europe originally contemplated by the Western allies was not a corresponding Western orbit on the Soviet border, but rather the organization in Europe as a whole of a political system independent of either Soviet or American influence. Whether it was through the European Regional Council proposed by Churchill when he visited Washington in May, 1943, or through the United Nations Charter drafted in its original form on the instructions of Roosevelt, the Western allies hoped to see in both Eastern and Western Europe the restoration of states that were independent, peace-loving, and as democratic as their capabilities permitted. With such a system it was hoped that the very atmosphere of Europe would encourage those political forces in Eastern Europe which favored democracy and social progress, and that the security of the Soviet Union would be assured by the absence of organized power in Europe and by the international regime of the United Nations.

That the Western democracies, and especially the United States, delayed so long in recognizing the threat of Soviet domination in Eastern Europe may be attributed to several factors. The outcome of the inter-allied wartime negotiations regarding strategy had been presented to the public as agreed decisions, and the Soviet position in Eastern Europe was at first accepted as part of an allied plan blessed by Churchill and Roosevelt. Moreover, many persons in the West were so poorly informed regarding the Soviet system as to believe that it would bring great positive gains to the peoples of Eastern Europe. Even more influential was the paradoxical view held by many that, although Soviet power was too great to be resisted in Eastern Europe, there was no reason to fear its extension beyond that region. In fact, the very opposite was the case. Although the establishment of an Eastern European orbit was certainly a major objective of the Soviet leaders in 1944-45 and in fact they made efforts to gain control in Western Europe as well, there is much evidence that they would have accepted a great deal less if they had been required to negotiate with determined British and American counterproposals. As soon as they perceived that the Western allies had no intention of backing up their diplomatic notes of protest, they proceeded to exploit their advantage to the full both within and beyond the region. The Soviet leaders thus established their controls over the power structure of Eastern Europe during the first two postwar years. Only when they tried to extend their political influence from the southern periphery of their orbit into Greece and Turkey did they finally provoke British and American countermeasures.

The United Kingdom had been a vigilant guardian of the

balance of power during the war, and only American objections had prevented the launching of at least a limited campaign from Italy into the Danubian region in 1944. After the war the position was reversed, and the United States found itself assuming the role that the British, through lack of means, were reluctantly forced to relinquish. It was an arduous course in adult education that brought American policy to the point of accepting political responsibility in the Eastern Mediterranean, but once the decision was taken it was systematically implemented. During the period of containment, as American policy between 1947 and 1953 is generally referred to by friends and critics alike, the international position of Eastern Europe underwent important changes.

The policy of containment, in the words of its leading proponent, was "designed to confront the Russians with unalterable counter-force at every point where they showed signs of invading upon the interests of a peaceful and stable world." The belief that Soviet leaders would be restrained rather than provoked by such action rested on a careful study of their ideology and conduct. The gradual and ultimate character of Marx's world revolution as interpreted in Russia, the flexibility exhibited by Moscow's policy in the past, and the presence of inherent weaknesses in the Soviet system, seemed to justify the hope that containment would bring a halt to Soviet expansionism. In a limited sense a policy of containment had already been attempted in 1945-46 with respect to the Iranian question and other issues, and when American policy took a firm stand on well-chosen ground it met with unaccustomed success. When it was finally adopted in 1947, the policy of containment thus had a practical foundation in American experience as well as a considered basis in theory.

It is important to recognize that this policy was expected not only to bring the expansion of Soviet power to a halt but ultimately to contribute to the disintegration of that power in its home territory. It was believed that, if the United States could establish itself as a leading ideological force in the world by adroit propaganda and more particularly by adopting a vigorous and responsible approach to the myriad of problems that confront society in a revolutionary age, the source of Soviet strength would be greatly weakened. It was maintained that the attraction of communism in Russia and around the world would suffer greatly by this competition, and that the Soviet leaders might eventually be led by the frustration of their policies to make significant and permanent adjustments in their political system. In this sense, the policy of containment was considered by its proponents to be a positive though gradual policy in the field of political warfare and to be negative or defensive only in a military sense.

The policy of containment was evolved as a reply to the consolidation of Soviet power in Eastern Europe, to the aggressive attitude of the Communist parties all over the world, and in particular to the indirect Soviet aggression against Greece and the threats to Turkey. The new approach called for a reversal of the demobilization trend in the United States and for the initiation of a whole series of programs in the political, economic, and propaganda fields. By the very nature of the situation, this policy, or any other, could not be expected to bear important fruits for a number of years, and indeed during the period under discussion American policy suffered many serious defeats. In Asia Soviet power was in no sense contained and, if Soviet influence is not yet decisive in the Near and Middle East, conditions are favorable to its growth.

Only in Europe, with the reduction in influence of the Communist parties, the development of comprehensive plans for the economic and political integration of Western Europe and the establishment of NATO, did the policy of containment bear early fruit. Yet even the defeats in the Far East, serious though they were, contributed their share to the ultimate success of the new policy. The key to containment is the creation of a counter-force to Soviet power, and of all the events that spurred the American government and public opinion to a sense of responsibility, the victory of communism in China and Communist aggression in Korea were the most important.

It was the threat of Communist expansion in Eastern Europe that led to the announcement of the Truman Doctrine in March, 1947, and it was in northern Greece that the policy of containment met its first formal test and eventually won an important victory. In this instance, the first step in creating "an unalterable counter-force" to Soviet power was to establish beyond serious doubt the reality of the threat. This was accomplished through the machinery of the United Nations, and the report submitted by the Security Council Commission of Investigation Concerning Greek Frontier Incidents in May, 1947, served as an important rallying point for world opinion. The identification of the purpose and character of the threat facilitated the sending of aid to Greece, and after a bitter struggle the expansion of Soviet power in this region was halted.

The frustration of the Albanian, Bulgarian, and Yugoslavian forces that were serving as instruments of Soviet policy in Greece led to serious repercussions behind the Iron Curtain. The policy of containment was certainly only one of the factors that led to the break between Tito and Stalin, and it cannot claim the principal credit for this important setback to Soviet policy. Yet it is difficult to see how Tito could have broken away in 1948, or at least with such relative ease, if the United States had shown no interest in the threat to Greece, if the Communist parties had not been forced out of the governments in France and Italy, and if the general atmosphere of international relations had been one of an unimpeded expansion of Soviet power.

It is probably also correct to credit the policy of containment with the important change that occurred in Soviet policy in Eastern Europe in 1948. Difficult as it is to know what goes on within the Kremlin apparatus, the available evidence indicates that in the first postwar years a policy was followed of aggressively exploiting every opportunity to extend the influence of Communism all over Europe. When Europe rallied under the leadership of the Truman Doctrine in 1947-48 to inflict defeats on the Communists in many quarters, emphasis was placed on a defensive consolidation of the gains already made. Although this process strengthened the Communist position in Eastern Europe in certain respects, it was accompanied by many actions that served further to educate Western opinion as to the true nature of Soviet rule. The Communist *coup d'état* in Czechoslovakia, the masquerade trials of many political and religious leaders and of an American businessman and a correspondent, made a great impression on the West. American opinion in particular took new interest in Eastern Europe. Refugee scholars and political leaders from this region were now encouraged by the newly formed National Committee for a Free Europe to rally their followers and define their aims, and propaganda directed to Eastern Europe was developed by Radio Free Europe and by the Voice of America.

All this represented a great change in the American attitude and formed the necessary background for more positive steps. Significant among these was the signature at Ankara on February 28, 1953, of a Treaty of Friendship and Cooperation between Greece, Turkey, and Yugoslavia. The conclusion of this pact reflects the rapid development of events since the initial extension of American aid to Greece and Turkey in 1947. The support of Yugoslavia as a member of the Security Council of the United Nations in 1949 against serious Soviet opposition and the extension of formal American aid to Tito in 1950, marked the transition of that country from a bitter enemy of the West to an associate, if not an ally. At the same time, the accession of Greece and Turkey to

NATO in 1951 brought these countries into a closer working relationship with the West. The Balkan pact of 1953 is not a military alliance, but an agreement to consult on all matters of common interest and to cooperate on questions concerning defense and on problems in the economic, technical, and cultural fields. The significance of this treaty, despite the many obstacles in the way of its implementation, lies in the creation of an alternative to the methods employed in the Soviet orbit. The treaty protects its members from Communist pressure and at the same time provides a rallying point for states desiring to break away from Soviet control should the opportunity arise.

III

The policy of containment, as a theory of foreign policy, aroused considerable public debate because it was initially presented in such general terms as to be open to many interpretations. If containment is interpreted as the policy actually pursued by the United States in the period between the announcement of the Truman Doctrine in 1947 and the inauguration of the new administration in 1953, few would deny that this policy resulted in a significant change in the morale and strength of the Western democracies. Acknowledging this vital gain, responsible students of foreign policy nevertheless questioned whether strengthening Western Europe was enough, and maintained that the role of Eastern Europe in the balance of power was such that the Soviet Union would continue to have a significant advantage in the struggle for Europe as a whole until its grip on this region had been broken. Although the policy of containment anticipated the ultimate disintegration of Soviet power, its critics thought this process too gradual and advocated the more dynamic course of liberating Eastern Europe from Communist rule by means short of war.

Insofar as the outlines of a policy of peaceful liberation have been suggested by its proponents, one may explore briefly its assumptions, the conditions necessary for its implementation, and some of the methods that it might employ. The underlying assumption of this policy was set forth by Mr. Dulles when, as Secretary of State-Designate, he stated on January 15, 1953: "We shall never have a secure peace or a happy world so long as Soviet Communism dominates one-third of all the peoples that there are, and is trying at least to extend its rule to many others." The purpose of a policy of liberation would thus be to guarantee the security of the free world. It would be a limited political offensive for defensive purposes.

Liberation by means short of war calls for the offsetting of Soviet power in Europe so that in eventual negotiations for a European settlement the U.S.S.R. could be induced to withdraw its military forces behind the Russian frontier. It also calls for the piecemeal winning over of the countries of Eastern Europe by the diverse methods of political warfare. In Soviet eyes, the withdrawal called for under this policy would not be regarded as a defeat but only as a strategic retreat, carried out while accumulating forces for a renewed political offensive. There is good evidence that such a maneuver is in accord with Soviet doctrines. The Western world has no reason to argue with this Soviet rationalization, although its own purpose would be to convert this temporary withdrawal into a long-term stability.

There is a great deal to be said for such a conception of peaceful liberation, but before it can be implemented the United States must assume a more vigorous leadership in the free world, especially in Europe, and clear-cut decisions must be made regarding a post-liberation program for Eastern Europe. The political and economic integration of Western Europe is directly pertinent to a policy of liberation. Important to building a position of strength in Europe is the continued development of NATO and the ratification and implementation of the various agreements relating to the European Defense Community. To the extent that these plans can be strengthened by adopting the proposed European Political Community, United States policy should assist such a development. Without a further strengthening of the Western democracies, little can be done in Eastern Europe.

Equally important is the reunification of Germany and the negotiation of an Austrian peace treaty. It is possible to imagine an occasional individual country, such as Albania, leaving the Soviet fold at some opportune moment before this is done, but it is very difficult to envisage a general liberation of Eastern Europe. The role of Germany and Austria in the Second World War has not yet been forgotten in Eastern Europe, and a solution of the problems that they represent would be reflected not only in Soviet military dispositions but also in public opinion in this region. If Austria and one or both of the two zones of Germany could be fitted into such patterns of political and economic integration as may be established in Europe, conditions very favorable to a policy of liberation would result. Even something less than this rather ambitious goal would have significant results. If, on the other hand, the ambiguous status of Austria and Germany continues without change, Russian political and military pressures on Eastern Europe will remain strong.

A further prerequisite of a policy of liberation, and perhaps a more important one, is the adoption of clear-cut United States objectives in Eastern Europe. Whether they be used as propaganda, as a basis for negotiation with the Soviet Union, or merely as a frame of reference for government officials, the range of possible terms must be thoughtfully considered. Such terms must meet many requirements. They must be acceptable on political and security grounds to the United States and to NATO. They must appeal to large segments of the peoples of Eastern Europe, although it is of course too much to hope that all can be pleased. Since the aim is liberation by means short of war, such terms would also have to be acceptable in the last analysis to the Soviet Union, if not today at least in the changed circumstances that may be created in the next few years.

The drafting of such policy objectives is a large assignment, and all that can be done here is to suggest a few of the problems. On the question of frontiers, for instance, the United States cannot remain silent if it is to implement a dynamic policy. Yet the difficulties in taking a position on this issue are great. If the United States demanded a Soviet surrender of all the territories in Eastern Europe that it has annexed since 1938, a demand for which a case in international law could doubtless be made, the leaders of the U.S.S.R. and of many other states would not take it seriously. If the United States insisted on returning western Poland to Germany, on the other hand, it would not only alienate France but would also place an invaluable propaganda weapon in Russian hands for use in Eastern Europe. It may be that the only recourse will be to support the frontiers as they exist today, although this solution would cause great anguish in Poland and Rumania, as well as in Germany.

Equally difficult questions would have to be resolved in other fields of policy. The question of a new regional organization for Eastern Europe, for instance, would be vital. Should the incorporation of this region into the Western European defense arrangements be demanded, or should the states of Eastern Europe be encouraged to seek a form of neutrality such as that enjoyed today by Finland and Sweden? Should the goal of a Europe united by a common political and economic framework be pursued, or should Eastern Europe be left out of the federal proposals under consideration if this seems necessary to achieve greater freedom of negotiation? Should Communist regimes of a Titoist persuasion be accepted in these countries, or should prompt free elections be required? If it were not desirable that these and other decisions be made public, at least the responsible branches of government should have a clear idea of the range of possibilities within which they are operating.

Similarly in the social and economic fields important policy decisons would have to be made. Eastern Europe is no longer an underdeveloped area in the accepted sense of the term, and in significant respects it is in advance of the Soviet Union. However, it is true that in the period between the two wars the countries of this region failed to work out satisfactory solutions to the major problems of agricultural improvement, industrialization, and international trade. This is not to say that Soviet policy in this region since the Second World War has succeeded, for it has not. Nevertheless, the Communists appear to have recognized some of the main problems and, at least in the fields of industry and trade, have done something about them in their own characteristic way. It may be questioned whether Western policy has in the past given these problems equally serious consideration.

IV

If a policy of liberation by means short of war is to be implemented, not only must Soviet power be offset but the individual countries of Eastern Europe must be won over by more direct means. The substance of this process in each country is the removal of the reins of power from persons acting under Soviet discipline. Essential features of this task must be accomplished on the spot by nationals of each country, but the United States and its allies in Western Europe would have important responsibilities. These would lie chiefly in the realm of propaganda and intelligence.

The purpose of propaganda in this process would be to keep the hope of freedom alive in the minds of the peoples of this region and to undermine the self-confidence of the groups that now hold the reins of power. Almost a decade has passed since the heavy hand of Communist rule was laid on these countries, and during this period their peoples have been subjected to relentless Communist propaganda. A great effort has been made to convince them of the benefits of the new rule, but the daily evidence of the burdens imposed upon them negates most of this propaganda. At the same time, an equal effort has been made to bring home to them the inevitability of communism and the hopelessness of resistance. It must be recognized that the peoples of Eastern Europe have had little evidence from the Western world of its interest in their fate or understanding of their problems.

The hope of freedom could certainly be strengthened in Eastern Europe if a genuine appreciation of the problems of this region were demonstrated in propaganda and disseminated by radio and other available means. As it became widely known that the West understood the political, economic, and social problems of this region and that concrete solutions within a democratic framework were under discussion, confidence that liberation was a feasible policy would be greatly increased. This propaganda should reveal a knowledge on the part of the West not limited to broad matters of policy, but including a most intimate acquaintance with the details of life in each country—information that can only be gained by the maintenance of direct contacts.

While the great majority of the peoples of Eastern Europe are well aware of the burdensome character of the Communist regimes, there obviously remain important groups in each country that are still wholeheartedly faithful to communism. An essential task of propaganda would therefore be to undermine the faith of these elements and to convince them that a better alternative is available. Much could be done to bring home to these people the distortions in theory and the practical tyranny of the regimes that they support. A vast arsenal of facts is available for demonstrating the stupidity of the Soviet way of doing things. Yet the conveying of this information alone would not be enough, and as a policy of liberation got under way it would be necessary to impress the supporters of communism with solemn warnings of the inevitable failure of their enterprise. At the same time, some moderation of their fate might be offered to those who changed sides in time. There is no more important task of propaganda than that of dividing, dispersing, and defeating the ranks of those who hold the reins of power, and in the last analysis they can be expected to succumb without a major counterattack only when the reality of Western strength and purposefulness can be brought home to them.

An indispensable requirement of both the propaganda effort and the conduct of other aspects of policy is intelligence of day-to-day events in each country of Eastern Europe. Developments within the government, the prisons, the factories, and the countryside must be followed in detail if a policy of liberation is to be a success. The use that can be made of such information in the field of propaganda is obvious, but it is of even more importance in determining concentrations of effort, maneuver, and timing in the tactics of liberation. Moreover, a reliable system of direct contacts, such as those which must already exist in some measure under the direction of the exiled political leaders and organizations, would be of great value in bringing pressure to bear on the vital and sensitive points of each government at the right time.

Even if these tasks in the field of propaganda and intelligence were successfully carried out, the substance of liberation would not have been achieved until the reins of power had been transferred to persons not acting under Soviet discipline. How this transfer of power is to be achieved by means short of war is one of the most debated features of a policy of liberation. Secretary Dulles has cited the defection of Tito as one of the forms that liberation may take, although he did not hold it up as a necessary prototype. Indeed, it must be recognized that Yugoslavia was unique in Eastern Europe before 1948, in its relative freedom from infiltration by Soviet agents. There appears to be no reason to believe that similar independence from Soviet policy now exists for any other Communist regime in this region. An armed popular uprising is also unlikely to achieve success, and Secretary Dulles has taken special care to point out that sponsorship of such uprisings forms no part of United States policy.

If Titoism and popular uprisings are to be discounted for the foreseeable future, the transfer of power must be expected to occur principally as a result of splits and defections within the Communist elite and possibly, under certain circumstances, of *coups d'état* on the part of opposition groups. The feasibility of such actions can in the last analysis be evaluated only with regard to specific countries and situations. Suffice it to recognize that under the proper conditions such transfers of the reins of power are within the realm of possibility. The success of such efforts would depend both on the degree of stability of the Soviet orbit and on the way in which the situation had been prepared by creating a counter-force to Soviet power by negotiation, and by propaganda and intelligence. The task of a policy of peaceful liberation is to make a success of these preparatory measures.

V

The policy of the Western democracies towards Eastern Europe since the debate of 1952 has shown few of the dynamic qualities called for by the proponents of liberation. The fact is that containment and liberation are not the dramatic alternatives that their proponents claimed them to be, for they have in view the same ends and in very large measure the same means. The difference in the two approaches lies rather in the estimate of what it is possible to do. The proponents of peaceful liberation envisaged the early development of opportunities in Eastern Europe and the launching of a vigorous effort to exploit them. Yet recent experience, despite many dramatic events, has led to a policy much more modest than that of peaceful liberation and in some respects more restricted even than that conducted under the banner of containment.

Of the many factors that account for this slackening of pace, the most obvious is the reluctance of the Western democracies to undertake the commitments that a more dynamic policy would require. The burdens of rearmament and the strains of the wars in Korea and Indo-China have taken their toll, and Western political leaders have found it difficult to confront their peoples with demands for higher taxes and greater sacrifices. In the United States, for instance, the trend has been towards a smaller budget and some reduction of foreign commitments, and the reaction of Congress to the Declaration on Captive Peoples, proposed by President Eisenhower in February, 1953, was not encouraging to proponents of liberation.

At the same time, developments within the Soviet orbit have not reflected a significant weakening of Soviet controls. The death of Stalin and the fall of Beria no doubt served to lower the morale of the local Communist elites, and popular uprisings in East Germany and elsewhere have provided fresh evidence of a fierce spirit of resistance. Yet the promptness with which they were suppressed was as impressive as the spirit that these uprisings reflected, and in their subsequent concessions to the peasants and consumers the Communist regimes appear to have relinquished none of their effective power. The situation is sufficiently fluid to permit expert observers to differ in their interpretation of events, but the preponderance of evidence seems to indicate that Eastern Europe is still firmly in Communist hands.

The Western "counter-force" has thus been slow abuilding. The goal of a negotiated settlement with the Soviet Union has not been lost to sight, but there are serious differences of opinion as to when the balance of power will have tipped sufficiently towards the West to permit it to take full advantage of its great resurgence of strength in recent years and hence to negotiate on a basis of equality. Contrary to the view of many European leaders, American official opinion maintains that until the unfinished business of Korea and of the European Defence Community has been settled the Western democracies will not be able to match the bargaining power of the Soviet Union.

In the meantime, the peoples of Eastern Europe are rounding out a decade of Communist rule and may well be asking themselves what they can expect from the West. In reply, the Western democracies can point with assurance to the great strides that they have made since 1947 in organizing their strength and in facing up to the realities of international relations. They can also point to their progress in establishing economic and political institutions designed to provide a federal structure in which both Eastern and Western Europe may find security and stability. The Western democracies cannot publish a timetable for the development of their policies, but they can make it unmistakably clear at each step that they will not consider their own peace and security assured until the states of Eastern Europe can freely participate in European affairs.

Index

Acton, Lord, 216

agrarian movements: Agrarian National Union, Bulgaria, 29, 42-3, 123, 127, 129; Agrarian party, Czechoslovakia, 29, 44, 123-4, 127, 129; Agrarian party, Serbia, 29, 42, 125, 129; Agrarian Union of Serbians, Croatians and Slovenes, 125; definition of peasantism, 109-12; Green International, 101, 127, 188-9; International Agrarian Bureau, 127, 188-9; International Peasant Union, 130; National Peasant party, Rumania, 29, 126, 129; Peasant party, Croatia, 29, 30, 42, 124, 129; Peasant party, Poland, 29, 38, 70, 124-5, 127, 129-30; peasantism in Eastern Europe, 109-31; peasantism, political philosophy, 117-21; Red Peasants International, 101; Smallholders party, Hungary, 126-7

agrarian parties, *see* agrarian movements

agriculture: collectivization, 101-8; Communist policy, 101-3, 107-8, 127-30; cooperative movement, 96-7; credit societies, 95-7; debts, 97; destruction in Second World War, 99-100; economic status of peasantry, 112-4; improvement, 18-9; in Eastern Europe, 93-108; intensive cultivation, 97; *kulaks,* 106-7; land reform, 94-5, 101-3; output, 134; population dependent on, 133-4; rural overpopulation, 93-5; serfdom, 112-3; tariffs, 98; *zadruga,* 114; *see also* agrarian movements

Albania: agrarian movement, 117-8; agricultural population, 133; authoritarianism, 51; Constitution of 1946, 79; land reform, 101-2; national movement, 13-4; role in Eastern Europe, 219-20; Second World War, 246-50; social structure, 138-41; trade, 162; trade with Bulgaria, 202; trade with Italy, 138; trade with Yugoslavia, 202-3

Alexander I, King of Yugoslavia, 40-2

All-Slav Congress, *see* Pan-Slavism

Ankara, treaty of, 24, 201-2, 256

Anschluss, 190, 240

Antonescu, Ion, 193

Austria: administration, 146; capitalism, 34; economic development, 32; member of Green International, 188-9; political trends, 40-5; role in Eastern Europe, 33, 219-21; Social Democrat party, 23; territorial losses, 184

Austria-Hungary: agriculture, 19; Balkan policy, 12; Compromise of 1867, 10, 23; industry in Bo-

Pan-Slavism, 21-2, 37, 198-200, 210
Paris, treaty of, 13
Pašić, Nikola, 32, 41
Pauker, Anna, 73
Paul, Prince, 40
Peasant parties, *see* agrarian movements
peasantism, *see* agrarian movements
People's Democracy, *see* Communism
Pestel, P. I., 40
Peter I, King of Serbia, 31-2, 41
Petkov, Nikola D., 78, 129
Piast party, Poland, 124
Pilsudski, Jozef, 32, 38-40, 43, 51, 70, 125, 127
planning, 158-60
Plato, 228
populism, 115-6; *see also* agrarian movements
Poland: agrarian movement, 117, 124, 129-30; agriculture, 19, 133; authoritarianism, 32, 51; capitalism, 34; Communist party, 69-71, 74, 77; conflict with Czechoslovakia, 187; Constitution of 1947, 80; Constitution of 1952, 80-1, 83, 85-6; cooperative movement, 96; destruction in Second World War, 99; education, 17-8, 142-3, 155, 169-73; elections, 72, 77; expulsion of Germans, 99; forced labor, 82-3; German occupation, 148; Home Army, 71; industrialization, 135, 139-41, 152, 154-67; invasion, 65; land reform, 101-2, 122; liberation, 62; Lublin Committee, 71; member of Green International, 188-9; minorities, 14, 143-4; Munich pact, 190-1; National Front, 152; nationalism, 7-9, 33; pact with Germany, 190; Pan-Slavism, 21; partition, 1939, 70-1; Poles in Austria-Hungary, 23; political rights, 16-7; political trends, 38-9, 40-5; role in Eastern Europe, 219-20; Second World War, 246-50; serfdom, 112; Social Democrat party, 69-70; social structure,

138-41; Soviet occupation, 60; Soviet orbit, 197-218; territorial changes, 100, 260; trade, 160-2; transfers of population, 100; treaty policy, 187-8, 201-6
Polybius, 49
Portugal, 112
Posen, 9
Potsdam conference, 196-7
Prague, 21, 127, 240
Prague, University of, 18
Pribičević, Svetozar, 42
proportional representation, 56-7
Protestantism, 39
Prussia, role in Eastern Europe, 9, 219-23; *see also* Germany
Pulaski, Casimir, 3

Radić, Ante, 117, 124
Radić, Stjepan, 30, 124
Radical party, Yugoslavia, 29
Radical Socialist party, France, 30
Radio Free Europe, 256
Radishchev, A. N., 40
Ranković, Alexander, 212
Rassay, C., 42
Red Army, 68
Red Peasants International, 101
Ribbentrop-Molotov pact, *see* German-Soviet pact
Roman Catholic church: influence in Poland, 39; *Quadragesimo Anno,* 120; *Rerum Novarum,* 120
Roman Republic, 49
Romanov dynasty, 3, 6; *see also* Russia
Rome Protocols, 187-8
Roosevelt, Franklin Delano, 248-9, 251
Rumania: agrarian movement, 29, 126, 129; agricultural population, 133; agriculture, 19-20, 97; authoritarianism, 51, 54; Balkan Entente, 186; Balkan federation, 24; Communist party, 73, 74; Communist treaty network, 201-6; Constitution of 1948, 81; Constitution of 1952, 81, 84-5; cooperative movement, 96; educa-